Retrospectives and Conclusions

RETRO-
SPECTIVES
AND
CONCLUSIONS

Igor Stravinsky and Robert Craft

Alfred · A · Knopf: New York

1969

...iary, *Faber and Faber Limited, London,*

...*'Stravinsky at 84: An Essentially Happy*

...*ginally appeared in* The New York Re-

"*Music and the Statistical Age*" *originally appeared in* Commentary, *September 1966.*

"*Stravinsky at Eighty-five*" *originally appeared in* The New York Review of Books, *June 1, 1967.*

"*Side Effects I*" *originally appeared as* "*On Manners, Music, and Morality*" *in* Harper's Magazine, *February 1968.*

"*Side Effects II*" *originally appeared as* "*Side Effects: An Interview with Stravinsky*" *in* The New York Review of Books, *March 14, 1968.*

"*Where Is Thy Sting?*" *originally appeared in* The New York Review of Books, *April 24, 1969.*

"*Some Perspectives of a Contemporary*" *originally appeared in Italian as the Preface to* Storia Della Musica, *Volume IX:* La Musica Contemporanea, *Fratelli Fabbri Editori, Milano, 1967.*

"*Die Meistersinger*" *originally appeared in the Bayreuth Program Book, 1968.*

"*Svadebka (Les Noces): An Instrumentation*" *originally appeared in the program book of the State University of New York at Stony Brook, April 27, 1969.*

"*Three Types of Spring Fever*" *originally appeared as* "*Stravinsky Reviews the Rite of Spring*" *in* HiFi/Stereo Review, *February 1965.*

"*A Realm of Truth*" *originally appeared in* The New York Review of Books, *September 26, 1968.*

A portion of the Diaries 1948–9 originally appeared as "*Stravinsky and Some Writers*" *in* Harper's Magazine, *December 1968.*

A portion of the Diaries 1966–7 originally appeared in Harper's Magazine, *October 1969.*

"*Virgil Thomson by Virgil Thomson*" *originally appeared as* "*A Selective Self-Portrait*" *in* Harper's Magazine, *December 1966.*

THIS IS A BORZOI BOOK
PUBLISHED BY ALFRED A. KNOPF, INC.

FIRST EDITION

To Christopher Isherwood

CONTENTS

PART I

Miscellanea

PART II

From the Diaries
of Robert Craft, 1948-1968

APPENDIXES

Retrospectives and Conclusions

INTRODUCTION

A Master at Work

Stravinsky again! (still? but yet?): eighty-four last week, still composing, still speaking his mind, still vital. It is precisely this actuality that distinguishes the festival of his music at the Philharmonic next month. Homage on such a scale is rarely accorded an active contemporary, for the reason that most artists at the homage-receiving time of life are still stranded in the period of their first flowering, hence have ceased to *be* contemporary. Moreover, few contemporary artists of any age have produced a variety of work rich enough to sustain an active exhibition of this sort as distinguished from a museum retrospective. But Stravinsky qualifies; he is one of the representative spokesmen of 1966 as he was of '06, '16, '26, and so on. And for practical-minded program builders he qualifies richly on other grounds as well. No one has illuminated larger areas of the past, or of the present in the past, and at the same time left so deep an imprint on so many successors, apostolic and otherwise. Stravinsky as a point of intersection is as much the theme of the festival as Stravinsky's music.

That the more permanent part of his activity takes place

in Hollywood must be well known, his studio there having been televised, still-photographed, described in tyrianthine prose. But the changes of recent years have not been recorded. The room is air-conditioned now, and often reduced to what seems like frostbite temperature, a surprising difference to friends who remember the composer's former valetudinarianism and his apprehensions of the slightest draught or breath of cool air; the transformation seems to be due to a blood disease which overheats him. Another difference is the display of honors: the mounted shofar from Israel; the silver-framed benison from the Pope; the Grand Cross of Santiago from Portugal; the Dresden ware from the Bürgermeister of Berlin, and the first edition of Lessing from the Bürgermeister of Hamburg; the "keys" to American and Canadian cities, and the plaques, scrolls, and medals from foreign ones. Trophies such as these did not exist a few years ago and would not have been exposed if they had. But there is another change, and one more likely to impress the visitor. This is the presence of so many reminders of death: the portraits of the composer by the late Giacometti, the photographs of Pope John, President Kennedy, T. S. Eliot, Jean Cocteau, Aldous Huxley, Evelyn Waugh, and of Celeste, Stravinsky's beloved cat. Eight of the composer's later pieces bear the subtitle *In Memoriam*.

Stravinsky still composes at the piano, but not exclusively, at least not in the preliminary stages. Music paper, or styluses and unlined paper, are close to hand on all of his peregrinations, and he seems to be visited with a great deal of what may or may not be inspiration on airplanes; perhaps the perfect composing conditions for him would be found on an interplanetary flight. Any scrap of paper—bit of an envelope, back of a menu or program, napkin, margin torn from a magazine —will do for notations, which is why the pages of the notebooks in which these sketches are pasted look like collages. Stravinsky dates each sketch and marks each choice of serial route in colored pencils, for the reason, he says, that it is so difficult to check errors otherwise, though obviously it is more than that, being in fact the manifestation of a powerful compulsion for order.

Stravinsky's composing procedures seem not to have changed in late years. He almost always begins with a melodic idea, which in the first writing may be expressed only by its rhythmic values. This single line is frequently extended, in isolation it seems, to a point at which larger shapes become clear to him. The piano is not resorted to in this melody-forging stage, I should add, but only when harmonic and contrapuntal relationships begin to appear; it is then that Stravinsky will say he has invented (*i.e.*, discovered) something which he now intends to compose (*i.e.*, develop). Inventing tends to occur in the mornings, and most intensively toward noon, whereas composition is largely postmeridional; at present Stravinsky leaves his studio before lunch only for a walk, a forbiddingly solitary exercise more for mind-limbering than, as his doctors have ordered, limb-minding. The work of instrumentation has no fixed hours. As soon as a substantial musical unit has been completed in sketch score he will work overtime to finish the orchestra score. This goes at high speed, or as fast as it is possible to write on transparencies; he does not use Xerox or a music typewriter. It is a function of the composer's daughter (another is trimming her father's hair) to arrange for the reproduction of these scores and post them to the publisher, sometimes virtually page by page, for Stravinsky never looks back, afraid perhaps that his Eurydice might disappear. His daughter is also the custodian of all work in progress during her father's absences.

Stravinsky's work goes beyond composing, as concert-goers, record buyers, book-review readers, and TV viewers hardly need to be told. As he has never lacked advocates among performers, and was over forty when he himself began to conduct, the financial motive he advances as the excuse for this career may be accepted, at least in part. Not being able to live on the income from his compositions, he became a summer composer—concert life was much less developed in that season then than now—and a whistle-stop guest conductor and touring recitalist in winter. In late years the concert appearances have been very rare, but they continue, nevertheless, and avowedly for the same reason, though the real one is simply the unrenounceable love of live music-making. In fact, the forty-year habit is impossible to arrest entirely, and the stimulation and pleasure to *him* (at least) from conducting seem visibly to sustain his age.

For a backstage glimpse of Stravinsky on tour I shall try to photograph him in his hotel room at the Lotti, in Paris, where he is reposing before a series of concerts; or, rather, as he dislikes being photographed, I shall attempt to snapshoot the room itself—it also says something about the man. Within a half-hour of occupancy, its character is entirely transformed. The medicines, toiletries, and sacred images neatly set out on the bed table; the clothes tidily piled in dressers and hung in closets; the immaculate arrangement of writing materials, business papers, letter files, dictionaries and other books: all of these exemplify Stravinskian order. The composer's individuating touch is also reflected in his replacement of the "Utrillo" and the "Van Gogh" with pictures from magazines Scotch-taped to the wall; and in the pile of extra pillows on his bed; and in the green beret on the pillows, for he sleeps in this *aficionado*'s headgear as if it were an eighteenth-century nightcap.

The files are extensive and as space-consuming as the books, which fill a small shelf. His daily tally of the economy will include such minute investments as the purchase of a postage stamp, and the medical bookkeeping is even more thorough. His weekly blood tests are recorded, together with a schedule of Sintrom and other anticoagulants which is the composer's lifeline in the most literal sense. His copious correspondence does not go untended during concert tours, either, and although his pen pals may reasonably be suspected of collectors' interests in their in-mail, *he* is rarely the party in arrears. Stravinsky on the road is his own clipping service, too; articles on science, art, archeology, and books are painstakingly scissored out and sorted away, often with initialed comment. But it is disturbing to discover obituaries pasted in the sketch-book calendar of his present work (photographs of Scherchen and Jean Arp were entered there only last week), disturbing to see that death is not only in the composer's everyday thoughts but also close to his creative ones. He appeared at breakfast a few mornings ago saying, "I dreamed I could walk normally again and I saw myself in a crowd keeping pace with everybody else. It was cruel to wake up."

Stravinsky the gourmet is always happy in Paris, though in his favorite restaurants, Ami Louis (the world capital of *foie gras*), the Boule d'Or, the Grand Véfour, the delights of the table are dangerously good. As I write, in fact, the composer's liver is giving him complaint. And no wonder. After unpacking, he sped to the second of these restaurants, ostensibly for its view of an old *quartier*, but was soon seated and consuming crayfish (apparently irresistible to Russians) at an alarming rate. He himself does not attribute his discomfort to gross quantity, however, but rests his diagnosis on a nicer point. As he had been shown the delectable monsters in the kitchen, still in the quick, he now believes that he is being punished for betraying them and for the sin of "eating a creature that one has already met socially." In truth, though, at eighty-four Stravinsky still has some of the appetites of a Pantagruel.

Let us return to the scene of that more permanent work still achieved principally in California. On a good day Stravinsky manages to devote four or five hours to composition, and more than that on week ends when there are fewer interruptions from telephones—which can be expected to split through thoughts and feelings about thirty times a day, normally, and on ten resonant extensions. And there are other rackets: a piano-practicing neighbor, very conscientious at scales; another neighbor, no less dutiful with a bugle and set of "traps"; birds, as dependably melodious in the middle of the night as the Hi-Fi canaries at Forest Lawn; ear-piercing smog-warning sirens (or are they Viet Cong warnings?); and helicopters, for which the Stravinsky residence appears to be an important marker on an aerial freeway. As no one could be more sensitive to these auditory tortures than the composer—he still flinches at any noise a full second faster than anyone else—it is a marvel that he can work at all.

The composer's entertainments are unexceptional. Reading is the most important; he reads as much as a book reviewer, and in range from the classics to the air-mail editions of several foreign weeklies. He seldom braves the cinema any more, but will turn on the "telly" sooner than you can say "Jackie Gleason" (and turn it off even sooner). Diversion is afforded by his flower and fruit gardens, and he takes great pride in, and pretends to prefer, the lemons, oranges, and avocados from his own trees. He is fond of animals, too, and even of the lizards that slither over his preserves in warm weather; I might add that the lullabies of that musical species of lacertilian, frequenting bedroom walls in the Philippines, enchanted him on his visit there, as they horrified me. He also relishes cruising about in one of his (two) Continentals, especially when Madame Stravinsky is at the wheel, for then he can indulge in some back-seat driving.

If I were asked which people share comparatively easy access to Stravinsky at present, I would have to say that Russian-speaking visitors are favored and that time will be found for a

Hurok, a Magaloff, a Joel Spiegelman, an Ussachevsky, an Isaac Stern, a Babin and a Vronsky when it will be denied to others; it is a relaxation for Stravinsky simply to converse in his mother tongue. He has begun to open his doors to historians, too, when their quests have tended to concentrate on his associates and to concern himself only indirectly. He promised, not long ago, to contribute to a BBC television documentary about Diaghilev, and he has recently entrusted his Cocteau material to Francis Steegmuller, whose biographies of Flaubert and Maupassant he admires. But of the old circle of really intimate California friends, only Christopher Isherwood survives.

Have the tempers of the man and his music changed in recent years? The chemical balances are different, to be sure, but more than that is hard to say. Stravinsky was and is an essentially happy spirit. Whereas the majority of his compositions might be described as *divertimenti*, the emotion of only a handful can be called tragic. His most profound moods (not the same as his most profound music) are generally found in his religious works, and it is there, too, that the shift in chemistry is most noticeable: Stravinsky seems to be more exclusively a religious composer now than before. At the same time, the moods of all of his music, the barbaric exuberance, the joking and leg-pulling (there is a fat Rossini imprisoned in this thin man), the exaltation, the anger, serenity (*Apollo*), and gentleness (the lullaby in *Perséphone*)—these cross the boundaries and are discovered in all of his forms. They are expressions of a humanity that has informed not only the musical sensibilities of our age but also its minds and hearts.

(R. C., June 1966)

PART I

Miscellanea

INTERVIEWS

Stravinsky on the Musical Scene and Other Matters

"Where is any certain tune or measured music in notes such as these?" ELIZABETH BARRETT BROWNING

NEW YORK REVIEW OF BOOKS: Did you fly in from California, Mr. Stravinsky? How was it?

I.S.: If you mean Los Angeles, as sunless as a mushroom farm. If the flight, well, at least the Muzak is no longer compulsory, speaking as one who prefers the aching void. But I will not complain about airplanes. I am unable to walk around the block any more, yet I can fly around the world. Some "turbulence" interfered with the in-flight movie, and the pilot made an announcement that has stuck in my mind ever since. He said that the IBM flight plan had chosen 33,000 feet as the favored altitude, but that in his opinion we should be higher. This touchingly obsolete criticism of computer authority shocked me, I confess, and I sincerely hope that the relationships of men and their computerology (and, conversely, the computerology of men and their relationships) become more trusting. Part of my shock may also have come from the contrast of computerized flight control itself, and my memories of the Homeric air age of Saint-Exupéry and his contemporaries, who were guided at times by little more than their own apprehensions. But the principal part was due to the circumstance that in my own work I regard my feelings as more reliable than my calculations.

N.Y.R.: Would you explain the distinction, Mr. Stravinsky?

I.S.: It was probably an empty one or, like the distinctions between analytical and empirical truths and learned and innate behavior, one not admitting of a very sharp line of separation. Our calculations and our feelings obviously overlap, or are congruent. I will persist, nevertheless, and say that I trust my musical glands above the foolproofing of my musical flight charts, although the flight charts are formed in part by the same glands; and add that I prefer to exercise the "free" option of my ear, rather than submit to a punch-card master plan. If, however, I were to assert that the supreme authority of mathematics in the arts at present were the result of a deep-rooted modern superstition, that would be mere *ipse dixit* talk: it says something only about myself. But, now, at my age, that is the kind of talk I prefer. I do not have to use so many escape words, for one thing, and for another, the subject—myself—is closer to home.

N.Y.R.: You have criticized option-of-the-moment arguments in the past, Mr. Stravinsky. Are you reopening the doors?

I.S.: I have criticized them not in composition but in performance—though this is an unacceptable distinction to the "happening" school—and my views on performance have hardened rather than changed. Happenings are compositions too, however, at least in retrospect. Soon someone will discover that they can be more interesting by being compositions before and during their performance as well, with which the cycle can begin all over again with Bach or Tubal Cain. Already the German orchestras are refusing to participate in happenings or perform unwritten or incompletely notated music, though I take this not as a portent of the next step but simply as the reaction of good soldiers in need of explicit orders. What, then, does "next" mean? Even while I am talking the "next" will have become the "former," and conformism is so hot on the heels of the mass-produced avant-gardes that the "ins" and the "outs" change places with the speed of Mach III. Gone are the days when art movements existed together with political ones (and fell with them as, for example, total serialization disappeared with de-Stalinization, and *musique concrète* with the unpersoning of Khrushchev). Who can say, any more, at any exact moment, whether it is Nono who is holding up sinking Venice or the other way around?

N.Y.R.: What is your view of the present state of traditional performance, and how do you think the increased quantity of our music and the greater competition affect qualitative standards?

I.S.: Let me begin with a comment fresh from my own experience. We all know, or should know, that America breeds some of the finest instrumentalists in the world, though the reasons are mysterious, orchestra players being as ill paid on the average as poets or school teachers. This knowledge did not prepare me for the abundance of high-quality performing talent that I have discovered of late on visits to colleges and music schools such as Oberlin, Eastman, the University of Texas. That said, I must add that I found not only talent but a sensible new generation of human beings. Last spring I saw my *Oedipus Rex* produced at an agricultural college in Indiana by students whose other time, for all I know, was occupied with lectures on fertilizer. And only a few weeks ago I heard the Eastman School orchestra play to perfection, on a minimum of rehearsal, some of my most difficult later music, including parts of *The Flood*, which at least one world-renowned professional orchestra could not manage after a week of rehearsals and a dozen performances. The flexibility of the young *versus* the rigidity of the *routiniers* is an old story, of course, but you can hardly imagine the pleasure this student orchestra gave me.

As for quantity, quality, the effects of competition, I suggest that Veblen's classic criticisms of these capitalist concepts may also be applied to music. The prior questions are the same, at any rate. Competition to what end? What standards, and in what ways are they improved? I have just heard a conductor improve a work of mine with beauty treatments, daubing the music with lipstick and smothering it with face powder. Such things are both a form and result of competition, but of conductors' competition about conducting, or call it the performance of performance: they are in no wise a musical matter. In recent years the performance of performance has developed to such an extent that it challenges the music itself and even threatens it with relegation. I have seen performances (of performance) as fully worked out as a sonata, as neatly contrived as a fugue. The new conductor, X, for example, controls every stage of the operation as completely as a cradle-to-grave social-welfare plan, from the first entrance exuding just the right amount of artistic mystique to the final few dozen exhausted bows. I will not attempt to describe the performance that X employs with the music except to say that its most winning features are a crucifixion, the extended arms motionless, the hands limp in frozen passion; a pelvic thrust, used at climaxes and coordinated with a throwing back of the head; and a great deal of profile work, not just *toward* the first violins but beyond them and out to the audience. Most of the other repertory is composed of stock mirror-the-music '"expression movements" (Lorenz's

term for the same thing in goose ethology), but another in-
novation is promised before the show reaches Broadway, and
according to rumor it will be handstands during inverted
counterpoint. Yet the high point is none of these but the
after-performance performance. It begins with a tableau
modeled on the Descent from the Cross. The arms are life-
less, the knees bent, the head (hair artfully mussed) is low,
and the whole corpse itself is bathed in perspiration (warm
water, one suspects, squirted from hidden atomizers). The
first step down from the podium just fails to conceal a totter,
but in spite of that the miracle worker somehow manages to
reappear forty-six times. It *is* a great performance, too, and
could be topped as an advertisement only by skywriting.
Only a musician would not be swept away by it.

N.Y.R.: What new music have you heard recently, Mr. Stravinsky?

I.S.: New to me was the *Fanciulla del West,* a remarkably
up-to-date TV horse opera, with a Marshall Dillon and professional Indians like the lobby Indians in the Fonda Hotel at
Santa Fe. These aborigines are characterized, if you can call
it that, by some ineffectual reminiscences of Debussy, but
most of the score is back in the land of *Butterfly:* the opera
is really an Eastern Western. No matter what the geography,
the music—self-parodying arias, a Roxy Theater overture—is
bad, and plain bad, not interestingly bad. Why? The absence
of people with whom the composer could identify (they
could not identify themselves, for sure)? The unsuitability
of the subject to that genius of sentimentality which in *La
Bohème* is so perfectly matched to the dramatic substance and
so superbly deployed that even I leave the theater, when I
can get a ticket, humming my lost innocence? The one conspicuous success in the *Fanciulla,* however, is the attempt to
make it American—*i.e.,* simple-minded. This is achieved by

having the gold miners sing in unison and by repeating a Grofé-type trot rhythm to the point of incandescence.

No doubt you mean newer music that that, but I am so out of touch I can scarcely tell a musical mobile from a musical stabile, let alone distinguish their splinter groups. I only hear what comes my way, moreover, and that is rarely of my own choosing. *Couleurs de la cité céleste* came my way recently. It seemed to have been inspired by J. Arthur Rank, and its *force de frappe* is so great I wonder the marimbas, xylophones, cymbals, and gongs did not collapse from metal fatigue. At about the same time I heard the same composer's *La Rousserolle effarvatte*, which proposes to do for the Reed Warbler (twenty-four hours in the life of) something of what Joyce did for Bloom. (Well, I heard *some* of it.)

I attended a program of electronic music, too, but only one composition seemed to exist in and because of the medium, the others being translations, of which the best I can say is that they probably would have sounded still worse in their native tongues. The very thought of the paper work involved in fabricating these noises depresses me, for though I can sympathize with a Van Eyck laboring for months, with the aid of a magnifying glass, to paint a beetle (and my sympathy is *not* for the reason that he didn't just drip or blot), I cannot understand musical composition that takes place outside of music. Better, now and then, one of those exhibitions of Anti-Music, though I have also failed to keep in touch with developments in that department, if there are any; the only sounds (at least) that reach me are the breast-beating and ax-grinding of the Anti-Musician claqueurs themselves.

I have lately been exposed to an amount of window-dressing new music by Polish composers, and can report that its surface qualities are often attractive, for example in Tadeusz Baird's unprovoking (in the sense of the title) *Erotica;* here feelings seem to have entered into calculations. More recently I have heard some striking scores by new French composers:

Guézec's *Architectures colorées,* Éloy's *Équivalences,* Gilbert Amy's double-orchestra *Antiphonies.* There is a new French School, and a good one, judging by levels of skill. Boulez is its father figure, naturally, though he has steered further and further away from the question of Dada.

One of my two most impressive recent musical experiences —the other was *Jacob's Ladder*—I owe to the late Noah Greenberg and the tapes of polyphonic singing recorded by him in mountain villages near Tiflis. Greenberg's discovery of an active performing tradition of music ranging from tenth-century conductus and organum to High Renaissance was a major find, contributions to performance knowledge being even more valuable than acquisitions of more music, and this time the line *can* be drawn. The yodeling, *kriman-chuli* as it is called in Georgian, in the performance of *trecento* hockets, is one of the most virile vocal performances I have ever heard. This exhumed treasure, being both foreign and religious in origin (and therefore embarrassing to progressive historicism), and polyphonic (and therefore subversive), is unwelcome in the Soviet Union, needless to say, and unlikely to be preserved. It will no doubt be ploughed under again for good and replaced by Moscow-manufactured party-slogan songs. The decline of culture, in musical terms—if you will pardon my own simplistic historicism—is the devolution from polyphony to monophony.

Hollywood, California
1 April 1969

To The EDITOR
The *Composer*

Sir:

I have just read Mr. Geoffrey Bush's "footnote" to my *Dialogues and A Diary,*[1] in the Autumn number of the *Com-*

---

[1] Faber edition, 1968.

poser. Mr. Bush says that a "point of considerable musico-ethnological interest is involved," and he offers "to try to put the record straight."

In fact Mr. Bush's elaborations have little to do with musico-ethnology. What does concern him is my attribution to the late Noah Greenberg of a "discovery," near Tiflis, of "an active performing tradition of music ranging from 10th century conductus and organum to High Renaissance." That my word was misleading, Mr. Bush's misconstructions prove. But surely Mr. Bush is being wilfully naïve in taking it to mean universally unknown, and in supposing that I had thought an Intourist could be in a position to uncover anything of so unsecretive a nature not already known at least *in* the USSR. (In fact I had heard of the existence of the tradition during my visit to the USSR in 1962.) Mr. Greenberg's discovery was purely his own, obviously, and that of the other musicians with whom he shared it on his return to New York.

Now Mr. Bush supplies a new link, explaining that Mr. Greenberg's discovery was the result of his encounter with Mr. Bush and Mr. John Gardner, two "much less interesting curiosities" (Mr. Bush's phrase) than the music itself. Messrs. Bush and Gardner had merely invited Mr. Greenberg to, well, "tag along" and hear the music with them. I cannot think why Mr. Greenberg failed to mention Messrs. Bush and Gardner to me, but clearly no slight was intended.

Yet Mr. Bush's assumptions do not "set the record straight." One obstacle is that they are not exhaustively logical. He asserts that Greenberg "cannot have discovered and transmitted to Stravinsky anything that the three of us had not already heard; for Stravinsky's remarks are an exact description of the music which had been played on tape and performed for us that morning . . ." Then what about the music I did *not* describe?

Nor do I understand why Mr. Bush is so nicely precise

about matters of which he is not certain—saying that the claim of the "discovery" was "not necessarily advanced by Greenberg himself" (then by whom?)—but so casual about the New York Pro Musica Antiqua: the statement that "Greenberg had with him a party of singers and instrumentalists" sounds more like a reference to Mr. Greenberg's namesake in the train of the Duke of Mantua.

What Mr. Greenberg *did* say, to the best of my recollection, was that the music performed by his New York group, and the resemblances noted in it to the music of the local tradition, had excited the interest of Georgian musicians. Then, as I understood it, after his concerts Mr. Greenberg and two or three members of his ensemble were taken to villages near Tiflis, where they performed for the villagers and the villagers for them.

But my recollection is rickety, and it is several years since Mr. Greenberg played his tapes for me. In fact I would be inclined to believe in Mr. Bush's doubts and call the story a daydream, except for one circumstance: I am positive that my wife and Mr. Greenberg compared notes about two villages near Tiflis in which she had lived and which Mr. Greenberg most certainly had visited.

Mr. Bush cavils at the "anti-Soviet inferences drawn from the episode by Stravinsky" (they were drawn from a great many other episodes as well, of course), though he finds them natural for a "White Russian" with a "built-in prejudice against Soviet Communism"—as if it were possible to be unprejudiced about Soviet Communism, and as if the classification accounted for my emigration, for artistic reasons, long before the existence of a White Russia. "As anyone at all familiar with the USSR knows," he continues, "it is Party policy to stimulate . . . manifestations of local culture." I daresay I am "at all" familiar with the USSR, but apart from that, Mr. Bush's contention is by no means self-evident, as he seems to think; in fact, *pace* Mr. Bush, the USSR's policy of *suppressing* manifestations of religious culture (notoriously of late in the case of the Jews) would be, I think, far more generally conceded.

As it happened, only shortly before I heard the tapes, Mr. George Balanchine had visited his brother, the Georgian composer, in Tiflis, and Mr. Balanchine's expression of his views on his return undoubtedly influenced my own remarks. As a native Georgian, Mr. Balanchine is at least as prejudiced as I am, or as Mr. Bush is. Which is why his report, reflected by me, of the intense dislike of many Georgians for a Party policy many of them described to him as one of cultural containment is as valid (insofar as opinions of the sort have any validity) as Mr. Bush's impressions of beneficent Soviet stimulation.

May I add that not long before his death, Mr. Greenberg gave me some additional tapes of the music, and that my pleasure was as great at the later date as at the time of the first experience.

Respectfully yours,

Igor Stravinsky

Igor Stravinsky

Jacob's Ladder is described as a "sketch" and a "torso," and both words are correct but misleading. The notes are Schoenberg's but not the color, though enough of that, too, is the composer's own to guide the mixtures by another hand. Where the instrumentation *was* completed by Schoenberg, as in the latter part of the music of "One Dying," the difference is enormous. It follows, then, that when the composer's instrumental indications are sparse, as in the music of "One Wrestling," the realization is hopelessly conventional and the rate of change in orchestral combinations too slow. There are some obviously wrong interpretations, too, as in the accompaniment to the word *Rhythmus* at the end of the music of "One of the Called"; here the voice-leading indicates that the same timbre could not have been intended for both the top line at the beginning of the measure and the third line at the end of it. Yet in spite of the orchestration and the incompleteness, the existing segment is a peak of our music.

The multiple orchestras and speaking choruses are responsible for a great deal of special-pleading Schoenberg Crusade talk about the prophetic nature of the score, but the reincorporation of tonality, which Schoenberg himself had excommunicated eight years earlier, is more remarkable. The association of tonality with the words of "The Indifferent" and "The Resigned" is pointed, of course, but tonality is integrated in other places as well, and throughout the score, while octave doublings occur regularly and in parallel form, as in the introduction to Gabriel's speech "This Either or this Or." Whether or not in consequence of these levities, the harmony is exceedingly rich. *Die glückliche Hand*, together with the *Four Orchestral Songs*, supplies a rudimentary context for the opening, but Schoenberg does not tarry at past points of connection, and the music unfolds in continuous upward progression until, on the threshold of a new world of sound, the manuscript comes to an end. (At this juncture Franz Joseph had gained a conscript.)

❋ ❋ ❋

N.Y.R.: You said it was easier to talk about yourself, Mr. Stravinsky. May I ask what it is like to be eighty-four?

I.S.: There is no triumph in it, I can tell you, and hardly any exhilaration. I am forgetful, repetitive, and slightly deaf, for which reasons I read more than I talk, and prefer Russian-language conversation. *When* I talk, therefore, I talk too much, as you see, which is an irony, because I do not believe in words, as I believe in music, and if I had the power would erase all of my own. A still greater difficulty is the diminishing of my working day. My working speed has not slackened, I think, but the time allotted to it, due to the slower tempo of all of my other activities, and to the greater demands on my time from lawyers, merchants, and doctors, evaporates more quickly. I suffer from polycythemia, and am obliged to have a blood test every seventh day, as well as bleedings— shades of the eighteenth-century barber shop—every two months. The containment of the disease by radioactive phosphorus is no longer safe in my case, but I used to swallow capsules of this alarming substance in a glass of fizz that was fed to me from lead-tipped calipers held by a technician in an asbestos suit and a mask like a bee keeper's. The cycle of the thickening and thinning of my blood has imposed a rhythm on my temperament, and on my whole creative life.

I suffer, too, as never before and as I have never admitted, from my musical isolation, being obliged to live now at a detached and strictly mind level of exchange with younger people who profess to wholly different belief systems. I am also, and for the first time in my life, bothered by a feeling of loneliness for my generation. All of my contemporaries are dead. It is not so much old friends or individuals, nevertheless, and certainly not the mentality of my generation, that I regret, but the background as a whole, and the habits of the home, and even the social intercourse. This homesickness is very recent, I should add; until a decade ago I fled at the mention of Russia and from every reminder of the past.

N.Y.R.: What do you mean by your musical isolation, Mr. Stravinsky? No composer in musical history has had a greater influence, received wider recognition, been more widely and frequently performed in his lifetime. Is there no triumph in that? And have you never felt the sense, not of isolation but of the very opposite, namely, that you as much as anyone in the world are in powerful communication?

I.S.: Thank you, but I can hardly afford to see myself in that light. And my catalog of past works does not interest me as much as my present work, which the catalog tends to over-shadow and for which, in any case, it has never earned me any credit cards. Certainly it is gratifying to see loudly con-demned new scores such as *Agon* and the *Movements* quietly taking their place among earlier regularly performed ones, but I do not think of it as a victory. And what I meant by isolation was at the professional level. I do not regret not belonging to a movement, still less the failure of the music I now compose to answer to any commercial demand. But I would like to exchange more than a few rapidly crossing glimpses with my colleagues, and as it is now, I see eye to eye with no one.

N.Y.R.: Surely this is the result only of your own eminence, Mr. Stravinsky.

I.S.: To hell with eminence! I can hardly cross the street any more without a convoy, and I am stared at wherever I go like an idiot member of a royal family or an animal in a zoo; zoo animals, by the way, have been known to die from stares. "This is probably the last time we will see *him*," the eyes all seem to say, though I dare say a few of those onlookers may go on a bit ahead. A limbo of uncertainty surrounds any name that has been around as long as mine has, and if the middle-aged are unsure, hearing it, whether it belongs to someone still in the quick, young people must assume auto-matically that a man with my *fin de siècle* connections would naturally be dead.

N.Y.R.: What did you mean, a moment ago, by saying you do not believe in words? Is it a question of their exactness?
I.S.: Rather their metaphoricalness. They are not so much an-other form of notation as an irrelevant and unedifying form. Sometimes I feel like those old men Gulliver encounters in the *Voyage to Laputa*, who have renounced language and who

try to converse by means of objects. (See Ruesch and Kees: *Non-Verbal Communication.*) A composer is always in that position, having no verbal control over his music. He tries to talk about it in graphs, symbolic codings, and other devices, which may be more efficient—they are certainly more trenchant—than his statements in ordinary verbal syntax, but which bring him no nearer to the music. The only true comment on a piece of music is another piece of music.

N.Y.R.: May we ask what you are working on now, Mr. Stravinsky?

I.S.: I can give you no more than a label; as I have just explained, the music says what it is and I am unable to enter my work with words. In fact I have just completed the *Rex Tremendae* of my pocket *Requiem.* I call it that both because I use only fragments of the text, and interlard them with instrumental music (though there is precious little lard in it), and because most of it was composed in notebooks which I carry in my pockets. But I am superstitious and do not like to talk about any work in progress, let alone a monument ordered, like Mozart's, by a "mysterious stranger." I will be greatly relieved to be done with it and get on to something else.

At times during the composition I have been comforted by the knowledge that my great-grandfather lived to 111. And I have wondered what he was like at 84. He did not compose music, I know, but—so family tradition goes—he was doing something very like it, which is making love. In fact, the old gentleman, bless his hormones, died in consequence of a fall while he was trying to scale a garden fence on his way to a rendezvous. What a way to go! as the Americans say. Better yet, what a time of life to go that way.

I.S.

March, 1966

Music and the Statistical Age

COMMENTARY: How do you view the statistical life generally, Mr. Stravinsky?

I.S.: With misgivings. But I have not arrived at anything so solid as a view, being at best dimly, and not for that reason unprejudicially, aware of certain effects of the quantifications of society that have already taken place. The quantifying of the entire mental world that is now in store, and that supposes a new type of mind, or way of thinking, is a development I am powerless to imagine. Still, the incapacity for it has not prevented the question from invading my mind a good deal of late.

c.: Why "of late"?

I.S.: It is difficult to say for certain. Small encroachments of statistical philosophy take place all the time, but we notice them, concern ourselves with them, only when we suddenly notice that a new area has fallen. It was like that with automation. I had read about it inattentively during the last few years, then a month or so ago some firsthand experience jolted me like a judo throw. This occurred, surprisingly, in a tatty, down-at-the-heel Midwestern hotel. I called to order my *petit déjeuner* before going to bed and was answered by a recorded Mother Superior voice: "This is your breakfast robot. After you hear the dial tone please give your name, room number, breakfast order, the time you wish it served. . . . beeep." A silence followed, just long enough—it was sealed by a terminal "beeep"—to encompass a statistically averaged recitation of the requested facts from a properly organized customer. But I could not remember the sequence of the questions, did not *know* my room number, neglected to say how to prepare the eggs, forgot to specify the time of service.

Moreover, that final "beeep" so exasperated me that when I did get "organized" I promptly recorded an order for two hundred pieces of burned toast to be sent to the three hundredth floor at 4 A.M., which is "feedback" with a vengeance.

c.: But do you not believe that improved automation techniques directed by ever more sophisticated tools of statistical analysis can effect a more efficient channeling of resources?

I.S.: I can say that recent errors in my bank statements have promoted no confidence on at least *this* individual level. We should of course expect more equal distribution of certain kinds of wealth, in the totally synthetic civilization of the totally automated future; and a consequent rise in the living conditions of so-called under-privileged peoples; and improvements in everyone's animal living habits, as the new science of ergonomics promises (see the survey just published at Cornell on the mutual misfitting of the human anatomy and most bathroom appliances); and new techniques of conservation (not merely blood banks everywhere, but banks of frozen superior sperm as well, though to me this sounds depressingly like the whaling industry, in spite of the one-sided amusement that the banking process may afford the eugenically selected depositors). Nor are some of the new kinds of mentalizing efficiency difficult to imagine, the propensities of the literature of our own period being clear enough in such current bestsellers as *The Cybernetics of Sexual Positions in Relation to Socio-Economic Status.*

But I wonder about that new mind. Will it, in turn, conform to its own statistical findings? More people than Francesca and Paolo have been seduced by books, after all. We know from nation-wide demonstrations, too, that trend analyses of vote tabulations in the Eastern States are able to influence voters in the Western time zones. Even from this example, supported by, as in my case, a stealthy skepticism of most individual judgment and, correspondingly, an infinite faith in the powers of statistical persuasion, wish-imagining suggestibility, mass attraction, it is possible to envision the future. In fact, one foresees the statistical philosophy becoming more and more circular, untidy figures being polished and rounded out, and trends being pushed to their conclusions, "to make the crooked straight" ever having been one of the most ruthlessly compulsive propositions in the history of our ethical geometries. Thus when people are being informed by their statisticians that they might be developing cancer at a certain age—unless they have already died from the effects of strontium 90 at an earlier age—will they not, poor lemmings, do their best to oblige?

One also wonders about the faculty of observation when exact prediction is a rule of life. Won't the observing mechanisms occupy an ever smaller place in that new mind, on the analogy from physics according to which prediction by mathematical theory can precede observation, as in Yukawa's discovery of one of the meson-type particles? (This is simply so much prattle on my part, of course, for I know nothing about such matters myself, and in fact still think sequentially, as the McLuhanites describe certain until-recently-respectable mental operations.)

c.: What will be the effects of quantification in music, Mr. Stravinsky?

i.s.: It will come to the same thing: on the one hand, greater efficiency in such useful but peripheral endeavors as the computation of all sound elements, the discovery of a precise and economical notation, the formulation of a statistical musical theory equipped with a tangible terminology; and, on the other, the control at the heart of the matter by a statistical conformism, whose measurements will be stamped in the structure of that new mind. But I am crystal-gazing again, and I have no gift for it. Unlike those shades in the Tenth Canto who see the past and the future but *not* the present, I see only the present. Besides, what I wished to suggest was that a backward look might be more instructive. Statistical philosophy in music seems to have been discovered some sixty years ago by Ives.

c.: Have you heard Ives's Fourth Symphony yet, Mr. Stravinsky?

i.s.: Yes, with considerable but uneven interest. Ives was not a symphonist; the *Three Places in New England* are more of an entity than any of the symphonies, besides which they contain much better music than the Third and more consistently good music than the Fourth. But the second movement of the Fourth is an astonishing achievement. The inclusiveness which is at the root of Ives's genius ("all things in their variety," as he quoted Emerson) reaches saturation point in these seemingly free-for-all pages; "seemingly" because while this or that tune suddenly bursts out for no other apparent reason than *joie de vivre*, it cannot be extricated from the skein of the composition. But I will say no more. I know too little of this no doubt soon-to-be-overrated composer, who was exploring the 1960's during the heyday of Debussy. Polytonality; atonality; tone clusters; tone rows; multiple orchestras; perspectivistic effects; micro-intervals; chance; statistical composition; permutation; rhythmic dimensions that maintain a lead on the avant-garde even now; add-a-part, practical-joke, and improvisatory music: these were Ives's discoveries, patented by the silence of the musical world of a half-century ago; in fact, he quietly set about devouring the contemporary cake before anyone else had even found a seat at the same table. But to me personally these innovations are of less moment than my discovery in him of a new awareness of America.

c.: What was this discovery, Mr. Stravinsky? And since you have lived almost as long here as in Russia, and longer here than in Western Europe, would you tell us some of your feelings about us? Do you have any sense of identification with America? What in America do you like most and dislike most?

I.S.: Identification, yes, but I am not certain where and how it obtains. I feel no identity with the military version of the Manifest Destiny, and therefore no sympathy with the victims of peace scares (*i.e.*, stock-market investors), but as I do not wish to provoke a visit from the CIA, I will heed the advice of the Devil in my opera when he says, "Let us not speak of that." I do not identify with American music either, close as I have felt to individual American composers, and at one time to musical life in America. The American music that attracts me most is the kind that does not try too hard to promote itself as homespun. Yet Ives was written off as Americana precisely by the colonials of "neo-classicism" and the "12-tone system," and he seems to have survived only by crawling into that interesting New England woodwork.

But I am at a loss to describe that personal discovery and can only point to a vague general direction. Some of Ives's music has told me more about what I think of as a distinctly American feeling of isolation than either Whitman or *Walden*, Miss Dickinson or Tuckerman (who felt "the dark wind strain"), or the outdoor novelists whom I used to read in France. The qualities of it, like the dominant qualities of Ives, are alien to me, but they are an identifying link all the same, as I realize in Europe where differences of culture bring previously unnoticed feelings into relief. In Europe, nowadays, I often feel that I belong to the American side, and I even admit to brief onsets of topographical nostalgia there, though more for the reflections of clouds on tall glass buildings on Park Avenue, than for those Midwestern parallelogram cities designed to be passed straight through. But to return to Ives, I think the time has come to turn criticism around and rather than continue to emphasize his isolation, consider his share in the ideas of the century.

As for the compilation of my likes and dislikes, that would merely constitute a string of disembodied prejudices. I could say, for instance, that a salutation last year by the Mayor of Muncie (Indiana) touched me more than that of an eminent European Minister of Culture, because, the degree of musical innocence being equal in both, it seemed more excusable in the former. Then to tip the argument the other way, I could protest the American demolition mania, that neurotic need, now in peak phase (I hope), to repudiate the past. Some of the destruction, including the impending demise of the Metropolitan Opera House, the laying of whose cornerstone postdates my own birth, strikes me as a personal offense. Not that I had very fond feelings for the Met, but now that it is empty I feel as if a part of New York itself had died, and that a junior colleague has disappeared.

c.: And the *new* Metropolitan, Mr. Stravinsky, what do you foresee for it?

i.s.: Difficulties. It has lost most of its aura, a large part of its alibi, and practically all of its identity. But what *are* the reasons for centralizing a city's art commodities into shopping centers, or, in a word, supermarketing the arts? Is no one afraid that, lumped together, the characters of the individual institutions will tend to blur? And since when has environmental diversity been a discredited idea?

c.: Do you feel the same way about the Kennedy Arts Center?

i.s.: I have no feelings about it, but I foresee huge buildings— the more marginal the contents of the art, the larger and more stolid the containers—tumbled about like blocks in low-scoring Stanford-Binet tests. The two largest of them must inevitably be the "Research Laboratory for the Readjustment of Acoustics in New Concert Halls," and the "Hall of Fame for Heroes of Public Relations"—impresarios, patronesses, orchestra conductors, and other *maîtres d'hôtel* of the arts who have won or purchased a momentary place in the annals of publicity, and are here paid off with monuments in appropriately "soft sculpture" (doomed to dissolution if the air conditioning should fail). In short, the art centers emphasize performance and exhibition at the expense of making and creating. And that is the last sour note, toned down as it is, I intend to blow today (though I cannot guarantee not to backslide). For a minority group of one I am much too vocal.

c.: To return to the question of the new media, Mr. Stravinsky, won't they offer new resources as well?

i.s.: So one would expect. But I am not convinced that greater resources are what is needed. It seems to me that the possibilities are already rich enough, or too rich. A good artist will not be stopped by a want of resources, which are in the man himself, in any case, and which time makes new every day. The so-called crisis of means is interior.

c.: Lévi-Strauss observed recently that "if electronic musicians sought to understand what music is instead of trying to produce it, we would make tremendous progress toward solving the problem which music sets the science of man."

i.s.: Electronic musicians, at least the ones I know, are not unconcerned about the nature of music, but they would scarcely think of turning to the philosophy and science of what they are doing instead of just doing it, definitions of art being not only of no use to artists but possibly some encumbrance. I would expect in my own case that when the computer had quantified my musical characteristics I would try to avoid them, and though I think I can survive the exposure, I do not welcome it. Lévi-Strauss's inquiries should be supported to the full. He is the first major philosopher to have understood that the true position of music is at the center of human culture.[1]

c.: Do you agree with Messiaen that Nature (he writes it in upper case)—its sounds, colors, forms, rhythms—is the composer's supreme resource?

i.s.: Only if you allow the word the scope of the small *n:* the large one signifies a mere countryside or landscape, personal perhaps, but not new in kind. In fact, Messiaen's *oiseaux exotiques* differ only in genus, not in musical intention, from Beethoven's homely cuckoo. This is not to deny the legitimacy of Messiaen's imitations, or the fertility, to him, of "Natural" resources. What I do say is that no matter how faithful these imitations may be, they are necessarily expressed in, cannot escape being contained by, the harmony, rhythm, instrumental color, and volume—on which I lay some stress in Messiaen's case—of the contemporary musical language.

c.: Do you think of art and nature as two realities? Do you believe in transmutations of the one into the other?

i.s.: There are any number of realities, dualisms, pluralisms; concepts of this sort can be set up merely by installing the convincing word-furniture in the available empty idea-flat. For me, music is reality, as I have said before, and like Baudelaire, but unlike Messiaen, "*J'aime mieux une boîte à musique qu'un rossignol.*" As for transmutation, I do not admit the idea because I am unable to understand what the cognates would be. Obviously the phenomenal world is refractable in music, or represented in it. My point is simply that I don't understand the mirroring, or transforming, chemistry. (Try Lévi-Strauss.) It must also be obvious that composers are partly formed by interactions of choice with the

---

[1] I first met Lévi-Strauss during the war, incidentally, when he was cultural *conseiller* in New York, attached to the French Embassy.

phenomenal world, and no less obvious that the entelechy of these individual choices has made them different composers. But my picture of the phenomenal world, as citizen if not as artist, probably differs in no very significant way from that of other scientific illiterates; or perhaps I should say that while the differences are comprehensive, the resemblances conform in enough "gritty" facts to permit the establishment of a statistical society—which brings us back to our starting point.

c.: What has been your experience of the generation gap, Mr. Stravinsky?

i.s.: The long-haired ephebes attract me, but I am too square to belong to their Big Daddy elect myself. And what is so new about the Age War? Isn't it a tendency of old people of all periods to see everything absolutely and too moralistically, and haven't they always narrowed the issues to their own ever-shortening sight? Haven't they—we—always been puzzled by the enthusiasms of the young for things that we have outgrown, and no less puzzled by their lack of sympathy for things that we continue to feel enthusiastic about but that the *times* have outgrown? I wonder if any aged person has voiced the feelings of the old more honestly than Tolstoy. Here is an observation by him quoted in Anatol Koni's memoirs (*Vospominaniya O Pisatiliach*, Leningrad, 1965), and it speaks for me as well: "Old people dislike the fact that young people talk so much and seem to know so much without having had their experience."

c.: Generally, as well as in your own case, Mr. Stravinsky, is it more difficult to compose music now than ever before?

i.s.: It is certainly more difficult now, and it always was. Speaking for myself, I can say that my ideas come as fluently as ever, and even that my new opus promises to be the most easily digestible of all my recent music; it was *not* easier to compose, and in fact the difficulties in manipulating two series were sometimes extremely inconvenient. At the same time, as the form is that of a *retablo* of small panels, rather than a large-scale fresco, I did not have to carry a large plan about with me but could work in small doses and tap my "inspiration"—which is portable, whatever else—only when it seemed full. I am able to appraise music, while I compose it, only on a technical level, however, and am no evaluator of my functioning mind.

c.: Have other composers written music of value at your age, Mr. Stravinsky?

I.S.: Schütz was older, supposedly, when he wrote the *Requiem*, and Richard Strauss was a year older when he composed the last songs. But your wording implies that *my* new music has value, and I am grateful for the confidence, though unable to participate in judgments about it (which does *not* mean that I am willing to entrust them to a Professor Auld Lang Syne). Men of my age are touchy and vain of their hoard of years, you see, and probably thirstier for meeds of praise than they will admit. They like to see themselves as the end of culture, too, and to dramatize themselves as the last defenders of true art—in a tone, furthermore, which suggests that their own passing is likely to bring on a winter of Pleistocene duration. Perhaps I have nurtured some such stage conception, with a Lear-like part for myself as "the last composer who does it all alone, without an orchestrator, even without a computer." But a "beware" to whoever else sees me that way. There may be a song or two yet to come before the one which will be called my "swan."

I.S.

June, 1966

Stravinsky at Eighty-five

"I turned the tuneful art
From sounds to things . . ."
An Essay on Man

N EW YORK REVIEW OF BOOKS: We read that you had canceled your European tour, Mr. Stravinsky: I hope not because
of illness?

I.S.: Not illness, thank you, though if I sneeze nowadays you
may count on the newspapers reporting it. In fact I have just
returned from a concert tour, a *via dolorosa* further darkened
by some unscheduled glimpses of the Culture Explosion (the
violent arts), in so far as this phenomenon may be said to have
reached Miami, Beverly Hills, Seattle, and Honolulu.

N.Y.R.: What were the local detonations like?

I.S.: Pfft. Miami might at least be expected to possess a first-
rate orchestra. But nothing in the city seems to be propitious
to the arts, apart from the hotel I stayed in, which had a
Venus de Milo with the arms restored. Certainly the sun-
worshipping life—the entire population looks as if it had been
fried in butter—is against it, and so, apparently, are the
musicians themselves, a description that in some cases appeared
to mean anyone with the knowledge that a violin is more or
less held under the chin.

   Nor did a sampling of the condition of culture in Beverly
Hills force the imagination to travel as far as Florence or
Athens in search of adequate comparisons, even though it did
make me change one of my own tunes. Heretofore I have
belabored the policy of building more and bigger halls for
bad and worse performances. Now I say, at least *halls*. The

boudoir-pink ballroom of the Beverly Hilton was an absurd environment for *The Rite of Spring,* and the switching off of the lights while I conducted—it did not help that the music we fizzled through during the blackout was the *Fireworks*— made a concentrated performance even less possible. The management must have thought that the long overdue air raid had finally begun.

In Seattle, my *Histoire du soldat* was embellished with panel backdrops by Saul Steinberg, but they were indecipherable without telescopes beyond the first row. Even on stage I had to squint to make out the pagoda-like first scene (Vietnam?), while the Soldier—who may have had weak eyes, since he was surprisingly ready to weep, a degree of fortitude being expected in his profession—seemed baffled by the "Royal Palace" at a distance of only a few feet. (A penthouse? condominium? space needle?)

N.Y.R.: And Honolulu?

I.S.: I enjoyed it more than my last trip there, which was in 1959, shortly before the islands became a state. There were annoying airport formalities then, including a health inspection for which I tried to look sober and refrain from blowing my nose, but the standards must have been extremely low: the inspector strode by so quickly that he could have noticed no more than whether anyone was actually dead or unusually green. The new state is easier to enter, in spite of the strangulation and asphyxiation threats from the *leis* of the hula welcoming committees. And once it is entered, the only perils, that I was aware of at least, are those of the deep. I watched a "native" fisherman haul in a net of crustaceans at the very place where I had been dipping my toes an hour before, but in Hilton's Honolulu even the crabs could be smarmy; besides, the scene was too picturesque: the catch was probably planted.

There is a pineapple problem, too. It is practically impossible to obtain any form of food unmixed with *ananas* (the French sounds like a Biblical sin). Nine days passed before I found an unpatriotic waiter to whom I could risk saying: "Now take this ten-dollar bribe and please try, this once, to smuggle the spaghetti in without any pineapple." The day I visited Pearl Harbor, incidentally, the tourists were mostly Japanese, which made me wonder about the monuments our descendants will be visiting in Hanoi in another twenty-five years. "Ah, so, Perarber, Perarber," they were saying, wistfully as it seemed to me, though I doubt we can expect a film *Pearl Harbor, Mon Amour*.

N.Y.R.: What did you think of the "mod" *Rake's Progress* in Boston last month?

I.S.: I didn't see it, but I gather that the opera was able to sustain the "mod" apparatus, and I have even heard that the staging and the music managed to turn each other a few compliments. I also noted a change in the press: no more rallying behind the idiotic prejudice that the conventional must be the feelingless, and the experimental the expressive. It is obvious of course that leather jackets and motorcycles, psychedelic and strobe lighting, Stravinsky sweatshirts and discothèque dancing, pin-ups of Allen Ginsberg and Tim Leary in the Rake's pad (is *he* queer?), have no connection with the opera, although mutability *is* one of its themes. But I would have objected to them only if they destroyed the intimacy of the music. (I suppose the argument *for* them was that as the music parodies and time-travels, why not the surroundings?) The staging was said to offer a novel solution to the problem of Baba the Turk, and on that account I regret not having seen it: Baba opens the opera's largest credibility gap. The motivation for the Rake's marriage to this "freak of nature," namely freedom from "the twin tyrants of appetite and conscience," can seem a little makeshift, and the absence at this point of any thought of his betrothed may appear a little unlikely. "Do you desire her [Baba]?" asks Shadow. "Like the falling sickness," answers the Rake. "Then marry her," Shadow rejoinders, and his words provoked a scream from a woman in one of the audiences, an effect that could be written into the score. After being sold as an object at auction, Baba reappeared, like a *dea ex machina,* on closed-circuit TV. Her revelation in Act II was staged in rain, moreover, which justifies the brevity of the scene, and allows for the display of some pretty brollies.

N.Y.R.: Your basso profundo has been rather noticeably absent from the cheering section of the culture boom, Mr. Stravinsky.

I.S.: That is because the cultural prosperity, like the missile-rattling economic prosperity, seems to me inflated, naïvely quantitative, misdirected in emphasis. The inescapable illustration is the reopening, in flashier quarters, of the very old Met. Here, one would have supposed, was yet another platinum opportunity to overrate the growth of the arts in America. This time, too, the cover stories could be devoted to a real, live, local artist, instead of the usual paeans for tax-deducting patrons, and budget figures for the gross national product. Mr. Barber *had* been entrusted with the baptismal score, after all, and he *was* the maker in the musical community, which includes the operatic community, no matter how low the present musical standards of opera. What Mr. Bing and the anonymous middle-opinion glossies knew, and were not saying, was that Mr. Barber had been chosen for a sacrificial role by the same people (namely themselves) who had pampered him in the days when his brand of music had not yet become bad news. The Great Society being short of great composers, he alone satisfied the indispensable requirements of being at the same time home-grown, well-known, efficient and reliable, and unnoticeable in musical tendency; in short, he could be counted on not to divert publicity from the house, the staff, and the social event, or otherwise detract from the occasion.

What I find more difficult to explain is the installation of Mr. Bing as a culture hero, not *how* it came about, of course—he has virtually no competition—but *why*. Why mythologize an artistic director who denies the possibility of a new opera, as his commissions for the new house show; who supports the now generally discredited star system, which in effect contradicts the idea, at last gaining circulation elsewhere, that opera is drama; and who keeps the tiniest inventory of operas of any company of its class in the world? Mr. Bing disingenuously justifies his repertory as box-office taste, knowing full well that taste must be created, and anyway, that a good salesman should be able to sell good merchandise as well as bad. With the advent of new interest in Wagner wouldn't a new *Tristan* better have befitted the celebrations of the new house than the revival of a moth-eaten comedy like *La Gioconda?* Or a progressive novelty, for example a double bill of *Curlew River* and *Suor Angelica?* But in spite of *Gioconda* and *Cleopatra* and *Adriana Lecouvreur* and *Cav* and *Pag*, Mr. Bing is one of New York's top swingers (old-fashioned, innocent sense). No doubt he will be made into a musical, which is a cultural achievement of a sort.

N.Y.R.: You were courted by the Musical Establishment yourself, not long ago, Mr. Stravinsky. What, may we ask, were your morning-after reactions to the New York Philharmonic Stravinsky Festival?

I.S.: No hangover. Nor did I feel scathed, whatever I looked like. Perhaps I was spared by the circumstance that all of the concerts except my own were group shows. Would-be assassins were not lacking, of course, but all except the one dispatched by that society of failed newspapers, the *Trib Sun Telegram Post News Mirror*, seemed to have lost heart; and he backfired; a collection is now going around to put up a small public lavatory to his memory in some plumbing-poor neighborhood of his native city.

N.Y.R.: Do you think that the audiences in general were attracted more by what was being played, or by who was playing it?

I.S.: The latter, but the ad men can give you factual answers, and to the metrics-of-taste question (Bentham's idea). Lincoln Center audiences are probably exceptional in that some percentage of the people might still come as much to see the buildings as to watch Mr. Bernstein, as was once the case with the Music Hall and the Rockettes. It seemed to me, at any rate, that of the 2,000 customers who attended the Festival's chamber music concert, not more than a tenth could have come with foreknowledge in kind expressly to hear what they heard. This was apparent from the initial giggles of the captive majority, who, however, when the dynamics were conducive, tried to settle down and make the best of it; I have never seen so many eyelids at half-mast. As for the program, it was an error to relegate Milton Babbitt's electronic composition to the lobby during intermission. At a time when silence pollution is reaching saturation point, a time of pocket transistors, processed classics, and round-the-clock mood music (music for mealtimes, music for meditation, music for everything in fact except undivided listening), resistance to intermission subconcerts, at least on *my* indifference curve, is very strong.

N.Y.R.: And what did you think of the programs, Mr. Stravinsky?

I.S.: Some g., some n.g., but my lips are sealed. Besides, I am no judge of programs; I go to concerts myself to hear only one work. My early music was favored, but not that audience lollipop, *The Firebird*. And my neo-classicism—in which the slump seems to be lifting—was well represented. *Apollo*, the U-turn itself, was missing, but *Oedipus* and *Perséphone* were there, as well as *Pulcinella*, the first of my purported raids on the past. As for my later music, which is no less neo-classical, the only considerable example was *The Flood*. The trouble it gave the orchestra partly explains why. The title episode itself was so unweatherable to them (what did they expect, sea chanties?) that I was tempted to cut it to only a few measures —a flash flood, in fact. Music sociologists might note that for whatever reasons of rehearsal time and morale, it was the orchestra, not the audience, which required larger diets of familiar music.

N.Y.R.: And the other performances?

I.S.: Well, frugging is apparently *de rigueur* for Philharmonic conductors. Even Kondrashin did it. (Where did he learn *that* in the USSR? Do conductors study films there, like secret agents?) But Mr. Bernstein is unflappable in competition, and so glittering a performer [1] that he could get a dozen curtain calls out of the National Anthem. (Not, however, out of *my* version, which needed a more tightly cranked-up performance.) The character of articulation in my music eluded most of the conductors, even in so simple a point as that the metrical lines are constituent to the rhythm, not mute, inglorious markers which the conductor is invited to ignore for the sake of something he calls the phrase. But the performance standards, both bad—*Oedipus Rex*—and good—*Histoire du soldat*, the high point of the summer's revels thanks to John Cage's *opéra-bouffe* Devil—were determined by extra-musical antics. As for the standards of the music itself, July was too hot even for a soft look. I did notice, however, that whereas

---

[1] He was much less effective on TV a few days ago giving his endorsement of rock 'n' roll (which seemed not to have the remotest need of it), and expressing the sophisticated musician's wonder at such prodigies of invention as the Beatles' use of a three-beat measure in a four-beat song.

the "Ragtime" in the *Histoire* is as smoothly integrated as a minuet in Mozart, the one for eleven instruments is as dated as a coonskin coat.

The curtain-raiser concert of *Le Sacre* and American beneficiaries was a fine gesture of homage to Mr. Bernstein's youth. Even the peculiarities of *tempi* and *rubati* in the *Sacre*—a more hand-wringing reading than I am accustomed to— were derived, as he told me, from Stokowski's performances in the Thirties. Of the other pieces, Copland's *Dance Symphony*, a very precocious opus for a composer of twenty-three, would have been equally serviceable in a festival of Ravel, while Revueltas's *Sensemaya* offers several composers for the price of one and would do as an influenced piece in any number of surveys of the sort.

N.Y.R.: But do you think Revueltas would have developed, if, like yourself, he had been given another thirty-five years of working life?

I.S.: I have no opinion. I can answer only in the other direction, telling you about people who might better have disappeared thirty-five years sooner.

N.Y.R.: Have you any late-hour prescriptions for a young composer, Mr. Stravinsky?

I.S.: If he can turn an honest million outside music he might seriously consider neglecting his talents for a time and turn it. Otherwise, and untempted by all lesser sums, he should go directly underground and do nothing but compose: that is, not strive for Foundation awards, academic prizes, college presidencies, foreign fellowships; not attend culture congresses; not give interviews; not prattle on the radio about music appreciation; not review new scores (except his own, pseudonymously); and not push, promote, maneuver, advertise, finagle, operate.

N.Y.R.: Some composers borrow structural patterns from the

sciences; Xenakis, for instance, uses Bernouilli's Limit Theorem, and his *Metastasis* was derived from the same blueprint as the architecture for the Philips Pavilion at the Brussels Fair.

I.S.: I admire the economy. And I look forward to the days when Mr. Xenakis's successors are writing music that can at the same time compute taxes and regulate urban renewal. Meanwhile, I confess that I would be frightened to enter some of the compositions I have heard of late, in their forms as buildings.

N.Y.R.: Now that computer programming is our fastest-growing profession, do you foresee a larger role for computers in the service of the creative arts?

I.S.: When the computer has become the electronic culture's universal knowledge distillery, artistic creation, if there is any, obviously will have been technically, theoretically, and teleologically overhauled. But I am undergoing a Luddite reaction myself and foresee very little. Like everyone else, I welcome the benefits of, say, the computerizing of medical information (which no physician could keep up with anyway), but unlike most other people, I am frightened by the prospects of, say, the IBM project for the direct conversion of information to speech; the very thought of millions of electronic voices indistinguishable from live ones ("Till human voices wake us and we drown") almost makes me jump the tracks.

N.Y.R.: Nowadays, Mr. Stravinsky, how is an upper-average (middle to high) Playbrow to know "what is art"? I mean, when is a crushed car sculpture, when are "ditties of no tone" music—that sort of thing?

I.S.: It is still generally thought of as art if it is shown in a gallery, and as music if it takes place in premises traditionally associated with concerts. Another way of knowing is by way of the dealers who are obliged to keep the racket going. Their formula is, and it seems to be working very well, "Buy now on the likelihood that it may later turn out to *be* Art." Speaking for myself, I could not begin to distinguish music and nonmusic in some of the concert-hall activity I have observed of late. Nor would I be at all confident of recognizing a new musical genius. If I were asked to fill Schumann's role today, in fact, and hail a new Chopin, I would probably have to modify his dictum to: "Keep your hats on, gentlemen, for all I know he may be a charlatan."

N.Y.R.: As the term avant-garde implies direction, in what direction do you think today's avant-garde is going?

I.S.: Not knowing what kind of music is looking ahead, or even what ahead means, I have no idea. If, for example, the Diabelli Variations seem to forecast so much, it is retrospective prophecy that enables us to say so. Compared with science, many of whose future conquests are known goals, even the areas in which musical developments might be expected to take place are not generally predictable. And whereas progress in science is measurable and even absolute, agreement as to what progress is in music rarely exists. Musical languages seem to develop by new infusions of emotion, or new emphases and combinations of emotion, in correspondence with shifts and changes—losses as well as additions—in vocabulary. But a new linguistic mode can also be more crude than the one it supersedes.

As to the actual avant-garde, I have had little contact with it in the last few seasons, and this is in a field where six weeks can count as an era, and ownership of an idea, at the present rate of "dynamic obsolescence," lasts about six minutes. It seems, however, that the trend is still to mixed media, corporate expression, the instant *Gesamtkunstwerk*, and therefore away from music by and in itself; and this is understandable, too, if only for the reason "The lyf so short, the craft so long to lerne." It is also a trend away from composition, in my fuddy-duddy view, for effects plotlessly stumbled on are very different from those that occur in the course and frame of an unfolding order. What I found of some, but less than inexhaustible, interest in the avant-garde of a few years ago was the exploration of minutiae of sensibility in a man alone and immobile. This was not entirely new (think of Gulliver, swarming with a *"Fourmillante cité . . ."*), but it did not become an all-out movement, I think, until Beckett. For a parallel in music we have to thank Mr. Cage for making us aware of our amplified breathing and swallowing (this sounds like Niagara Falls), and the crinkle of a single hair.

N.Y.R.: Are those changes of vocabulary and new infusions of emotion strictly interior musical developments or is there a relationship of a metaphorical kind with the real world?

I.S.: As I see it, the metaphorical alignments, symbolizations, reflected thoughts and feelings are purely the listener's, without any "real" basis in the music; or, in other words, the investing of the musical object with the listener's subjective responses is actually nothing more than a form of the pathetic fallacy. I doubt, furthermore, that the subjective regions of most metaphorically inclined listeners are as rich and varied as they suppose, most "free" association really being a comparatively narrow and patterned habit association. But this begs further questions which would eventually lead back to the postulate (it appears in Marx's *Contribution to the Critique of Political Economy*, I think, but I am not an answering service) that reality is not determined by our consciousness, but the other way around.

N.Y.R.: Surely pieces of music can have valid meanings beyond themselves?

I.S.: Certainly: your own. And you may look to them for

whatever you like: comments on the times, for example, as embodied in formal, substantive, and structural characteristics (the method of the "contextual interpretation" industry); or exercises in analogy—I could get up a Platonic dialogue myself on the proposition that good music expresses high truths, and bad music platitudes and lies. It is all up to—since it also begins and ends in—you.

N.Y.R.: But in your own mind, Mr. Stravinsky?

I.S.: My "mind" does not count. I am not mirror-struck by my mental functions. My interest passes entirely to the object, the thing made; it follows that I am more concerned with the concrete than the other thing, in which, as you see, I am easily muddled. And in the first place I do not regard composition as more of a mental function than a sensual pleasure. "Lascivious pleasing" is a famous description of the performance of a—very chaste, it would seem to us—lute song, and performances are but pale memories of creative acts. In music, as in love, pleasure is the waste product of creation.

N.Y.R.: Would you comment on Leopardi's claim that old age deprives us of every pleasure while leaving every appetite, but that men fear death and desire old age?

I.S.: Prefer, not desire, and the logical symmetry is also untrue: there are pleasures still, and in parity with appetites. But if old age is hardly more appealing today than it was in the time of Leopardi, who died too young to know anything about it, we treat it cosmetically now and it may at least look better. Under the slogan of senior citizenry, in any case, it is being sold as a vocation, its salesmen likening senility to a late, more effulgent, phase of the moon, and pretending that our loss of momentum, when too evident to be denied, is the price of a compensatory larger wisdom. They even find substitute love affairs for us in our own illnesses, whose progresses they teach us to follow as if "we" were hardly involved.

Reality is different, and it *could* be like a mental Deep-freeze. A doctor recently prescribed a new tranquilizer for me on the recommendation that it had worked wonders for his grandmother, meaning that it had probably kept her in a semi-coma and out of his way. But did the venerable lady also write music? I asked, and the shocked answer implied that if *I* did, I should stop immediately for the sake of my own tranquility—which, I now know, is no longer a place where emotion is recollected, but a near-vegetable state.

N.Y.R.: May we inquire about age in your own thoughts, Mr. Stravinsky?

I.S.: If you mean the knowledge that in a half-decade at the most, but probably sooner, I will be dead, that has little effect on me: the possibility of death is always present, always in the cards, after all, and it is only the likelihood that has increased. If, on the other hand, you are inquiring about changes of mind and character, then I will have to admit that I am aware of some of them only from other people. They tell me when I am being too suspicious and refractory, for example, but surely faults of this kind, life being what it is, are independent of questions of age. One change that is apparent to me with no outside help is the tendency to magnify my smallest bruises. No doubt a simple biochemical explanation exists, but I cannot control my bile count. In the past I constrained myself against the complacency of all judgments with exemplary charity ("They have ears but hear not") and the thought that while death *is* there is hope. But now I know that while there is death there is succession.

Like childhood—my childhood—old age is a time of humiliations. For me the most disagreeable is that I cannot work long at sustained high pressure and with no leaks in concentration. But there are others. My slips in writing are frequent now, and my manuscripts have to be vetted. This is "understandable in a man of his age," people say, but it disturbs me, understandable or not. So is my hide-and-seek memory, now in hiding more often than not. I have orchestrated the same page twice, greeted perfect strangers in Russian, and performed other equally scatterbrained acts. Coué would have said that Nature is protecting me, in reducing my power to retain the nugatory. But I prefer not to need the shelter.

One night last week I dreamed a new episode of my work-in-progress, but realized, when I awoke, that I could not walk to my desk to write it down and that it would be gone by morning; in that instant I wondered for the first time how much longer it will be before I shall have to close down as a composer altogether.

N.Y.R.: Have eighty-five years strengthened your belief in the continuity of life and art, Mr. Stravinsky?

I.S.: It seems to me, on the contrary, that discontinuity must be only a short way ahead. Certainly in another four score and five the "clones" bred by genetic engineers to the specifications of Bureaus of Human Uses will differ from me far more than I differ from, say, the astronomers of Fowlis Wester and Stonehenge (who, it now appears, must have known a lunar movement later "discovered" by Tycho Brahe). I lack confidence in genetic and other utopias, as you see, and am tired of analogies based on successful demonstrations in frogs. But, then, the present has already begun to make me giddy—that discovery at Cambridge, for instance, showing that in certain insects the sense of time itself is encoded in two or three cells. (So, then, time *is* ontological?) But do not misunderstand me. Though I would refuse any Faustian bargain, I am far from content with myself. I simply want to go from here on out trying to do better what I have always done, and in spite of statistical tallies telling me that it must be getting worse. And I want to do it in this same battered but long-lived-in *Identikit*. "Myself I must remake," Yeats's poem says. And so must we all.

Side Effects 1

I

"To avenge the wrongs of our time . . . the wounds of Igor."
The Song of Igor's Campaign (NABOKOV translation)

Harper's: Your New York appearances have become rare, Mr. Stravinsky. The cancellation of the recent Carnegie Hall concerts was a great disappointment to us.

I.S.: The city itself is hazardous for me now. I started out on a walk one afternoon during my last visit, in May, but the wind was so strong I had to lean against walls and hold on to No Parking signs. A Meter Maid was soon watching me censoriously, probably thinking I was drunk. Then a young man approached, not to offer help, but to ask for an autograph. To oblige him I inched my way like a mountain climber out of the Sixty-first Street wind tunnel and back into the hotel lobby, where I duly signed my name. But the absence of a sense of the absurd in this collector, or dealer in disguise, left me so out of spirits I did not try to resume my wind-blown promenade.

HARPER'S: Newspaper accounts of the cancellation said you had been in the hospital.

I.S.: True. I was in for two weeks because of a gastric ulcer, a "benign" one, in medicalese, but if it isn't "benign" you are as good as dead. The doctors blamed the lesion on too much alcoholic vasodilation, but of course their report mentioned only the alcohol part and omitted the virtuous intentions. I was not worried at first, and my presentiments that the real trouble might lie further upstream and that I might be headed for the rapids, were aroused only by the sudden bedside manner of certain music critics. But it *was* only an ulcer. And I recovered more quickly from it than from the hospital for ailing philanthropists to which I was sent. There the meters started to tick when I broke the electric beam of the front door, the pills came with my name on them, and the bill may still have to be paid by a charity ball.

But seriously, penitential orders—Desert Fathers and such —seeking to update their mortifications could hardly find more ingenious exemplars than in a modern hospital. My day began at *ca.* 5 A.M. with an urgent and for some reason unpostponable mopping of the cell, and once it began even earlier, when the television started by itself. From then until "lights out," when I was regularly awakened and told it was time to sleep, I remained constantly, ulceratingly vigilant to avoid being injected with someone else's medicines, nearly having been fatally so injected during another hospital siege some years before. As it was, not many fakirs can have been so often stuck, jabbed, poked, punctured, perforated, and considering that loss of blood was the reason for my incarceration in the first place, the further withdrawals seemed remarkably copious and frequent. I also swallowed, was pumped with, breathed, absorbed through the pores, an impressive variety and volume of medications; and was betweentimes tourniquetted for blood pressure, radiologically sensitized, laxitized, squeezed, thumped, and subjected to much "laying on of hands."

The hospital was partly audio-tactile; the patient addresses his pleas to wall tubes sieve-ended like the speaking grills in confessional boxes, then waits for the answers to boom back at him, like flight announcements, from the ceiling. This ceiling voice reminding me to drink my milk was a torture worse than the milk itself, I might add, my tongue becoming ermine-coated, as it might have done with one of Pavlov's hounds, at the first crackle of the sound system. Some of the humans, moreover, were as automated as the automata. One of them brought Jello three times a day and another yogurt, but so far as I could discover, neither did anything else. At first I thought this arrangement had been devised to safeguard easily overtaxed brains, but now I suspect that there weren't any (brains) and that all cerebral zones except those controlling Jello and yogurt deliveries had been surgically removed. I now wonder, since these automata had been programmed to clear away empty but not unconsumed dishes, how long it took to discover the forty or so uneaten jars of Jello in my closet.

My own nurses were not yet automated, and in fact one of them was so old-fashioned that she drew a curtain around my bed before giving me B₁₂ shots *in the arm!* Her sense of delicacy was less exacting in keeping me informed on the new diseases caused by the new medicines, but she *did* teach me an effective sleep-inducing formula: gamma globulin, hemoglobin, the threshold of pain, the front door of pain, pain itself . . . zzzzzz.

My love of painkillers has now been confirmed, incidentally, and if I had been a "terminal" patient I would have opposed the anti-drug lobbyists who claim to be "entitled" to their deaths. A mere three doses of morphine were enough to "hook" me, and to raise my allowance of Demerol I began to "put" the doctors "on." I have been able to "kick" the colchicine habit—shared by gophers, incidentally—only because of the disquieting knowledge that it splits chromosomes in plant cells; but Darvon is still prescribed, and I am still, therefore, at least temporarily, a legal addict.

I still feel like Amfortas, too, and still feel giddy at moments, as if I had stepped from a Ferris wheel. I have become a milk dipsomaniac, too, and pharmacology continues to be my "life style". Worst of all, the retreating ulcer left a booby trap of digital gout. The pains are both erratic and pedantic, hence difficult to accustom to. They are so strong at times, too—I do not believe Aubrey's account of Milton singing in his "gout fits": he was more likely howling—that I am no longer certain of being "an artist to my fingertips." It is almost impossible to hatch any new music for the moment, as you see, and absolutely impossible to do so at the piano, the gout having deprived me of my dexterity.

HARPER'S: Only "almost," Mr. Stravinsky?

I.S.: I am composing a set of pieces provisionally titled *Etudes, Inventions, and a Sonata.* Only two selections, both ante-ulcer, are completed. I hope the plural is not over-optimistic.

2

"*Of Paradys ne can I not speken propurly for I was not there.*"   SIR JOHN MANDEVILLE

"*. . . for months together, vast, wet, melancholy fogs arise and come shoreward from the ocean . . . it is always sad.*"

R. L. STEVENSON on California, 1880.

HARPER'S: Why do you live in Los Angeles, Mr. Stravinsky?

I.S.: I came there for my health, originally, or in other words for the same reason I am now advised to leave, the effects of smog, and the phlegm in this interview is among them, currently being estimated as the equivalent damage from two packs of cigarettes a day; the poet's "Fear death?—to feel the fog in my throat" has a literal meaning in Los Angeles. I had been considering La Paz as the next step, not because I had a message for Guevara, or anyone, but because gastric ulcers are almost unknown there, owing to what is thought to be the "benign" influence of altitude on the gastric enzymes.

HARPER'S: But is Los Angeles really so different, or is it merely that certain forms of social behavior are developing there a few steps ahead of the rest of the world?

I.S.: The latter, unless by ahead you mean in the *real* sense, *i.e.*, retrogressing faster. Los Angeles is well ahead (meaning behind) in, for example, such relatively minor developments as the cinematizing of politics, and in such fads as, currently, decal tattooing and silicon rejuvenating (with which, to adapt Eliot, most over-forty faces that you meet have been prepared). But the city is undeniably ahead also in such fairly important developments as the change-over—men to women, women to men—and in the elimination of death.

Dying in Los Angeles is only remotely connected with death. According to notices of burial bargains all over the city, the question is merely one of tidying up a few problems (namely your remains) which, thanks to certain altruistic business services, can be arranged by a telephone call and then put out of mind. In the past these advertisements struck me as merely ribald, except in the center page of Philharmonic program books where they were usually quite fitting and on bus-stop benches where, buses being the transportation of elderly poor people, they are cruel. But I see them now as the logical end of the local philosophy of life (meaning death). By taking the funereal out of funerals, and with it the nonsense about bereavement, as well as the sense of a "supreme irony" and any lingering superstitions about a "victory over the grave"; by substituting the movie-style fade-out for the baroque-style celebration with trumpets, elegies, and marble tombs; in short, by connecting the transaction to negotiables, and reducing it to a supermarket service, death itself is made in some measure less unknowable. This, I think, is the reason why the moribund take such a lively interest in ascertaining the relative advantages of cremation *versus* Pharaonic preservation ("keeping up appearances") and in securing the most favorable installment ("pay now, go later") terms.

A late-lamented friend of mine, shortly before her own final collapse, told me that a salesman in the mortuary "studio" she first visited had tried to persuade her that satin was the most becoming material for her casket lining. This so annoyed my friend that she had to remind him who was dying, that it was *her* funeral and not *his*. She also said that the musical resources of this atelier included, in addition to the usual assortment of Japanese electronic canaries, a choice of "cremation blues," one of which really did make her flesh creep. Next year's advertisements will no doubt offer to present our corpses not only in their daily habiliments (Polaroid glasses are *de rigueur* in Los Angeles) but in "not quite living color" as well.

The transsexual trend, or switching of sexual roles, is hardly less interesting but more difficult to follow because the sociological point of view is switching as well. At first the new *Nacktkultur* was classified, by unvested interests, as merely the latest manifestation of the visual-tactile revolution. But now, under pressure from the Garment Industry, the same experts tend to see it as a reactive phenomenon. The nude waitress is a sexual suffragette, the new argument runs, a diehard demonstrator in the cause of the old-style binary design of the sexes.

However that issue is decided, the sexual acculturation of the rest of the country sags far behind Los Angeles in the free exposure of the American former-male's mammary fixations. And by this I mean not only the topless restaurant, but the ice cream parlor as well, for at the time of day when the Gaul is downing his *marc* or his Pernod, the adult male Angeleno, a parent, it may be, of consenting daughters majoring in suntanning or surfing at UCLA, is himself ensconced in a milk pub sucking an ice cream soda. (Let me remind you that my own present incontinencies in the matter of milk do not stem from the same cause, which is that of not being properly "fed-up" as an infant.) But what of the mammalogical future? After a few centuries of natural selection, what

will the Supergirl foldout of A.D. 2500 look like, taking as outside measurements of progress the Eves of a Cranach or Clouet
and *Playboy?*

(Is *au naturel* restaurant service beneficial to digestion, or
does simultaneous emotional involvement have a disturbing
effect on the digestive juices? Does anyone ever inadvertently
order a tomato or a fig leaf? Music appears to have entered
the bottomless era, too, incidentally, not in the sense of pro-
fundity, of course, but, as in the film *Night Games,* in the
actual use of the anatomical surfaces for musical notations.)

3

". . . a few are riding but the rest have been run over."
                                              THOREAU

*"A personal God . . . who loves us dearly with some ex-
ceptions for reasons unknown."*   *Waiting for Godot*

*"Is it possible that Shakespeare should be forced
to accuse himself of ignorance of the 'ism'?
Is it possible that Stravinsky should be dragged
through screaming streets with a pail of gar-
bage on his white hair?"*
                          VOZNESENSKY, March 1967

HARPER'S: Are you aware of a "gap" between yourself and the
young, Mr. Stravinsky?

I.S.: Judging from a news program that I happened to watch
for a moment last night, an Arizona-size canyon divides me
from practically *everyone* else. The telecast began with an
announcement about overpopulation that included statistics
like "7.2 people"; by the end of the century the expression
"joined the majority" will mean born rather than died. Then
in that alternately serious and facetious, man-to-man and
man-to-woman (and denture-setting-on-edge) tone, the news-
caster read the latest toll from "anti-personnel" (*i.e.,* people)

bombs. This count included some non-Communists killed by mistake, though happily, in their case, their families are to be reimbursed, the announcer promised, at the $34 going price *per* non-Communist corpse. And so far from any trace of doubt underlying this specious recital, the price-fixing on lives and the paying for them as hunters are paid for pelts was made to sound like a matter for handshakes all around. I switched off at this point for the sake of my ulcer, though in truth the promise of a "round-up" of cultural events, meaning a movie closing and a prediction concerning tomorrow's smog, did not tempt me.

The gap between myself and the protesting young, to return to your question, is only as deep as my furrows compared to the chasm separating me from the people who can be so mendaciously mouthed to. In fact, as the Sunset Strip, that dry Ganges for hippie holies (immersions in water not being in their line) is only a few steps from me, I shall probably apply for membership among the young Hindus myself. As for their elders, it hardly seems to be worth asking whether they know what became of humanity. (*P.S.:* Voznesensky must have been thinking of Stokowski. I am bald.)

4

*"Claudio Monteverdi, in moving the affections . . . becomes
the most pleasant tyrant of human minds."*
AQUILINO COPPINI (1608)

HARPER'S: A picture of Monteverdi is conspicuous in the photographs of your workroom, Mr. Stravinsky. What does he mean to you in this quatercentenary?

I.S.: Obviously I feel very close to him, but he is probably the first musician to whom we *can* feel very close. The scope of his music, both as emotion and as architecture (aspects of the same thing), is a new dimension compared to which the grandest conceptions of his predecessors, as well as their most estrual ardors and dolors shrink to miniatures. The man himself, as he emerges in Goretti's description of his habits of composing and conversing while at Parma, and in his own moody letters, with their anxieties about shortness of time and complaints of migraines, sounds not only strikingly contemporary *to* me, but even, if I may say so, rather *like* me.

To me the progressivist sense in the labeling of the great composer's First and Second Practices has been reversed, as the forward-looking and backward-looking have sometimes done. I mean by this that the older polyphonic style, with its explorations of rhythm and contrapuntal tensions (the suspending seconds in the *Gloria* of the *Magnificat à* 7), sounds even newer now than the harmonic novelties of the declamatory style. Yet the most modern effect of all did undoubtedly occur in the Second Practice. One of the composer's letters, newly (1966) published, indicates that he must have had something very like *Sprechstimme* in mind for a scene in a lost dramatic work. At any rate that is how *I* read his phrase "*a parlar nel modo come se l'avesse a cantare.*"

If I marvel at Monteverdi's rhythmic inventions first, it is partly because I have worked all my life in some of the same directions (at least) myself, and because they are part of my psychometrics as a composer. I know of no music before or since the *Sonata sopra Sancta Maria* which so felicitously exploits accentual and metrical variation and irregularity, and I know of no more subtle rhythmic construction of any kind than that which is set in motion at the beginning of the *Laudate Pueri,* if the music is sung according to the verbal accents instead of the *tactus* and the editor's bar lines. On the other hand, listeners gratified primarily by rich harmonies naturally find the almost purely rhythmic interest of the *Dixit Dominus* monotonous. I relish that canonic monotony myself, and to me the drop to G minor at the *"Gloria Patri,"* after the long A minor, is as powerful as the three unmodulated plunges in tonality of the first theme of the *"Eroica."*

One of the greatest honors of my life was the invitation to introduce two of my own works in rooms hallowed by their association with Monteverdi: the *Canticum Sacrum* in the Basilica of San Marco, and *Threni* in the Scuola di San Rocco. (*"I Treni,"* *The New York Times* called the opus, perhaps confusing it with *Pacific 231.*) In Mantua, however, what impressed me most was Isabella d'Este's study, that monument to the high condition of music in the Gonzaga court both of an earlier time and as a whole; miracle that the occurrence of Monteverdi was, developed tools awaited him. But, then, no musical association of that most romantic palace in the world is as haunting as the Gonzagas themselves, at least in Mantegna's frescoes, where Lodovico seems to be on a poppy mandragora "trip," and unable, for sheer drugged drowsiness, to retract more than half of his eyelids.

5

2ND MUS.: *"I say, 'silver sound,' because*
musicians sound for silver."
—*Romeo and Juliet*
"The third, doubtless a serving-man,
Carries a musical instrument."
Lapis Lazuli

HARPER'S: What can we borrow from art patronage systems of other times, Mr. Stravinsky?

I.S.: Little, except to try to improve individual taste, for example by teaching the piper payers some of the tunes. Patronage systems are not abstractable from social systems as wholes, of course, and it is pointless to compare the ruling-class culture of, say, Monteverdi's time and our own. Nevertheless, art was important, in fact near the center of life, to the heads of church and state who were Monteverdi's patrons, and who —though this is a subordinate differentiation—were able *as a class* to exercise trained judgment on the qualities of architects, sculptors, painters, poets, composers. Now certainly no one would dare accuse any high officeholder today of even the slightest interest in art, at least not without incurring the risk of libel action. Art, to middle-class millionaire politicians, is something to be collected and dowered. And this is part of the reason why our yachting millionaires and racehorse millionaires include so many French Impressionist millionaires but so few musical millionaires: the resalable musical artifacts are comparatively insignificant.

Nor are the cultural economics of other societies more instructive, except for drawing still more invidious comparisons. We can learn from them that musicians have not always been starvelings or in such undemanded supply as they are now. In Sophoclean Greece, for example, musicians' salaries were fixed by law (*cf.* Sifakis's *Studies in the History of Hellenistic Drama*). And in Greece, as well as at Mantua, and Esterház, and Monticello (Virginia), they seem to have been regulated by merit. To recur to the trained-judgment question, if Haydn was hired help, at least his employers did him the honor of knowing something about his work. Jefferson was musically cultivated, by the way, and though he was probably a difficult source of income to his orchestra players, demanding that they should also be gardeners, and so forth, he spent a far greater share of his money on music than the "eleven cents out of every hundred dollars of disposable income" (according to the Twentieth Century Fund survey) that his fellow countrymen are now squandering on the "performing arts."

HARPER'S: What do you mean by musical artifacts?

I.S.: The marketable commodities. Publicity is the largest, but the manuscript trade is brisk, and letters and such "associational objects" as soap from hotels where the artist has stayed, are starting to come along. This transference of the price tags from the functioning talent to souvenirs of its penmanship (my own manuscripts have always fetched far more than I received for writing the *music* in them), from the actual delectation of a piece of music to a collector's association with its author through an autograph album, accounts for a large part of art commerce. And composers are valued now less for their actual composing function than as committee sitters, meeting attenders, and teachers. In fact most of them, including one great one, have been and still are too poor to afford the time from teaching to compose. The great one illustrates the first part of my argument, incidentally, in that a university has recently put up a museum to exhibit his pocketknife, underwear, and last cigar ash, no doubt having paid more bounteously for the least of these relics than the living composer received for all of his music. When you consider what a thousand dollars won't buy nowadays, think about that thousand-dollar commission which a good composer must work for a year or two to satisfy.

As for "associational objects" of my own, not long ago I tried to give away a fur coat which I had worn for a number of years, but which was in good condition. I could not find anyone chilly enough, however, and even the Salvation Army turned it down. At this point a Foundation scout heard about my garment of no *useful* value, with the issue that my old *shuba* is now enshrined at the Paris Conservatory (its conveyance there doubtless having incurred several substantial entries on a number of expense accounts). And it is the same with my music as with my overcoat. My next composition will serve musical commerce less for its real value of musical content than for its consumer value as publicity, meaning its use as a première. For the new artist, in fact, publicity has become almost the only value; he must be a publicist himself before all else.

HARPER'S: And Foundation patronage, Mr. Stravinsky?

I.S.: Foundations are tax-escape systems whose money has been diverted from society as a whole; there *must* be more pressing social needs than *some* Foundation-supported art activity. Yet it seems unreasonable to complain about that, in view of other wastes, compared to which all expenditures for art are trivial. And, anyway, money is not the only ingredient; to have subsidized a Bach, or Fulbrighted a Beethoven would have done no good at all. Money may kindle but it cannot by itself, and for very long, burn. (Conscience money may smolder for a while, though.)

HARPER'S: Do you think that society undervalues artists?

I.S.: For their art, yes. Otherwise, it is the contrary, which is why their opinions about matters beyond their competence are publicized (*viz.*, this interview). Intelligence and virtue do not occur together in natural incidence with artistic talent, as is sometimes popularly supposed, nor can a good artist have the time to know very much about anything except his work; nevertheless, the political wisdom of painters, actors, cellists, composers continues to be disseminated. In sum, artists and "intellectuals" can be as foolish and dangerous as professional politicians, and so far from being morally superior to other people, they are, often, owing to their exceptional vanity and egotism, a shade worse.

6

"To occupy the sense of hearing . . . with many noises."
The Imperfections of Modern Music (1600)

HARPER'S: Is there a talent famine, Mr. Stravinsky?

I.S.: Not of small talent, if sheer volume means anything. But

I must hold my tongue. I am a dropout myself, no longer being able to attend the picnics of those small, ingrown, and not very saturnalian new-music groups through whose efforts, nevertheless, a talent of any size would most likely *have* to appear. My opinions are formed from the tapes and scores I receive in the mail. (The scores, by the way, are for the most part verbal descriptions and diagrams, some of which I suspect of being fashion-market research charts in the literal as well as graphic sense.) The yield has included nothing enticing of late, though I *have* learned something about certain operations of chance, namely, that it is not so much that it doesn't make any difference, but that in not making any difference it still sounds very much the same. In other words, the infinite range of possibilities between those *à la mode* landslides of noise which neither man nor beast can unscramble (I say nothing about machines), and those equally *à la mode* silences is in practice a small and patented area of cliché. And I say this not forgetting that the harvest of my mailbox is also an aleatory. But do I hear that way merely because I still require music, not just sounds, and because "open-ended" art does nothing for me, or "minimal" art (already leaning indistinguishably flatly on "no" art), or that glare of publicity and high commerce which calls itself the "Underground"?

What, may I ask, has become of the idea of universality—of a character of expression not necessarily popular but compelling to the highest imaginations of a decade or so beyond its own time—and which artist in any medium born in the last fifty years has come within a Mars shot of it?

HARPER'S: But do you find nothing to applaud in the young art, Mr. Stravinsky?

I.S.: Apart from some slow handclaps for aleatory, I hail the new invisible sculpture (Takis's *Radar*, for instance, which the "viewer" is supposed to "energize" in an "environment"), and all forms of throw-away art and self-exploding art are surefire with me.

HARPER'S: May we ask why you tend to disparage the "expanding possibilities"—quarter-tones, multiple sound systems, and so forth—of the new composer's arsenal, Mr. Stravinsky?

I.S.: But I haven't. I only question their use, for they often seem to kill even the possibility of art: *parvo in multum*, to reverse the slogan. The use of the new hardware naturally appears to the new musician as "historically imperative"; but music is made out of musical imperatives, and the awareness of historical processes is probably best left to future and different kinds of wage earners. At the same time it is obvious that mathematical machines will soon be making something that will be called art. (How will art be defined, anyway? What was *"le bonheur,"* in Holbach's *Traité mathématique sur le bonheur?*) Whatever *I* think about the composer's new hardware landing him in an impasse cannot count, in any case, for I have no title to an opinion, and even the exact nature of the problem is as remote to me as the Gluck-Piccinni debate. The only musical hardware I have examined of late was a musical typewriter which I found to be marvelously suited to the needs of . . . Bach.

HARPER'S: You have named Messiaen as a dominating influence of the decade, and at the same time criticized important elements of his music. How do you appraise his music generally?

I.S.: High. In fact, one of those great hymns of his might be the wisest choice of all our music for the deck-band concert on the *Titanic* of our sinking civilization; among other advantages, rescuing vessels—other planets—would have a good chance of hearing it. I unrashly predict, as well, that his more recent works will last as long as any music of the time. But I still can't "make it" with *Turangalîla*.

So far as criticisms are mere likings and dislikings, they define the critic more than his subject. Even the antinomical definition I attempted to draw between myself and Messiaen said more about my brand of convention, my way of holding the mirror up to nature, than about his. (Unlike him, for example, I would accept the *shang* in the pentatonic scale as an autumn symbol, but not the description of the note itself as autumnal.) But my main reservation was founded in a personal, even perhaps a neurological, disability. Our ever more Noise-Energized Environment, which includes highly dangerous inaudible noise, has made me ever more nervous. I have lately had nightmares of new Jerichos, and dreams of being trapped with a hearing aid that I cannot turn down. Acoustic wattage of a certain intensity can be lethal.

HARPER'S: In connection with your remark concerning universality, Mr. Stravinsky, do you believe that all of the great emotions have already appeared in music?

I.S.: Until new ones appear to prove that they haven't.

7

"Everything must be learned, from talking to dying."
                                                    FLAUBERT

HARPER'S: Apart from your new composition, what has most occupied your thoughts recently, Mr. Stravinsky?

I.S.: The ultimate *force majeure*, naturally, for in spite of all those little capsules, "mood raisers," to shoo away the truth, a hospital bed provides an abundance of both time and "motivation." The darkest thoughts have been dispelled since then, and I feel as if I had been reprieved from, say, one minute before twelve to eleven thirty (I hope it is no later than that!). But I look and feel like the Seventh Age of Man. Stiff, creaky, slow, I am hardly certain at times of being "in possession of all of my facilities."

The chief mental problem in being eighty-five, though intelligent people are afflicted with it already at twenty-five, is the realization that one may be powerless to change the *quality* of one's work. The quantity can be increased, even at eighty-five, but can one change the whole? I, at any rate, am absolutely certain that my *Variations* and *Requiem Canticles* have altered the picture of my whole work, and I seek the strength now to change that completed picture just one more time.

By some unlucky circumstance I happened to reread *The Death of Ivan Ilytch* a few months ago, and, as every reader of the story must, I have been seeing myself in it ever since. (For similar reasons Groddeck's *Das Buch vom Es* should be avoided by anyone with an overactive auto-suggestivity.) While identifying with Ivan Ilytch, however, I admired the skill with which Tolstoy projects his hero's consciousness of growing separateness, and of the irrelevance of himself and his condition in the lives of younger people. As for Ivan Ilytch's awareness of the transparency of doctors' professionalism, of the diplomatic dishonesty of his family, and of such subtleties as the feeling that a goodnight kiss must be under-expressed to avoid a collision of unsaid thoughts—of these things my recent experience has equipped me to be an ideal literary critic. No less brilliant, as my experience has also taught me, is Tolstoy's delineation of the awareness of transitional stages; of the alternation of struggle and acceptance; of the need for sympathy and the rejection of sympathy; of the onslaughts of childhood memories; of the attacks of philosophy in endless interior dialogues about the meaning of life; and, above all, of the sick man's acute sense both of the nature of his destiny and of the terrifyingly accidental aspect of life (and how much of it *is* accident if, as Rank claims, our birth history—

instrument landings and so forth—is the all-important event in it).

But thank Heaven it is Ivan Ilytch I am talking about! As for myself, let me say: "To be continued, I hope."

I. S.

October 1967

Side Effects II

I

"One of the difficulties in assessing the skill of the medical practitioners of the time is the almost complete absence of any records of the patients who had come for treatment."
From a review of *Medicine in Medieval England*, T.L.S., 11/1/68

NEW YORK REVIEW OF BOOKS: We were sorry to hear you had to go to the hospital a second time, Mr. Stravinsky.

I.S.: I appreciate the sympathy. And I need it, too. It has seemed to me lately that the greater the medical advances the narrower the patient's chances of surviving doctors and hospitals. Until this last adventure I was unaware of the extent to which medicine men, like generals and politicians, enjoy the right to be wrong; and unaware of the breach between medical science for its own disinterested sake—"operation a success, patient dead"—and medical practice for the sake of interested people. Some of the publicity concerning the late Mr. Washkansky's new heart helped to obviate the distinction by too blatantly showing that the man's life was less important than the symbiotic experiment for which it provided the opportunity. Freshly primed by my own experience, I worried not only about Mr. Washkansky but about his news-unworthy fellow patients as well. While the nurses were posing for *Life*, and the doctors talking to the cover-story team of *Time*, who was distributing the digitalis?

My second confinement was twice as long as the first and, the so-called maharajah care notwithstanding, a hundred times more harrowing. I was too drugged, luckily, to have been aware of most of it, but clear enough to realize that a great deal was going wrong quite apart from what was wrong with me. My confidence in doctors had begun to dwindle, too, though the preoccupation with status in their profession—the AMA must harbor many a *"Médecin malgré lui"*—had already disaffected me, even more than the surgical *Schadenfreude* and the pill-pushing indifference (equanimity, if you prefer, but I am smarting from my experience). Nor was my confidence in routine hospital functions on the upswing. I was fed the wrong X-ray dye on one occasion, and on another nearly perfused with the wrong intravenous fluid; when the right bottle was found, moreover—about to be piped into a visitor—and finally attached to my arm, the needle slipped out and inflated the skin like a balloon. I "blew my stack," as one of the nurses used to say, with less reason, but this protest could not have been stentorian enough, for the spigot on the next bottle was too loose and I was soon so over-irrigated that I began to wonder how much of the deleted me was the erstwhile me and how much the synthetic.

Identity problems of this type will become increasingly common as more and more brains are washed, and as—overcoming complications of histology and apartheid—spare-part banks and surgical mergers ("grafts" and "transplants" in the horticulturalized, antivivisectionist terminology) become more efficient. Another eventuality to allow for is the accidental transference of the soul and the id. This could lead to a revival of Eleatic divisibility/indivisibility arguments (the One and the Many); to theological tangles concerning prevenient grace; and to forensic medical arguments in personal property suits (*very* personal property) as to the exact contents of a "me" or a "you," the settlements of which could end by hyphenating the donors' and the donees' names. Since molecular biologists activated the laboratory-made DNA, after all, former definitions of "life" itself have become obsolete. But I am straying.

N.Y.R.: You were talking about the harassments of the hospital.

I.S.: Most of the other incidents were excusable. In any event, it would be difficult to fix responsibility for the invasion of my floor by an escapee from the neuropathic ward on the neuro-warpath, or for the replacing of my broken window-shade one night by a black screen so that I was uncertain in the morning whether I *had* awakened or had already gone over. (Hospital beds are peculiarly bier-like, from between the railings.) Nor is it reasonable to blame the staff for a mis-aimed "pain-killing" injection that would have won me first prize for the horizontal high jump if the hospital had been a sports arena instead of a Circus Maximus. The psychological technique of the staff in dealing with pain, incidentally, is to coax the victim into classifying its intensities himself, according to a scale of euphemisms ranging from "very slight" to "somewhat severe." No headway was made with this martyrizing appeal in my case, needless to say. I am insusceptible of masochistic enticements, and I recognized long ago that the arrows in most of those Sebastians of the Godward-rolling eyes are really Cupid's *flèches d'amour*. ("With Phoebus' amorous pinches blacke," as Cleopatra says.) To me all pain is extreme, and the question is not how much but how long.

It also could not be helped that my dose of radioactive phosphorus had to be consigned by the Atomic Energy Commission and transported, like money, in a kind of Brink's armored van. But guilt feelings at the thought of burdening the war effort were less unnerving than the jitters of the administering technician who seemed to regard me as a one-man test site, or human atomic atoll. Perhaps I shall find consolation in the knowledge that I am magnetic to fireflies and glowworms, if not to mine detectors, but this has not happened yet.

The worst of the hospital, nevertheless, was the musical frustration. My pilot light may not be very gem-like or hard any more, but it is still burning even when the stove is not in use. Musical ideas stalked me, but I could compose them mentally only, being unable to write at the time and unable to remember now. And the mind needs its daily work at such times, not the contemplation of its temporality. To be deprived of art and left alone with philosophy is to be close to Hell.

N.Y.R.: And your convalescence, Mr. Stravinsky?

I.S.: My nurses and "physiatrists" are flourishing, I assure you, and if my rehabilitation continues at the present rate for long, I will soon be obliged to apply to the Rolling Stones or Von Mehta for a loan. But *I* don't flourish. And in spite of protestations by the medical moguls that I have recovered (what else, after those prices, *could* they say?), I feel like a centenarian, am as thin as Kafka's Hunger Artist, and as pale —in spite of being kept in the garden, apparently for photosynthesis—as the afternoon moon.

But I complain too much, and too splenetically (which is reasonable, trouble having been found in that department as well); if my caducity were as bad as I make it sound, some College of Fine Arts would have rushed in by now with a last-minute doctorate. Besides, positive cause for elation has been found in my encephalogram, which seems more important now than ever for the reason that I am not permitted to sit for long at the piano and must compose, most of whatever I *can* compose, in my head. This is hampering because the instrument helps to push my imagination into position; and ironic because I am writing my first solo-piano piece since 1925. Yesterday I worked at the piano for the first time in five months (the "feel" of dust on the keys was unpleasant), beginning with a C- to B-flat trill, very slow, like the vibrato of a prima donna on a farewell tour. The trilling impulse came, I think, from exposure to a Christmas-present canary (someone had overestimated my fondness for *The Pines of Rome*) whose finest fioriture appear to be mating responses to our electric juice squeezer.

2

"Neue Kraft fühlend"

N.Y.R.: Have you noted any fresh developments in the musical world, Mr. Stravinsky?

I.S.: The Ivesian vogue of "simultaneous strands," the musical equivalent to multiple-projection films, is at high tide. So is pop, to the extent that the record companies spend most of their resources panning, like old-time prospectors, for pop hits. Certainly there has been no "breakthrough" in the classical establishment. Conductors are still the lap dogs of musical life, and the laps are still not much like "the gods'." The most dazzling instrumental virtuosity hardly counts in comparison. It may be true that an infant phenomenon playing *Turangalîla* in an arrangement for the left hand could make a certain *bruit d'estime*, but the histrionic range of infant phenomena playing instruments is naturally more constricting than that of grown men playing themselves. Furthermore, instrumental mastery is acquired at an expense of time and work, whereas the *musical* training of conductors—who before all else must be experts in jet schedules, international tax laws, body English, hair styling (the expression "the silver-haired Karajan" having attained a myth-like status comparable to "the rosy-fingered dawn" in Homer)—is briefer with each season's increasingly rapid turnover in the *stupor-mundi* market.

But I have already "made my representations" against the visual standards of an activity that is contiguous to music without always being of it. It may even be time now to redress the criticism slightly, pointing out that while amateurism is deplorable, so is too much professionalism. In the sense of technique the most admired conductor in the country —by me too, though I often wish his *tempi* were a heartbeat slower—is the ombudsman-elect of the New York Philharmonic. But what about that goal toward which conducting is hardly more than a necessary evil? Is it not possible that a *chef* with lesser technical powers but a wider and deeper scope might make better music? a musician such as Von Mehta, for instance, who can give humid and intensely suffered performances of Dvořák symphonies, and ingenuously felt and at times even searing ones of Rumanian, Hungarian, and other rhapsodies, including some with different titles by composers who did not actually intend that sort of thing.

Part of what I mean by scope is simply a larger stretch of sympathies. But in the first place I fail to see how a musician based almost exclusively in last-century repertory can ombudsmanize the affairs of the fast-getting-on present one. Imagine my pleasure therefore in the discovery that at least this sort of limitation no longer impedes the swell of progress in the Quaker City, the conductor there having proclaimed the new state of enlightenment (see my italics below) while lifting the veil from the long-cherished secret of his acquaintance with Alban Berg. "At that time I was not as well versed in the twelve-tone school of music *as I am now*," he says, and goes on to praise Berg for having given "logical, intelligent, and understandable" answers to his questions. I like that "understandable." As for the Philharmonic, I think it might do better in the Yellow Pages.

N.Y.R.: Have any new developments on the critical front caught your attention, Mr. Stravinsky?

I.S.: I am in arrears, but the new thing seems to be the critic as hero. A recent advertisement in the *Times* for a new Broadway play featured a photograph not of the author, or director, or set, or leading lady or animal, but of the *Times* reviewer who had given it a rave. This should help to restore a sense of importance to a function heavily inroaded by the pre-reviewing of producers' and publishers' blurbs.

Mostly, however, reviewing is the unabated *old* thing, music, dance, drama still being treated primarily as means of easing unemployment among roving all-purpose journalists, rather than as fairly specialized assignments. I used to blame the "intellectual community" for the failure to demand better, and in fact have only lately realized that no such community exists, or even much respect for the individual voices who might have formed it. An appeal on behalf of an American Jean Genet (unthinkable as the equivalents may be, not only to Genet but to the appealers, Gide, Claudel, and Sartre) would receive no acknowledgment, let alone result in effective action. And the press would most likely deride the petitioners, as *Time* derided Mr. Lowell for declining a certain invitation to dinner. But if the "intellectual community" has no representation in public affairs, it cannot claim a great deal more in the public arts. One wonders whether any student, or artist, or writer has ever ventured among the tiers of bankers, stockbrokers, and board chairmen who comprise the "public" of New York's ghetto of the performing arts, granting, of course, that *Martha* and *Hänsel* are deterrents as formidable as the ticket prices.

As for my own PR, I have seen no sign of a suspension of normal uncouthness for the sake of defunct traditions about courtesy to older people. But *I* have no intention of calling a moratorium either, or abiding by rules of games I neither made up nor agreed to play.

N.Y.R.: Debussy predicted that you would "tolerate no music whatever as an old man," Mr. Stravinsky.

I.S.: But I love more music than ever before. If I seem to stint unduly on the Smetana tone poems, Mendelssohn oratorios, and the type of concerto employed at pianists' Olympic Games, the reason is simply to have more time for the Beethoven quartets. I have revisited a great deal of music lately, some of it after sixty- and seventy-year interims and, therefore, heavily buffeted by past involvements, and discoveries of radical differences between remembered and renewed experiences. Certain songs and piano pieces by Schumann, for instance, have jolted me sharply. Schumann is *the* composer of childhood (first childhood; I will not say who I think is the composer of second childhood), both because he created a children's imaginative world and because children learn some of their first music in his marvelous piano albums. In fact, I have just realized that the reason I dislike *Carnaval* is not, as I had supposed, that my musical personality lacks identities corresponding to the Florestan and Eusebis archetypes of all of Schumann's music, but simply that I was told to like it as a child; and the force of these childhood atavisms is such that I am not old enough to dislike it independently even now.

I must have been insufferably proscribing when Debussy projected that estimate of me. He also referred to me, I think in the same letter, as a "primitive" and "instinctual," rather than a "schooled" composer. And he was right. Like Ramanujan, who did his mathematics without formal mathematical education, I have had to depend on "natural" insight and instinct for all the learning I would have acquired if I had taken a Ph.D. in composition, except that I would have flunked the finals and never taken it.

N.Y.R.: What is the outlook for the Ph.D. composer at the moment, Mr. Stravinsky?

I.S.: I don't know. He used to plead allegiance to either of two totalitarian banners, the one pro-science, the other anti-, to the extent that the scientific pieties of the data-processed society were its main target. But now the lines of these affiliations have crossed, "infighting" has ceased, and the bitterest factions have linked up, perhaps under the influence of the Maharishi, for the one commodity everybody is willing to buy comes from the Royal Liverpudlian Academy of Music. Well, not *quite* everybody. At least a few of the tougher-minded scientists have resisted the general washaway into mixed-media pastimes, as I learn from their announcements of new reductions in encoding time, and in the development of new systems able to accept both digital and analog input. In short, the final goal, computer facilities for all, is getting closer.

But I am no bellwether myself. I am losing patience with music that does not sing or dance (the day has long gone by since we have had very much of that) and that makes no other gesture I can understand except to reflect mechanical processes that quickly set me adrift. Nor am I satisfied by the promise of "consequentiality" in these processes; I am only interested in, at my age I can only afford to be interested in, content. A further, personal, handicap is that I am more of a craftsman than a computer or an engineer, and I find no common ground of craftsmanship in most new machine-made art products; which may be similar to the way an easel painter of my epoch feels about the latest creations in liquid fiberglass.

I further admit to a need to go from a beginning to an end,

through related parts. Perhaps in sympathy with my body's diminished mobility, my mind no longer seems to be willing or able to jump from isolated "present" moments to other isolated "present" moments. I have been listening this week to the recorded piano music of a composer now widely esteemed for his ability to stay an hour or so ahead of his time, but I find the alternation of note-clumps and silences of which it consists impossibly monotonous, and I long for the leverage of Beethoven's timing, to say nothing of harmonic and other leverages. The *matter* of the music is so limited in effect, too, and so solemn, that I was sustained only by the hope, during each longer silence, that finally the pianist might have "had it" too and shot himself.

N.Y.R.: Would you amplify your remark about "consequential processes"?

I.S.: It is progressivist jargon. Of course it *sounds* better to be consequential than not to be, the promise of higher development in forthcoming stages implying superiority. But the true purpose of linear historicism is simply to open up more Midwestern territories of the mind to Ph.D. candidates.

The more consequential is often simply the better sited, the more easily seen or heard, and the inconsequential (historical sense) simply the less accessible, often owing to internal and external innovations of thought and communication. Works of the highest value of all, the Beethoven quartets for instance, are naturally inconsequential, though incalculable in these terms anyway because a value-history would move cyclically at times and wholly out of chronology at other times, skipping generations and even centuries in both directions. One might conclude that fashion plays the largest role, apart from the biological law that beginnings are naturally consequential and endings the other thing. But such speculations only lead to more historicity, whereas what I believe in is the unpredictability, rising above period, style, school, context, historical circumstance, of Beethoven.

N.Y.R.: An essential quality of your own work is the balance in it between past and present, and the continual discovery of the one in the other.

I.S.: Thank you. But it is precisely that debate of yesterday and today that is now relegating *me* to the past, to an annex of the nineteenth century, as I have been told, among less flattering rulings. "Nothing happened before us," the post-contemporary composer proclaims, and he is perfectly right. The nonexistence of the past is a necessary hypothesis to any-one proposing to start from scratch, and protection from annihilating comparisons is no less necessary to a *modus vivendi;* amusements that wither along with the giggles they provoke should not have to suffer exposure next to music that is without a wrinkle after a century and a half.

Post-contemporary composers are modest or hermetic con-cerning their materials and origins. I have been able to dis-cover little about either, apart from "no content," a backward limit of three years, and an explanation that all school-taught traditions are out, though it is some time since there *was* any school worth flouting. But the youngsters' own platform, the "celebration of 'now,' " presumably by spontaneously com-bustible means, seems a little lacking in sustenance; before it is too late they should apply to the science musicians for in-struction in *im*probability theory. The next three years and the three after that will soon be over, just as telephone-booth packing, panty-raids, hamsters, and Batmania were soon over. In short, the "no-past" will soon be a part of the "non-past," except that, to begin with, the past is difficult to deny, the *tabula,* however looked at, being a long way from *rasa.* I have a growing suspicion, in fact, that the pot at the end of this particular rainbow contains only pot.

N.Y.R.: Have you ever tried any drug yourself, Mr. Stravinsky, perhaps during your association with Cocteau?

I.S.: I use a very ordinary drug, procured chiefly from Scotland and France in the forms I favor. Cocteau's opium taking, at least when I knew him, was of a kind with Mr. Plimpton's percussion- and football-playing, in other words, bookmaking.

The late Max Reinkel of MIT was conducting his pioneer experiments with LSD when I became his patient in 1953, and I was aware of the drug at that time. Soon after that my friends Aldous Huxley, Gerald Heard, and Christopher Isherwood, who were among its first white-collar users, invited me to try it, to see its effects on my experience of music. But I am a square. Increased sensory intensity, time dislocation, the altering of consciousness: these are the very last sensations I am looking for. I have never even had a "bennie," let alone smoked a "joint," and the one "mind-bending" artificial paradise I care about is the ataraxia—or is it acedia? —induced by the aforesaid law-abiding potations. Society being what it is, however, and drug dependency certain to increase, legalized control is urgently needed, an opinion I formed after seeing a disturbing film of teenagers on the way down from "glue-sniffing" trips.

3

N.Y.R.: May we return to the question of the ineffectual, or nonexistent, intellectual community? What is your notion of the "intellectual" in the first place?

I.S.: *Not* the literary men, the philosophers, and the artists that my remark implied, but someone more like Gramsci's "Everyman who outside of his own job shares a conception of the world, has a conscious line of moral conduct, and so contributes toward maintaining or changing that conception and encouraging new modes of thought." (Elsewhere Gramsci forgets this Marxist idyll, noting that "Intellectuals have been produced in numbers beyond what is justified by the social need.") The poems of the *Manyōshū* were written by "Everyman" or at least by a representation of people extending from beggars to the Empress herself.

My remark was provoked by the kidnapping, in West Germany, of the Korean composer I Sang Yun, who was returned to and condemned in Seoul as a communist spy. I was unaware of the evidence, and even unaware of Mr. Yun, who could have been the ghost composer of *"We Love Chairman Mao"* for all I knew (Mr. Yun's first names are good for a musician, less good for a spy). I signed a petition to reprieve Mr. Yun, nevertheless, for the reason that I do not believe in judicial murder. (Or any other kind; I should add that I am not a scrutator and that I tend to shirk my social duty of agreeing on one matter with people concerning whom I am in permanent disagreement about virtually everything else.)

Mr. Yun was spared, but whether because or in spite of our protest I have no idea. The only acknowledgment I have seen that the protest ever existed is a note from the American Academy of Arts and Letters, to whose care the cablegrams were mistakenly directed. It said that Academy policy excluded it from taking a hand in such recommendations; I hope that a "policy" of that sort is a nuisance-avoiding expedient rather than an attempt to preserve the "neutrality" of arts and letters.

N.Y.R.: And your idea of community? Do you agree with Durkheim that society, as a moral body, should be "qualitatively distinct" from the individual bodies comprising it?

I.S.: No such society is making itself very conspicuous at present, in any case, nor is the perfectibility of the collective mini-mind showing greater signs of success than the perfectibility of the individual one. But I would be content with lesser ideals myself, perhaps with a *less* "human" and *more* mechanical system, but one capable of achieving a balance between the safety in numbers and the danger in numbers.

Whatever the relationship between the collective morality and the new instruments of communication, the double standard is now the one and only, at least in public life. No statement by any public figure not made under sodium pentothal or hypnosis can be taken as entirely candid, so long as the said figure is primed by popularity polls. As we are already in the second generation of "lip service," moreover, the public figures of the near future will soon be unable to tell the difference, even under truth serums, between their own true opinions and their blue-chip political investments, much less understand the fate of Ananias or the idea that silence can be a lie. Mr. McNamara's sudden change of occupation, for example, set me wondering whether a measure of personal victory might not have been salvaged from the defeat on the grounds that if it is impossible both to say what one believes to be true and to survive politically, then one should get on with the political suicide. To give Mr. McNamara the benefit of the doubt, he appeared to be merely dumbfounded, but it would have been so interesting to know what a "peace offensive" is really like, too, and who could have been in a better position to say?

And who now, what telegenic younger senator, will remind us that our judgment against the Nazi war criminals, a judgment independent of the differences between Nuremberg and now, was that even soldiers under orders are responsible for "crimes against humanity"? That, after all, is what Dr. Spock, Captain Levy, and others have had the courage to say. And somebody more highly and safely placed had soon better say it, too. In view of the vindictiveness toward Mr. LeRoi Jones, it begins to look as if we may have some Daniels and Sinyavskis of our own.

While and if we were about it, incidentally, the same

spokesman might well repeat the no less pertinent question of Marlowe's Machiavelli: "What right had Caesar to the empire?" Was it, I wonder, the right of self-defense?

4

> *"Since we are deprived of acquired experience and former practice by each new case, we do not know what to do."* AMIEL
>
> *"And age, and then the only end of age."* PHILIP LARKIN

N.Y.R.: Do you ever think about the future of your works, Mr. Stravinsky?

I.S.: No. I have already seen some of their "posterity"—as soon as a work is performed that is what it becomes, after all—and the more I see of that the less I care about it. Of course it is satisfying to see settled estimates unsettled, and the removal of interdicts from works of unfashionable periods. But I care less about my "works" than about composing. This is partly because one never composes exactly the piece one sets out to compose, just as I am not now saying exactly what I had in mind to say but what the extenuating words that come to mind as I go along lead me to say. But the threat of posterity is worse now than it used to be for other reasons as well. I have changed my mind, for example, about the advantages of embalming a performance in tape. The disadvantages, which are that one performance represents only one set of circumstances, and that mistakes and misunderstandings are cemented into traditions as quickly and canonically as truths, now seem to me a greater price to pay. The Recording Angel I am concerned with is not CBS, in any case, but the One with the Big Book.

N.Y.R.: And your own future, Mr. Stravinsky?

I.S.: I will have to stay closer to home, and my object world will be more limited. But I have been thinking of how Vermeer was able to reflect a world and live a life of perfect making in his own studio; and of how Chardin could display a richer representation of life in his kitchen than other painters managed with all Versailles. So I must try, in my smaller way, to look more closely close by, and to bring more life to my own still life. One difficulty is that I am regarded as an object now myself, some priceless piece of porcelain, as it may be, and this crockery is my greatest enemy. I hope nothing else befalls it for a spell, but if something *does*, that it comes "during office hours." As for the "contents," our talents are not given to us with any tenure, and "we" may well outlast them; I know, nevertheless, that I have more music in me. And I must give; I cannot live a purely receiving life.

Of the two greatest problems of age the first is simply the lack of preparation, the lack of a natural or acquired provision of experience. All our lives we observe other people in the condition, but fail to learn biologically from the spectacle, and even fail to believe that the same thing can and will happen to us. When it *has* happened, the suddenness is like Levin's awareness, in the peasant village, that the sky had changed and that this change, like the transformation in himself, was unnoticeable as a process.

The more difficult problem is inevitableness. It is put very gently by Augustine in his last sermon, and I would prefer to have him say it for me, as Mr. Peter Brown describes the scene in his *Augustine of Hippo*. After appointing the priest Eraclius as his successor, Augustine reminds the congregation that:

"As boys we can look forward to being youths; as youths to being grown up, and as young men to reaching our prime and, in our prime to growing old. Whether this will happen is uncertain; but there is always something to look forward to. But an old man has no further stage before him. Now I have grown old."

But the end of the story reminds *me* of something, which is that I have been talking too much:

Eraclius stood forward to preach, while the old Augustine sat behind him: "the cricket chirps," Eraclius said, "the swan is silent."
I.S.
Hollywood/Feb. 1/68

Where Is Thy Sting?

I

CRITO: *The attendant who is to give you the [hemlock] wants me to tell you not to talk too much . . . talking is apt to interfere with the action of the poison.*   Phaedo, 63

NEW YORK REVIEW OF BOOKS: When you went to Europe recently, Mr. Stravinsky, we heard that you were intending to go for good.

I.S.: For the better, anyway. At the time I left Los Angeles it already seemed too late for a phased withdrawal. The smog was like Mace, but then, the air, apart from radioisotopes, must be better anywhere else now, even in a coal mine. A major earthquake was predicted, too, not merely by seismologists but by the religious protection rackets, which were transferring east to pray out the millennium and to await the second option of chiliasm there; self-centered as it is to say so, in view of the probable devastations to and from atomic and bacteriological stockpiles, I would fall like Humpty Dumpty now, and being unable to make a "soft landing," break unmendably. A tidal wave was expected also, and since a few heavy showers can turn much of the city into "slide areas" necessitating helicopter evacuations, a really sizable inundation would wash the whole "songdom" and "gemurrmal" out to sea. Yet despite these and other catastrophes, actual and impending, no one got around to designating the State a disaster area until the midwinter monsoons.

Even so, the most immediate hazard was the state of society. Whatever they were "on" about then, "speed," "soul," the recent invention of "youth," people with anti-astronaut hair styles were milling about my street in such numbers that the ambulances—which siren by every few minutes normally, curtains raised, presumably to give the emergency patient a last look—had to find another route. Welcome as this was in terms of noise abatement, it attracted still more of the armed and uniformed men who were already so conspicuous that the neighborhood felt like occupied territory. Or worse than occupied territory. The xenon beams that search the Stygian gloom of the polluted upper sky ("the smog is lofting"— *Finnegans Wake*, 593) and that supposedly "send up" film premières, actually give one the impression of being near, or in, a concentration camp.

High barriers exist, in any case—and not only figuratively, the fencing of at least one private estate hereabouts apparently having been modeled on the Berlin Wall. A social war foments around them, moreover, and it could easily break into a shooting one, *did* break into one shortly before I left, when the police outgunned a man hardly three hundred yards from my house. At about that time, as well, the American Legion opened its campaign against my San Diego neighbor Professor Marcuse, an action I read as a warning to keep my peace about the war or risk being dealt with Chicago-style myself.

All the same, the final decision to leave came from a very different consideration. It was simply that I had begun to fear some city or state official might find out that I live there. This would almost certainly lead to an award, such as I have been receiving during the past sixty-five years from other cities, states, countries, kibbutzim, and tribes; and entail a ceremony, with a presentation speech by Miss Long Beach, perhaps, or one of the Beverly Hillbillies. Something had to give, obviously, and it was me. I took the least frequently hijacked run to New York, and then to Zurich.

N.Y.R.: What did you do in Switzerland, Mr. Stravinsky?

I.S.: Saw friends. *They* came not only to see but to touch me, though, as if I were a talismanic relic; I supposed that they were only double-checking, and remembering that the Great Leap Forward had checked on the tangibility of Chairman Mao by obliging him to swim, I did not complain. In lawful, orderly, and quiescent Zurich, however, and with distance lending enchantment, I began to miss not only the last-few-minutes-of-the-Roman Empire aspect of Hollywood, but also the commotion ("Come to America, where the action is"), campus "unrest" (*i.e.*, tanks, bombs, guerrilla warfare) and all. In fact, the sound of hunters' rifles in the woods near the hotel one afternoon made me so nostalgic for Sunset Boulevard on a Saturday night that if I had had an oxygen mask and enough bulletproofing. . . .

N.Y.R.: Where *did* you go, Mr. Stravinsky?

I.S.: To Paris, to see more friends. I walked quite regularly, too, as much as I *can* walk, in Le Nôtre's paths at Chantilly and, less bracingly, in the corridors of the Trianon Palace Hotel, where some of the boarders might have been making an early Chaplin film: a white-gloved cigar smoker; a spats-wearing walker of a small, compensatorily ferocious dog; an alcoholically roseate old woman talker-to-cats. I did not go to concerts but did hear some new music on tape, including one very fine piece (a lot of glib music is being written nowadays) by Gérard Masson, whose acquaintance I made as well. And, yes, I saw *Le Sacre du printemps*. This frolic was held in the Opéra, but it belonged at the Folies-Bergères.

I was in Paris during the monetary crisis, by the way, and was greatly impressed by the contrast between the success of the international bankers and the failure of the international peace negotiators. What is really important to "the comity of nations," or at any rate to the people who really run the world, can and does get instant action.

N.Y.R.: We read that you had talked with French television officials, but did you see any television there?

I.S.: No, which must be why it strikes me as even more echolalic and mind-jamming back here than before. But I have noticed changes in televisional *moeurs* since then, too. One is that the close-up of the dead and dying, of the accident and murder victim (locally as well as in Biafra and Vietnam), has become a feature of the medium. Another I cannot describe, but it is exemplified in yesterday's announcement by a color-video commentator, part green, part third-degree sunburn, that "Although General Eisenhower's condition has improved, plans are going ahead for his funeral."

Television sells more than that which is so disastrously rated next to godliness, to be sure (in fact, it sells vicarious existences), but the predominating advertisements seem to be those which imply that a dirtless, odorless, and inconvenience-less society is the ultimate goal of civilization. These somehow inadequate aims must be near fulfillment, furthermore, at least in the home, thanks to socially up-to-date detergents ("DRIVE eats blood stains") powered by "ultrasonic activated bubbles." The "technology of false needs" has turned to Nature itself, in any case, and is already spraying it with defoliants, denudants, desiccants, deodorants, herbicides, germicides, pesticides, nitpickers. A play about Adam in contemporary undress would be obliged even now to represent the Garden without a leaf, let alone an apple. Now, too, the punitive and expiatory needs of puritan sanitation insanity are arousing expectations of cosmic retribution in the contamination of other planets with terrestrial microorganisms and of our own with lunar spores.

Which reminds me of the video highlight on my return, the Christmas-pageant space show reconciling missile technology and Genesis. In fact the space capsule itself was turned into a teleological argument as the Three Wise Men astrobards, guided by earthshine, read Bible poetry to Sabbatarian earthlings. *Gott mit uns,* the Space Program was assuring us, but it must have been worried that a more prestigiously remote orbit had been destined as a pulpit for readings from *Das Kapital* on Marx's birthday.

N.Y.R.: What did your European friends think of our elections?

I.S.: They were unable to imagine the visage of the new President on Mount Rushmore, so they said, and not only because of the sculptural obstacles. And some of them questioned whether actual voting need take place any more, on the grounds that computerized public-opinion polls are reasonably reliable now, and, in effect, have already done the job; one friend, probably thinking of my own welfare, suggested that the saving in time, money, and fresh fertilizer, properly converted and applied, could be used to make Los Angeles inhabitable. Certainly an election by opinion survey would not destroy the illusion that by dropping a ballot in a ballot box and proclaiming the winner the people's choice (which he or she could be only by a concatenation of choices several million links removed), the body politic is exercising its freedom and democratic rights. Even so transparently supposititious an operation as the Democratic convention could not undermine *that* fantasy, after all.

Vested-interested legislators may be an old story, but some of the territory they are now obliged to administer—the management of the scientific future, for one rather estimable precinct—is alarmingly new. Consider the field of genetics, with its limitless power and short timetable of disaster. Assume, too, that the "new-mandarin" race-improving committees are "humane," "well-meaning," "responsible," and that they can be entrusted with the elimination of diabetics, cleft palates, stutterers, the color blind and the tone deaf. But what about mental defectives, and especially borderline cases?

Consolation of a sort is offered by the certainty that the administration of science by scientists would be even worse. When a debate opened up at the recent Congress of Genetics in Tokyo as to whether science could afford to be bound by ethics, one pro-ethics delegate clinched his argument with the epiphany that "Although man consists of molecules he is not a molecule himself"; and a like-minded colleague added that "The evolution of every species is certainly being modified very greatly by the presence of man." That, at least, deserves a prize for litotes.

But this is high science, still for the moment unapplied. What is transpiring meanwhile with some of the applied kinds, with for instance the grafting, transplanting, implanting of those thirty-five spare body parts? (What a relief to be too old for gardening of this sort!) Will those life-prolonging utilities be available to rich and poor alike, to the queue-forming as well as the well connected? And by what means will donors be found? Euthanasia? Black Markets in dismembering? Body snatching (of the still living)?

N.Y.R.: What were your friends' views of our Black Separatists?

I.S.: I have not worked out my *own* views yet. "Now there are only the blacks and those who dislike them," says Mr. Bond. But this is untrue and unhelpful. Nor will it help to ban Monostatos, and the Moor in *Petrushka;* Manichean characters they are, of course, but their absurdity apart from their music can only animadvert on white culture—they are little white lies—not on black. (Incidentally, the "racial" motivation in Monostatos's account of his rape attempt resembles Mr. Cleaver's account of the same thing in *Soul On Ice*.)

Since I cannot be certain that it mattered, I am no less rhetorical than Mr. Bond in mentioning that the man outgunned near my house was black. Yet the origins of the black man's crime were to some degree rooted in the inequities which that circumstance introduces. The point is irrelevant in the nearsighted and compartmented eye of the law, which does not admit or apportion any dependence of the particular on the general, and which is only beginning to accept the idea, as old as the Encyclopedists, of diminished responsibility. But the law, after all, is a large constituent in the moral dilemma.

The shooting was a consequence of petty larceny. But was it necessary to kill? Can trained marksmen do no better? Or are the Los Angeles Police (as they might at times appear to the incompletely manumitted people of Watts) deliberately under-practiced at certain targets partly because of over-specialization in the upholding of a prejudicial system? The system I mean is the non-distribution of wealth, thanks to tax shelters and other privileges whereby the rich may pay less taxes than their chauffeurs—which is why possession should be taxed rather than income, why we need an Onassis tax, and Rockefellow and Rothschildren taxes, and a tax on tax expatriots, and a not-likely-to-pass-through-the-eye-of-the-needle tax.

❋ ❋ ❋

The solution to racism is genetic, but I no longer remember my Mendel and whether fusion can be achieved quickly or only after a long interregnum of sexual roulette. I wonder, too, if when it *has* been, racism will disappear, or whether it will then be a question of

> ... *I swear Beauty herself is black,*
> *And all they foul that thy complexion lack.*

2

N.Y.R.: How would a contemporary musician paraphrase Mendelssohn's "what a piece of music expresses is not too vague a thought to be put into words, but too precise a thought"?

I.S.: He might say that music is a non-analogous system—or several non-analogous systems: it is more of a Babel than a universal language. And if he had said that, he might add that the basis of intelligibility (since it is not an encoded something else) is presupposed, self-contained, innate. The epistemological problem would thus be the same as it is with verbal language. The mode of knowledge is untranslatable but not private: it depends on other users. Which is Descartes' (superseded) "other minds" argument: "... *qu'ils usent comme moy de la Parole ... qu'ils le sont comme moy.*"

But *would* "he" have said it, subscribed to the nominalism, in the first place? A sociology of music, the correlating of music and the whole of life, does not exist as yet; but studies in specialized areas—in psychiatry, for instance, where patients who will respond to no verbal approach (*trust* no verbal approach?) both respond to and participate in music—prove that it *is* understood in correlative terms.

Does the world of the Beethoven quartets exist outside of music, then, and is it possible to discover a reflective system between the language structure of the music and the structure of the phenomenal world? No, to the first, but to the second, well, yes, perhaps, eventually. All the same, the music of the quartets, and of *The Magic Flute*, accedes to an in-extremis importance in the human consciousness beyond the pleasure principle, or divertimento principle, on which it nevertheless continues to depend.

My further, personal, belief is that the quartets are a charter of human rights, a perpetually seditious one in the Platonic sense of the subversiveness of art. The charter is obviously no solvent to the discarded humanity in Resurrection Cities, for whom, on the contrary, the accessibility of such treasures to other people must seem as unjust, and the use of them as tactless, in different orders of value, as the Burtons' *ditto* with their new yacht. Nor will it bring much balm to activists, for whom "art" is a cant word anyway, and "aesthetic examples" a run-around in the language game. (According to the Hindu *chakras*, the body-center both for the aesthetic feelings and the feelings of material affluence is—did Freud know this?—the anus, which may have something to do with the high incidence in aesthetes and collectors of a condition often if indecorously described as "tight-assed.")

A high concept of freedom *is* embodied in the quartets, nevertheless, both beyond and including what Beethoven himself meant when he wrote (to Prince Galitzin) that his music could "help suffering mankind." They are a measure of man (I am thinking of Professor Puccetti's extra-human "persons"), and part of the description of the quality of man, and their existence is a guarantee.

N.Y.R.: Why *The Magic Flute*, even assuming that you mean to limit it to the music?

I.S.: *Can* it be limited to the music? I believe in the entity myself. Certainly the *magic* is limited to the music, while the moral meaning—the entity I believe in—would hardly be worth stating, if it could be stated, apart from it. Still, the music is not "independent," and not "pure." In fact, it seems to me that the intentional meaning of the opera, the triumph of Life over Death, is reversed at times in the depths of the music; in the brave little parade of Music through the gates of Death, for example, the flute charms the Keeper into a stay of execution, but the piece is a funeral march, nonetheless. Death is just beneath the surface in much of the other music as well, especially Pamina's; and in the great C-minor fugato-chorale, which somehow succeeds in sounding Beethoven's *"Eroica"* note without Beethoven's display of superior will, the wings of the terrible angel are closer than they have ever been before in music.

Mozart's Masonic allegory-land is a more attractive country than the *dix-huitième* Establishment countries of his other operas, at least to me, and not only musically. It is morally more generous, for one thing, and for another the dramatic terrain ranges more widely, partly because of the new and diverse elevations of the religious, the mystical, and the super-natural. In fact, the greatest achievement of the opera is pre-cisely the entity, the unity of feeling that embues all of the music from sacred choruses and magic spells to the proto-Broadway duet—except in musical quality—concerning the future propagations of Papageno and Papagena.

Unlike *Don Giovanni* the opera does not include any ex-tended scene, but neither does it "lack" one. (It also does not include, or lack, any bore comparable to Masetto.) On the other hand, Mozart is more economical and faster-moving than ever, setting the stage for the final scene, for instance, with a single phrase. The simplest means are more effective, too, as in the device of the "false" relationship, which occurs in all of his music, yet here (most vertiginously in Pamina's *"Mir klingt der Mutternahme süsse"*) as if for the first time.

The most obvious anticipations are of Weber, Wagner, the Mendelssohn of the *Midsummer Night's Dream*. (The most obvious omission is Schubert, who had already been scooped in *"L'ho perduta"* from *Figaro.*) Wagner is everywhere, and all the way from *Tannhäuser* (the sixteenth-note violin figuration in the final *Andante*) to *Tristan* (*"Wann also wird die Decke schwinden"* and *"jeden Tone meinen Dank zu schildern"*). The Pamino-Sarastro scene is Wagnerian, too (though Sarastro's own music more strikingly resembles the music of Jesus in the Bach Passions), except that Mozart stops at the point where Wagner, already heavy-breathing, would have begun to overblow.

The forerunning, in any case and since I have somehow got on to this dreary subject, is more remarkable in the *Terzett* (No. 16) and in the accompaniment to Papageno's final aria, which plagiarize and improve upon *The Sleeping Beauty;* in the choral parts and instrumental bass-line of *"Bald, Bald, Jüngling,"* which have been lifted from *Rigoletto;* and in the introduction to *"Drei Knäbchen, jung, schön,"* which might have been borrowed from a rainy-day mood piece by Ravel.

❀ ❀ ❀

N.Y.R.: What are the outstanding tendencies in music today, as distinguished from a decade ago when you said that Boulez and Stockhausen represented them?

I.S.: Well, those two names are still an inescapable collocation, and Stockhausen is still on the crest of the *Nouvelle Vague.* In fact, most of the main rages of the moment were either begotten by him or else quickly taken under his wing. The one for the re-employment of the classics (an idea as old as the quodlibet) was popularized by his *Hymnen,* and the one for sustained sounds (". . . being all in one tone," says Hawthorne, "I had only to get my pitch, and could then go on interminably") by his *Stimmung,* a seventy-minute chord— Stockhausen's time scale is that of *Die Götterdämmerung*— which to me indicates the need of a musical equivalent to the parking meter; *that* idea, I might add, is as old as Purcell's *Fantasy Upon One Note*. The main lines of many other Stockhausen novelties are laid down in his own "concerts." One of them is the blurring of the termini both *a quo* and *ad quem*, or call it the blending of the aesthetic enterprise with "the world." Another is in improvising electronic accompaniments to the ascents of balloons, which is rather like bubble blowing, pictorially speaking.

The handiest index of comparison from the beginning to the end of the decade is not in the work of any composer, however, but in the status of electronic music. It has moved in that time from a corner of experiment to the center of the stage, from concerts for hard-core colleagues to soft-centered films like *Candy*. And it has moved into and conquered academe. The young musician takes his degree in computer technology now, and settles down to his Moog or his mini-synthesizer as routinely as in my day he would have taken it in counterpoint and harmony (see dictionary) and gone to work at the piano.

As for the *live* new music of the decade, the main power struggle was between the preordained and the lottery schools, even though, so far as the ordinary listener was concerned, this amounted to a stalemate, for no matter how polarized the differences, only score readers and initiates were aware of them. In practice, the *ad lib* timing, the unfixed notes in fixed range, the mechanisms of choice, were not recognized as the freedom gestures they were intended to be, but as effects that might have been as despotically "written" as any other.

Progress, or at least invention, might have been detected by the non-initiate in the new techniques for the movement of sound in space. But some of the other "pioneering" of the period must have seemed to him like paring closer and closer to nothingness: the engaging of choruses in varieties of pranks not including any use of the voice, for example, and the per-

formances on the woodwork of the piano (after the attractions of "topless" pianos had been overexposed), and the
exploitation of a principle of form based entirely on audience
suspense in guessing how near the actual *cul* of the *sac* the
promulgator really was. But the non-initiate may well have
been wrong, and he may really have been offered

> . . . *imperishable presences serene*
> *Colossal, without form, or sense, or sound*

Progress was also measured, incidentally, or not so incidentally, when, ephemerality was finally claimed as an objective. This may have seemed simply to be making a virtue of
necessity, but it increased production to the point where the
manufacturer could retire each new model to the used-car lot
even before it had been driven around the block.

N.Y.R.: Did you happen to read the Boulez-Liebermann dis-
pute on the present state of opera, or Ezra Laderman's letter
in the *Times* on the neglect of American efforts in this form?

I.S.: Boulez assailed his targets so convincingly that I all the
more regretted his reluctance to contribute his own example
of the requisite new opera. But whereas he rejects all contemporary operas except Berg's, Laderman does not even raise
the value question. American operas should be performed
because they are being written and because they are American.
And insofar as opera composers require even more help than
other kinds of composers, and American more than European,
who would disagree? Except that what is the point?

In 1937 the Met could have been doing *Wozzeck*. What it
did do was Damrosch's *The Man Without a Country*, the indigenous opera in an acceptably bland style by a composer
with the connections to get it performed. I did not hear it, but
being in New York for my *Jeu de cartes* at the time of the
rehearsals, I heard some tattle about it. (There was said to be
an unfortunate *fermata* on the first syllable of the last word
of the title aria: "The Man Without A Count . . . ry.")

Judging by its traces, the performance did little for the Met, the composer, or the future of opera, which in fact seems more and more to be in the past.

N.Y.R.: How do today's new-music audiences compare with those of your own early years?

I.S.: The question is unquantifiable, and anyway, as practically the oldest audience alive, I am hardly able to speak for young ones.

N.Y.R.: Then what are the incomparables?

I.S.: In my youth the new music grew out of, and in reaction to, traditions, whereas it appears to be evolving today as much from social needs as interior artistic ones. I am unable to evaluate this development, but I retract my former irrelevant objections, which were that if anything goes, then nothing *goes*, and if anything can happen, it cannot matter very much what *does* happen.

The status of new music as a category is another incomparable. It had none at all in my early years, being in fact categorically opposed, and often with real hostility. But the unsuccess of composers of my generation at least kept them from trading on success, and our unsuccess may have been less insidious than the automatic superlatives which nowadays kill the new by absorbing it to death. (By the same token, of course, the best hatchet jobs are done with pernicious praise.)

The largest incomparable is in the permissiveness factor. Twenty years ago, when Mitropoulos introduced Schoenberg's then still rather steamy *Five Pieces* to New York, one die-hard Philharmonic subscriber actually did die from the shock. Surely a response of *that* sensitivity is no longer possible now.

3

N.Y.R.: How do the upper eighties compare with the lower, Mr. Stravinsky?

I.S.: Very unfavorably. I probably seem like a "kid" to a Struldbruggian like Bertrand Russell, and in fact next to that redoubtable sage I do not look very arctic. Still, eighty-seven years can feel like, as of course they *are*, an incurable disease. At that time of life one's corporeality and what is bizarrely called one's health are too important. One must husband one's strength, and former mechanical body habits have to be programmed by the brain; at times even the simplest limb movements must be put through the mind. This is part of the reason why we no longer gallivant but only toddle—at the end as in the beginning, as I was reminded while posing for photographs with my two-year-old great-granddaughter not long ago. And this is the only certain "wisdom of age" I am able to impart.

My perimeter of pleasures, small as it was in the lower eighties, has shrunk further now, and whereas my one unimpaired epicurean habit, a liquid one, has been almost completely stanched, everything except a gavage has been used to try to revive its impaired solid, one-time companion, meaning food. Seek other satisfactions, they tell me, and one that I have very earnestly sought of late is the satisfaction of surviving their remedies. This is churlish, I know, but I grew up, and old, in the days of general practitioners who did not expect a stipend and humanitarian award for each house call, or require the invalid to diagnose his own ailments. Competent treatment is available even now, no doubt, especially for illnesses uncomplicated by the necessity of considering whole human beings. But I misdiagnosed one of my own maladies not long ago, and the doctors who likewise failed to classify it went about their search as if what they really wanted to determine was whether I would prove as difficult to kill as Rasputin.

The more acute pains are the moral ones, that "melancholy" (*i.e.*, the "spleen") which Dürer points to in himself, in the drawing evidently intended for *his* physician. But pain, in any case and from whatever source, quickly becomes what we believe in most completely. One of my most regular pains is induced by comparing my present exiguous output even with that of the by-no-means-bumper years of the mid-sixties. I am pained, too, by sudden memory blanks; this is like waking at night in a foreign hotel and not knowing where you are. And my memory taunts me; while I may be unable to find the right address in it for an event of a month ago, and while yesterday is vague and last week might have evaporated, a great deal that was etched there three quarters of a century ago seems to lie on the tip of the tongue. These memory failures are more disturbing than reduced engine power, a car being able to run on one cylinder, after all, and a little low-octane (not enough to flood the motor), so long as the transmission works and the chassis gets enough servicing.

At least I do not dwell on the future. (Unlike Prospero: "Every third thought shall be my grave.") In fact the "dying-trajectories" in the Glaser and Strauss book bothered me no more than an insurance company's annual statement of earnings might have done, even that vertical plunge at the end of each downward parabola marking the point at which the person represented by the graph had stopped creaking and, as the gerontophobes in my neighborhood so indelicately say, croaked.

❊ ❊ ❊

It may be that the past *can* be recaptured, in sudden regurgitations of memory with eidetic recall, provoked and abetted in old people by moments of chronological suspension and confusion. I must have been in some such bemused state myself in Lucerne one afternoon last fall, for I seemed to have re-entered an earlier time zone. I should mention that I have strong childhood associations with the city, and that its topographical changes are comparatively slight even today. Horses and charabancs have disappeared, of course, and the traffic police are young women now, ex-Heidis in white rubber coats, apparently weaponless though surely possessing secret ones, like Karate. But the geranium window sills, the swans waddling on the shore (not in the least Pavlova-like, in dry dock), the snow roofs and log stacks, and much more are wholly unchanged.

The time trick occurred, of all places, during a visit to Wagner's villa at Triebschen. The rooms themselves, the porcelain *pechka*, and the sash windows with pelmets, reminded me of Russian country houses I knew in my youth. Looking from them to the Lake (straight ahead because of encroaching factories and phalansteries), and hearing no sound but the wind—no juddering tourist boat, even no yodeler—I was transported to a similar and more naturally pristine afternoon on my first Swiss holiday four fifths of a century ago. I had returned from a walk with my father that day, and as we entered the lobby of our hotel, the Schweizerhof, he told me to look in the direction of a beautiful lady he said was the Empress Elizabeth of Austria. And he added, I think because it was only shortly after Mayerling, that she was *"neschastna"* (unhappy). The picture of the Empress, in any case, and of my father and the room, was as clear and as real as the picture of Wagner's villa in which I was actually standing.

Have I in fact remembered this because of my father's word, which I borrowed for my own miseries? *My* "unhappiness," so I have always been accustomed to think, was the result of my father's remoteness and my mother's denial of affection. When my eldest brother died suddenly, and my mother did not transfer any of her feelings for him to me, and my father did not become less aloof, I resolved (that resolution made at some time and for one reason or another by all children) that someday I would "show" them. But now that someday has come and gone, and no one remains to whom it would mean anything to be "shown" whatever is left to show, I myself being the last witness.

* * *

Restored to the present (and to resipiscence, if my "normal" mind can be described that way any more), I went from Triebschen to the Schwann Hotel for tea. (In 1890 it was tea and ratafia in, I think, the *Englischeviertel.*) Sitting there—where Wagner, not yet amnestied, followed with watch in hand the first performance of *Lohengrin* in Weimar—it seemed impossible that my own childhood could be so far away, and impossible that that world of feeling could be extinct, except in me. Yet not how far away but how close and how real; and how soon that question in answer to which, like Lohengrin, I must disappear myself.

I. S.
Hollywood/March 27/69

PREFACES

Some Perspectives of a Contemporary [1]

I have no synoptic view of our century's music to offer, at any rate none that I wish to impart or expound. The countenance I would put on the period must necessarily and too closely resemble my own, moreover, which means that among other limitations it would also and inevitably expose my deaf spots—such as that I know nothing whatever about electronic music, and about popular music only that all of it is very loud. Finally disqualifying myself beyond rehabilitation as a historian, I confess that my recollections of some of the many different stages of musical development since 1900 have become addled, not only in general but even in my own career. In consequence, I will restrict my remarks to what I see as the principal contrasts between the beginning and end—arbitrary divisions, but they conveniently define my own life in music—of the seven musical decades.

❊ ❊ ❊

[1] Preface to *Storia Della Musica*, Vol. IX: *La Musica Contemporanea* (Milano: Fratelli Fabbri Editori; 1967).

First and most important is the disappearance of the musical mainstream. (Whether it really *has* disappeared is a contention requiring analytical substantiation that I cannot furnish here, but I promised no more than a personal view.) The problem imposed by this absence is the same as the problem of man without God: irresponsibility. In the domain of art this is translated to that most unusable of goals, total freedom, as if the unserviceability of former laws and premises, of the techniques and systems embodied in the art of the past, invalidated the need to search for new ones. "Now will new *rules* arise through revolution," chants the chorus in a stasimon from the *Eumenides*. (My italics, to be sure.)

❀ ❀ ❀

Composers continue to be generated in and by traditions, nevertheless, however vestigial, splintered, and self-fabricated (by the free adoption of ancestors and the choosing and pasting together of assorted bits and pieces of the past). All works of art, and anti-art, must have antecedents, though these may not be readily apparent, and though connection may be created and discovered only after long periods of time. The *"beklemmt"* episode in the *Cavatina* from Opus 130, for example, acquired a new dimension a full century later because of the rediscoveries in rhythm by Webern and others. And this should warn me. The future will undoubtedly provide connecting links with what, to me, is most disjunct in the music of today.

❀ ❀ ❀

One cause of the evaporation, or fibrilation, of the musical main current is the dislocation of Western music from the West. Europe's musical boundaries have been continually and ever more rapidly crumbling during the whole of the seventy-year period, until now it is safe to predict that the promised symbiosis of new musicians and new media in the Future Welfare State is as likely to occur (if it does occur) in the Orient as in Germany or Italy. But the dispersion of the European musical heritage must also be attributed, in part, to the greater awareness, and increasing fusion, of East and West. Initiated in Europe and sponsored by Debussy (among more superficial investors), this fusion is exemplified today in Messiaen, who has been a dominant influence on the last decade of our period. (In the East it seems to have resulted mainly in such commodities as Japanese Bartók, but the region is beyond my competence.)

At the same time, nationalism in music has been as rampant as ever, though music is reputed by its nature to transcend its national imagery, and though many of the new techniques and new media are, by their nature, ethnically neutral. In fact, the new means of communication have achieved nothing by way of overcoming nationalism except to substitute an airport and motel culture for a stay-at-home one.

❋ ❋ ❋

It is this transcendent (or abstract, or self-contained) nature of music that the new so-called concretism—Pop Art, eighteen-hour-long slices-of-reality films, *musique concrète*— opposes. But instead of bringing art and reality closer together, the new movement merely thins out the distinction, at least to my mind. But then I regard the struggle between language and reality as mercifully unresolvable. To my thinking the most concrete art is simply the most perfectly made.

❋ ❋ ❋

Shorn of its historical tradition, will Western music come to an end? By any other name the music of the future will probably not sound any sweeter, certainly. But whether or not the Marxist argument of utility has been proved by the death of the creative tradition of Western music, Society certainly appears to prefer its new playthings, such as television, which is incontestably more interesting in itself than in any creative use of it. The ever-improving tools of reproduction in this age of the self-replicating molecule, and the exponential increase in reproductive art,[2] also support a forecast that the hominids of tomorrow will outgrow the need for creative art. To me, at any rate, it seems that the selling of the music of every era and culture in canned form—always in prettier and prettier cans, of course ("advertisements are truer")—can hardly encourage creativity.

* * *

The music of the 1960's—what I know of it—has been characterized by vastly greater diversity than the music of the first decade of the century; by a greater degree of experimentation; and by a facelessness, or blurring together, of its composers. It is characterized as well by new measurements, including a different specificity of time (and hence of the tempo of ideas), and the reflection of many ideas of the *Zeitgeist*, such as the attempt to incorporate elements of chance (which I understand not at all myself, for the reason that chance, being subjective, is noncommunicative at the level of causation, which is where my involvement begins).

But these impressions were formed under the sign of past perspectives. In another seventy years another observer may well characterize the same period as one of synthesis, of the comparative toning down of the experimental, and of the emergence of sharply delineated personalities. Even now, my

[2] See *The Work of Art in the Age of Mechanical Reproduction* by Walter Benjamin.

younger colleagues—and this is the measure of a gulf—are able to hear necessity where I hear only randomness, and to perceive an Ariadne's thread (as mollusks are said to perceive colors beyond the range of human awareness) where I find only broken bits of string.

❋ ❋ ❋

Do these seventy years constitute a period of high musical achievement? *I* think they do, and I would rate the highest flights of the time with the greatest achievements of the past. It is true that no great river of music comparable to the rivers of Bach, Mozart, Beethoven, has flowed from any original composer of the period (the adjective eliminating the many prolific reproducers in synthetic traditions), but then neither the age nor the nature of the new music is conducive to fluency.

❋ ❋ ❋

In spite of my title, and indelicate as it is to speak of myself, I must explain in conclusion that I have never thought in perspectivist terms concerning my own participation in the century's music. My activity—reactivity, my animadverters would call it—was conditioned not by concepts of history but by music itself. I have been formed in part, and in greater and lesser ways, by all of the music I have known and loved, and I composed as I was formed to compose.

I. S.
Hollywood, August 5, 1967

Gesualdo di Venosa: New Perspectives [1]

M usicians may yet save Gesualdo from musicologists, but certainly the latter have had the best of it until now. Even now he is academically unrespectable, still the crank of chromaticism, still rarely sung.

Two new publications, Professor Watkins's monograph and the CBS recording of the sixth book of madrigals, should help to scotch the prejudice of the scholars. Professor Watkins provides the composer with surrounding scenery not previously in view, and in which he does not fade but stands out more vividly, if in different colors, than before. The recording, on the other hand, corrects the view of the music as a case of samples, simply by providing it with its own context; the largely tendentious interest in Gesualdo had deprived him even of his own "normalcy." Together the two publications fill in the lacunae to the extent that apart from the continuing search for the lost book of six-voice madrigals, the major goals are reduced to two: the recovery of performance style (a by-no-means-impossible quest) and the recording of the complete music.

Seeking Gesualdo's origins in the Neapolitan school, Professor Watkins exposes Pomponio Nenna in the role of principal model. At least six of Gesualdo's texts, including *Ancide sol la morte, Mercè grido, Tu segui,* and *Deh, coprite,* were set by Nenna first. Apart from this coincidence, if that is what it was, Gesualdo appears to have helped himself to elements of Nenna's chromatic style and to have pocketed harmonic progressions verbatim. In fact, Gesualdo's imitations are so sedulous in some instances as to appear to us like

[1] Preface to *Don Carlo Gesualdo: The Man and His Music,* by Glenn E. Watkins (Chapel Hill: University of North Carolina Press; 1970).

plain light-fingering. Perhaps that was how they were thought
of at the time, too, but the ingenuous opinions of a powerful
prince's not-so-fellow musicians are unlikely to have been
committed to paper. And, anyway, apart from a missing credit
line in history, no monstrous injustice has been done. Nenna
never received the touch of Zephyr. He is as devoid of musical
interest, compared to Gesualdo, as Holinshed is of poetic interest, compared with the Shakespeare based on him.

It has been known since at least 1934 (Pannain: *Istituzione
e Monumenti*) that Gesualdo's sacred music (what was then
known of it) shared a style formed by Nenna, Macque,
Trabaci, and others. But *ante* Watkins almost nothing was
known of Neapolitan influences on the secular music. Its
radical chromatic tendency was linked to Wert, Rore, Luzzaschi, and other madrigalists of the Ferrara court, though
judging from the little I know of these composers, Luzzaschi
alone comes close enough to have been warrantably put forward as a stepping stone. Now, with Professor Watkins's
discovery of the Nenna examples—as with the discovery
of the Oldowan Fossil Cranium, the decipherment of Linear
B, and any other discovery involving contingent systems
of classification—the entire history of the subject must be
revised or scrapped. As discovery breeds discovery, too, Professor Watkins's should provoke explorations through the
whole of sixteenth-century Neapolitan music. For a beginning, one would like to know more of some of the shadowy
figures in Gesualdo's own circle: Luigi Tansillo of Venosa,
for example, and Giovanni Leonardo Primavera, whose
seventh book is dedicated to the Prince. And what of the
madrigal style of the *"infelice"* Troiano, who was not merely
shadowy but umbrageous, being the first of the composer-
murderers who were to enliven the peninsular musical scene
down to and through Alessandro Stradella, and whose frater-
nity was soon to include Gesualdo himself? Can any particular

of Gesualdo's settings of the word *"uccide"* be traced to him? For the rest, Professor Watkins surveys all of the forms, sacred and secular, as the composer inherited and bequeathed them. He ably anatomizes the complete music, too, and not only the music, but also the texts, for the musico-dramatic gesturing of the secular pieces depends on devices of oxymora, sexual symbolisms ("I expire," "I die" [2]), and other conventional insipidities. Further and finally, Professor Watkins newly maps the composer among the peaks of Mannerism, and concludes this first sensible study of him with a fully documented history of the misunderstandings of his music down to *ca.* 1970.

✻ ✻ ✻

As aforesaid, the most novel perspectives extending from the CBS account of Book Six are of the composer himself. Before the appearance of this admirably crammed grammy-award contender ("I am dubbed," says Shakespeare's Philip the Bastard), our musical bees had been extracting the composer's headier harmonic pollen as if he had cultivated only a single kind of flower. But the complete book shows him to be a composer of always strongly characterized and expertly made "normal" music whose special inventiveness lies in such other areas as rhythm and the intensifying of vocal color by means of unusual combinations in extremes of range. (I wonder whether some of these "normal" pieces are not more gratifying to sing than the chromatic ecstasies of *Moro lasso*, in which the demands of the ensemble must all but extinguish the performer's individuality?) Finally, Book Six, which rep-

---

[2] "Drowning" is a veil of the same sort in the Elizabethan madrigal—the seafaring English—and it may be one, too, for example, in Bennet's:

> *"O when, O when begin you*
> *To swell so high that I may drown me in you?"*

resents the apogee of the radical chromaticism of the era, also reveals the composer as anomalously conservative-minded, at least by the lights of those contemporary aesthetes and *précieux* for whom monody had gained the inside track and contrapuntally voiced harmony of Gesualdo's brand was disappearing from the course.

Whether Book Six was the most propitious choice with which to inaugurate a new Gesualdo series is hard to say, but the larger physical requirements of the other music may have borne on the decision: Books Three and Four include six-voice madrigals; Book Five varies more widely in tessitura; the sacred music uses five-, six-, and seven-part choirs. In any case, the stringencies of Gesualdo's madrigal form, in no matter which volume, may deter all except the doughtiest listener. Extraordinary absorptive powers are needed to digest a succession of twenty-three complete statements, each of great compactness—for if Gesualdo does not expand, neither does he dilate, and if his form is small, it is at the same time never elliptical. Another obstacle for modern listeners, if merely an implicit one, is in the limited possibilities of harmonic extension through key relationships. To a certain extent this is offset by novelties of sequence and juxtaposition, but the music will seem inexplicably static to some nevertheless, and as little satisfying to dumpling-lovers as a dinner of twenty-three canapés of caviar.

Nor are Gesualdo's most overt means of keeping awareness of formal limitations at bay invariably the most successful. In fact, the most completely satisfying madrigals tend to avoid contrast for its own sake (Pope: "The lights and shades, whose well-accorded strife"), and either confine themselves to a single mood or follow the free run of the composer's death wish, in which he certainly knew his way around, musically speaking. Monotony threatens, in any event, only when, pretending that matters are looking up, he pays too many courtesy calls on the happy ending. Finally it must be said that, as Gesualdo's mode of expression is dramatic, highly intimate, and very much in earnest, he weights the traditional madrigal of poised sentiments and conceits, of amorous delicacies and indelicacies, with a heavy load. But this is in-theory criticism. In practice, which is to say, while listening, no unoccupied faculty remains with which to question the balances and proportions of "form" and "content."

The extraordinary unity of character and style in Book Six —it would be impossible to exchange any madrigal with an example from the earlier books—opens the suspicion that the composer himself may have been responsible for the selection and ordering of the pieces. For one thing, the ingenious grouping in several kinds of pairs would seem to have been arranged by an "inside" hand. Thus the first two, and the first and last, the numbers four and five, eleven and twelve, thirteen and fourteen, eighteen and nineteen, are paired by "key". Pairing is likewise effected by tempo and mood; by the incidence of *ballo* meters (nos. 22 and 23) and pastoral modes (*Al mio gioir* and *Tu segui*); and by similarities in initial canonic departures (*Ardo per te* and *Ardita Zanzaretta*), final cadences (nos. 11 and 12), "instrumentation" (the two-tenor madrigals, nos. 18 and 19). Changes of tempo are managed by doubling or halving the unit of beat—the practice of the time—but rhythmic irregularity is introduced in about half of the madrigals by the use of meters of unequal length. An example occurs on the first page, in the partly-in-six, partly-in-four *Se la mia morte brami*, where the effect is strikingly similar to the effect of Wilbye's enlargement of the meter to drag the musical pace at the words "whereon man acts his weary Pilgrimmage." [3] The rhythmic inventions throughout Book Six are a match for the harmonic ones, in

[3] The "Ay me" in Wilbye's *Weep, Weep, Mine Eyes* is so like a Gesualdo "*oimè*," incidentally, as to suggest direct connection.

fact, and in such instances as the virtually meterless beginning of *Quel "no,"* and the lashing syncopations with the word *"tormenti"* in *Candido e verde fiore*, they are as "revolutionary."

* * *

The chief obstacle to the recovery of performance style is pecuniary. In a few hours' leave of absence from a bread-winning routine of taping television commercials and disposing of seasonal oratorios, even the most excellent singers cannot achieve the blends, the exactness of intonation, the diction and articulation that the Prince's singers would have had to master by edict and as a result of living with the music the year round. (And probably under threat of flagellation, too, though the composer, a votary of *le vice anglais*, seems to have preferred *that* in reverse—Marsyas flaying Apollo, so to speak.) In short, the world is in need of permanent madrigal consorts, and of Martha Baird Rockefeller Grants to sustain them. Only then can the styles be reborn, not only of the Prince of Venosa, but also of Marenzio and Monteverdi, Wilbye and Weelkes.[4]

In the case of the *Musica Riservata* style, edifying descriptions by earwitnesses abound. Thus, Cerone reports that "The madrigalist does not sing in a full voice, but artistically, in a *falsetto* voice or *sotto voce*"; to which I would add that pitch clarity in the denser harmonic coagulations can be attained in no other way, certainly not with woolly *vibrati*. Zarlino (whose theoretical writings influenced Nicolas Poussin [5]) affirms that "the madrigal singer must perform his part just as

---

[4] *Cf.* Gesualdo's *Beltà poi* and Weelkes's *Cease Sorrows Now*, at the words "I'll sing my faint farewell."
[5] As late as the eighteenth century, the architect Vittone was illustrating his exposition of the Renaissance ideal of proportion with analogies derived from music theory.

the composer has written it"—*i.e.*, without embellishments, and *a cappella;* the *concertato* madrigal introduced in Monteverdi's fifth book was without issue in Gesualdo. Padre Martini further informs us that "madrigals are to be sung softly" and that "bold dissonances were permitted in madrigals because perfect intonation was easier to achieve by a few singers than by the crowd of singers in church music." Finally, Mazzochi's reference to Gesualdo might be taken to infer that our composer employed *crescendo* (and the regraduation), as well as other dynamic shadings (*sfumato*) himself. The grounds for this illation are simply that Mazzochi had invented a system of notating dynamics, and that what he praises in Gesualdo is his exactness in notation. But the question is fodder for a thesis, and that is where I must leave it.

❋ ❋ ❋

My own attentions to Gesualdo between twelve and ten years ago led to a number of ramblings, musical and otherwise. Twice I visited the seat of the composer's family name, an unpicturesquely squalid town, the more so after Acerra and the other architecturally attractive villages of the Campania. On the first occasion, a listless day in July 1956, I had come to Naples by boat—my last such expedition, I resolved, the debarking ordeal alone taking longer than a transatlantic flight, not to mention (if I may be pardoned the apophasis) the simultaneous marathon concerts by competing brass bands, the continuous pelting by paper streamers, and the orgies of weeping by separating and reuniting Neapolitans. I remember that on the way to Gesualdo we visited the Conservatory of San Pietro a Maiella, and the fish stalls near the Porta Capuana; and at Montevirgine, watched the procession of a parthenogenetic cult, a parade of flower-garlanded automobiles led by boys carrying religious banners and running like lampadephores.

Gesualdo's castle was the residence then of some hens, a heifer, and a browsing goat, as well as of a human population numbering, in that still Pill-less, anti-Malthusian decade, a great many *bambini*. None of these inhabitants had heard of the Prince of Venosa and his deeds, of course, and in order to explain our wish to peek at the premises, some of his lurid history had to be imparted to at least some of the tenants. A result of my own attempts to do so was that I soon became the object of very alarmed looks, the audience having confounded the composers in the story (blame my poverty-stricken Italian) and mistaken *me* as the murderer of *my* first wife.

The castle is measly. Apart from the lion rampant emblazoned in the *sottoportico* and the well-known inscriptions on the courtyard wall, there was little evidence of occupancy at any time by an armigerous prince. The interior appeared to be furnished from the Apennine equivalent of Woolworth's, but as it was greatly in need of a dispersion of aerosol, I did not see much of it. In short, it was difficult to imagine the high state of musical culture that once flourished on this forlorn hill, the singers, the instrumentalists, the church choristers, and, not least, the great, if emotionally disequilibrated, composer whose last madrigal books were first printed here.

The portrait of the composer in the Capuchin church was dirty then but undamaged, whereas on my return three years later the picture had been cleaned but the lower left corner of it, just above the composer's head, was torn. (You can't have everything.) We were met there by a Padre Cipriano who said he was gathering materials for a biography of the composer, and that the most interesting of the documents so far turned up for inclusion were some verses by Gesualdo's ill-fated wife. I did not doubt this opinion; in fact if the lady's writings describe her amorous experiences in any detail, Padre Cipriano's book, if he ever wrote it, could become the first musicological tome to be published by Grove Press. The Padre served some thimblesful of the local liqueur, but while we were swallowing this furniture polish, complained of the American occupation of the town in 1944. His story has been repeated in kind a great many times since then and throughout the world, of course, but in the case of the Sack of Gesualdo, my sympathies were entirely with the G.I.'s.

I visited other sites associated with the composer after that, but not expressly, not on his trail. I was in the Este Library at Modena, and in Ferrara several times, but on behalf of the Schifanoia frescoes and the Etruscan Museum, and incidentally to drink Lambrusco. I even went to Mesola once, on an excursion to Pomposa Abbey and Comacchio, the latter loud with the clack of wooden shoes then, but now stranded in the ooze of the newly drained delta; other visitors be warned that Mesola, the Xanadu of the Estes, celebrated in a madrigal by Tasso and Wert, is now a very dreary town hall. As for Venosa, Horatian Venusiae, the city of the composer's principality, I have been no closer to it than Brindisi, perhaps not even that close, technically, as I did not leave the Greek ship— so overcrowded that tents were pitched on its main deck— which had called in its harbor, and on which I was bound for Venice.

The purpose of my next trip to Naples, in October 1959, was to conduct a program of my music in the Teatro San Carlo.[6] Neither Gesualdo the place nor Gesualdo the musician had any part in my itinerary. (Deliberate sightseeing was limited to Sperlonga, a pool shivering with eels in a grotto that surged like a sea shell.) But I *did* go to Gesualdo again finally, and, back in Naples, sought out the composer's tomb.

---

[6] Named for the composer's maternal uncle. The composer's paternal uncle was Cardinal of Santa Cecilia in Rome, and a witness to the notorious trial of the Prince of Mantua's potency, popularly known as the Congress of Venice. See *The Prince's Person* by Roger Peyrefitte.

It lies in the pavement of the Gesù Nuovo (whose *diamanti* façade is the most equable of pigeon roosts—a facet for each bird—whatever the pecking order), in the vicinity of some very grand mausolea. "Carolus Gesualdus," the epitaph begins, but it is entirely devoted to genealogy, failing to mention any contributions to music, or even that the interred was a musician at all. But then, very little attention has been paid to the music for four hundred years. And, come to think of it, that burial plaque is still in excellent condition. Perhaps, after all, "The Gilded Monuments of Princes *Shall* Outlive . . ." their powerful madrigals.

I.S.

Hollywood, March 7, 1968

Die Meistersinger

11 April 1968

Mr. Wolfgang Wagner
Bayreuther Festspiele
8580 Bayreuth, Germany

Dear Mr. Wagner:

I am sorry to be so late in acknowledging your letter, but I was in Arizona when it came, and have been exceptionally busy since my return. I am sorry, too, and ashamed, not to *have* any thoughts to contribute to your program book for the *Meistersinger* centenary; I have not heard a performance in a very long time. If you think the adjoining remarks worth printing, I am glad to give them to you, but I will certainly not mind if you decide against including them.

I still recall my excitement and pleasure in hearing the *Meistersinger* for the first time. This performance, which I attended with Rimsky-Korsakov, turning the pages of the score for him, was given in the Maryinsky Theater by a German company, and I remember that the accuracy of the musical execution, which far surpassed our St. Petersburg standards, amazed and delighted me.

Because I was following the score, my memory of my impressions of the stage is less strong than my recollection of the effect of the music. I had known it since childhood, but from the piano reduction, and the actual sound was a revelation whose force, all musical experience being "live" then, a young composer today is unable to appreciate. I was a composer myself, after all (not merely a listener), and each opportunity to compare my imagination of an orchestra score with its realization in performance had to be used as a lesson and a chance to acquire some skill of my own. And skill is a large part of what the *Meistersinger* is about.

It has been such a long time since I last heard the *Meistersinger* that I am unable to say what it would mean to me now. But I think I would still listen to it as an active composer listening to an active composition, for at the age of a hundred the *Meistersinger* is a very lively monument.

Igor Stravinsky

Svadebka (Les Noces): An Instrumentation

Hearing two of my discontinued preliminary versions of *Svadebka* (*The Wedding*) for the first time recently, I was reminded of a unique but long-forgotten experience of music-making fifty years ago. I am no longer certain how many versions I may have begun, or how extensive each fragment may have been; I have lately discovered a complete score for four pianos, without vocal and percussion parts, of which I had no recollection, and other scores and sketches may still be excavated among the manuscripts I gave to people in return for financial help during the war. Nor am I certain of chronology, except that the ensembles were pared down over the years from a super-*Sacre* orchestra (I still possess sketches for this) to one for two cimbaloms, harmonium, pianola, and percussion, requiring only five players in all.

This last version, composed in Morges in the winter of 1918–19, is the most extensive of the abandoned ones, and the most authentic, more so in some ways than the final score which, though streamlined, stronger in volume, and instrumentally more homogeneous, is also, partly for the same reasons, something of a simplification. (For other reasons as well, one being that the figuration in the unfinished version is generally more elaborate, and another that it reveals a contrapuntal tendency, *viz.*, the canonic treatment of the principal line at [54]; this seems wrong stylistically in the light of the final score, but might have seemed otherwise if the earlier one had been continued.) The manuscript is complete in detail to the end of the second tableau, except that repeated passages are not written out where the instrumentation is unchanged. At this point I was interrupted by the rush-order commission for *Pulcinella*, but I must also have begun to realize that the problems of synchronization with the pianola, and the near impossibility of finding competent cimbalomists, had made my instrumentation impracticable.

It is, nevertheless, the most practical score, in the technical sense, that I have ever written, every note having been sound-tested on my own proving grounds. I had packed all of the instruments into my little musical pantry and learned to play all of them myself, spending as much time practicing them, in fact, and tinkering with and tuning the cimbalom, as I did composing. But what I did write came directly from the instruments, while the sound was still hot. I am no mystic; I need to touch music as well as to think it, which is why I have always lived next to a piano, why in this instance it was necessary for me to manipulate the cimbalom sticks, familiarize myself with the harmonium registrations (a two-manual instrument: I still have my receipt for a year's rental), try out flams and rim shots on the snare drum, and even shake the tambourine ("raaaaaaaise your voices"). Risky as my memory is, too, in matters of dates and places, I am certain of the position of each of the instruments of this little orchestra in my room, which must be because my acoustical reality—bilateral in my case, not circular, as I am aware when hit in the nape of the neck by "spatial music"—is a part of my biological reality.

The instrumentation exposes lines of descent from *The Nightingale*, thereto unnoticed, at least by me. The music from the first entrance of the tenor, for example, seems to devolve from the opera not only in rhythm and harmony (parallel chords emphasizing fifths), but also in vocal style; and the twitterings in the pianola part during the bride's lament are unexpectedly revealed as an inheritance from the ornithological ornaments in the opera. Both works employ orientalisms, too, in *Svadebka* most conspicuously during that same lament, where the cimbaloms might be Japanese plectrum instruments accompanying a scene from a Kabuki play.

The pianola part was not intended for human hands but for direct translation into the punch-card language of the automated poltergeist. It exploits the superhuman (and multidigital) velocity of the mechanically programmed instrument to the extent that three pianists are required to encompass all of the notes—*if* all of them *can* be played, at strict tempo.

(My *Etude for Pianola* would require the same number of players, incidentally, if read from the six-stave original score.) I might add that I did not choose the pianola primarily for economy, but because the tinny, nickelodeon-like rattle of this primeval jukebox suited my scheme of sonorities; it compares with the glossy, emulsified "tone" of a Chopin recitalist's Steinway somewhat as a Model-T Ford compares to a six-door Cadillac. What defeated me, as I said, was the problem of synchronization, in pitch as well as tempo, for the instrument could make one's flesh creep, partly because of the spooky absenteeism of the player, but mainly because it was so grossly, irremediably, and intolerably out of tune.

The harmonium part was the most difficult to write. I did not trust the instrument acoustically, and in fact composed alternate versions for many passages, hoping to allow for the varying resources of different makes of instruments. Harmoniums were popular in that hymn-singing age, but are virtually extinct now, replaced by the electric organ, which I reluctantly admit as a substitute in my own ensemble.

No substitute, no thumbtacked or otherwise doctored piano, is admissible for the cimbaloms, the scarcity of which constitutes the chief obstacle to performance. It is a rare animal to begin with, and one that is even more rarely tamed—played by people who read music; and the chances of capturing two of the species, then of corralling a pair of competent players, are astronomically poor, comparable in fact to zoologists' chances with Chi-Chi and An-An. But its sound is so winsome that a society for the preservation of musical wildlife must be persuaded to endow one of the schools both with the instrument and with scholarships for its study. The music bounces, glittering delicately when articulated with felt sticks, and becoming more protrusive and as compact as billiard balls with wooden ones, which I prefer ordinarily. Both timbres are effective antidotes to the murky acoustical presence of the harmonium, and both combine ideally with the wiry playerless piano (as it should have been named).

The role of the *batterie* was another novelty, at least in 1918. Percussion sections had served the orchestra as arsenals and sound-prop departments, and supplied it with extra colors, articulation, weight. But before the *Histoire du soldat* and this *Svadebka* version, in which the percussion is a continuing and internally consistent element, the "drums" had never really been given their heads. The character of the music itself is percussive, moreover, and that character is part of me, another of my biological facts. To bang a gong, bash a cymbal, clout a wood block (or critic) has always given me the keenest satisfaction, depending on the resulting qualities of sound, and in fact I am still tempted at dinner tables to tap the drinking glasses with the cutlery. But surely this is natural in a musician, or at any rate part of a very old tradition. The first musician in the Bible, after all, was a hammer-and-anvil player (despite the façade at Orvieto, which portrays him striking bells suspended from a rack), and the music of the same instruments is supposed to have inspired the discovery of the relationships of intervals—by Pythagoras, another tapper of glasses filled to varying levels with water.

✻ ✻ ✻

My recollections of *Svadebka* itself are happy, but the associated ones are painful: all of my friends of the time are dead, and I am the only and ever-lonelier survivor. Stepan Mitusov comes to mind first; he was closer to me than anyone else at the time, and among other debts of gratitude I owe him the encouragement of my *Svadebka* idea. The thought of Mitusov reminds me, in turn, of Rimsky-Korsakov. We were together at Rimsky's nearly every day at one time, Rimsky being as fond of him as I was myself, while not accepting him as a pupil—which gave me my first better opinion of myself: I had at least been accepted.

I do not know whether Mitusov ever heard *Svadebka,* or even whether the music was repatriated during his lifetime. (Has it been now?) And the world is so different now that the name Korsakov is less likely to remind me of my old teacher than of the dreaded syndrome of defective time-memory. "Old men forget," of course, but they forget or remember selectively, like everyone else. These memories are a selection, then, but they are the only ones willing to be summoned today concerning a long-vanished episode in the making of my *Svadebka.*

I.S.

Zurich, October 22, 1968

REVIEWS

Three Types of Spring Fever
(Stravinsky Reviews *The Rite*)

A COMPARISON OF THREE RECENT RECORDINGS OF

Le Sacre du printemps [1]

BERLIN PHILHARMONIKER	ORCHESTRE NATIONAL DE LA R.T.F.	MOSCOW STATE SYMPHONY ORCHESTRA
Conductor: H. von Karajan	Conductor: P. Boulez	Conductor: P. Kpaøt
Deutsche Grammophon Gesellschaft	Internationale Guilde du disque	Amalgamated Unions Gramophone Studio

1 Introduction

A *ritardando* has been substituted for the written *accelerando* in measures 5–6. After 3, the differentiation of

The bassoon playing is effortless but too vibrato-shiny and saxophone-like, and the second *fermata* in the first

The beginning is un-propitious; the *tempo primo* is lethargic and the clarinet entrances are desultory. The tempo of

[1] Written in October 1964 for *HI FI-Stereo* magazine, partly out of annoyance with the useless generalities of most record reviewing. The complete text was first published in the *Süddeutsche Zeitung*, Munich, September 1965.

tempo primo and *tempo secondo,* if any, is imperceptible to me. The triplet, five before [13], is too slow. As a whole the performance is too bland, well blended, sustained: phrases overlap where they should contrast.

measure is too long. The *diminuendo* to [8] is expertly done, but the oboe should play *staccato* at [9], and the trumpet *ditto* before [11]. The tempo at the return of the bassoon solo is too fast, ignoring the written *tempo primo.*

the *più mosso* is good, however, and the trill of violins before [7], the clarinet triplet before [13], and the oboe articulation at [9] are better than in the other performances. The orchestral balances in this recorded concert are no match for the other two studio-made and obviously much-edited performances, but the disadvantages are to some extent offset by the feeling that it is a concert: at the beginning, some very dim applause followed by a deafening chorus of nasal and pharyngeal expurgations.

2　*The Augurs of Spring*

The oboe figure at [26] must be played *staccato.* The section from [28] to [30] is too smooth in this performance. At [31] the horn and contrabassoon are weak, and their syncopated notes (like all syncopated notes) need accents. Articulation would alleviate the plodding at [34].

This is much too fast, as well as ragged, especially at [15], at two before [20], and again at two before [21], where the strings are doubtful of the accents. The pitch of the tuba is muddy before [22], and from [23] to [28] the tempo is unsteady. The *crescendo* in the trumpets before [29] is unnecessary and unenhancing. More accentuation and acoustical presence from the horn and contrabassoon are desirable at [31], and a controlled tempo is needed at [33].

This is the best tempo of the three performances, and the steadiest from [31] to [37]. The octave in the tubas before [22] is more clearly in tune than in the other recordings, too, and the horn solo at [25] stands out more clearly. I would notate the strumming at [31] differently today, but am not certain how.

3 Ritual of Abduction

The fast tempo is good except when it *sounds* rushed; I suspect that it was facilitated by re-barring, but no matter. An important fault is the equalization of the 2/4 and 6/8 measures toward the end. The eighths, not the measures, have the same value.

This is much slower than the Karajan, and it slows still more before [44]. The 2/4 measure nine before [48] is too long, and the quarter notes in all of the 2/4 measures are *ditto*.

This is generally more distinct than the other recordings, but the horn at [44] is too remote and cavernous.

4 Spring Rounds

The bass clarinets and their *pizzicato* doublings are too weak at the beginning. Six measures before [54] the trumpets brutally violate the orchestral balance. At [54] itself, the metro-nomic 160 is slower than the metronomic 132 in the *Ritual of Abduction*.

The *ritardandos* before [49] and [57] are ugly solecisms. I prefer more separation between the quarter notes in the violas three after [50], and the silting *sostenuto* at [53] is definitely wrong. The downbeat at [55] is ragged.

This errs at the other extreme from the Boulez: there is too much separation between the quarter notes; they are the right length at [53].

5 Ritual of the Rival Tribes

The tempo falters in the first measure, but a more disturbing fault is the lack of *staccato* articu-lation. The daggers over the notes three before [61] call for an exag-gerated sharpness, and they apply throughout this section. The eighths thereafter are crisply and admirably played. At [66] and *passim* the horns are overbalanced.

The brass chords in the 3/2 measures are too short and the ensemble is ragged at [61]. At [65] and *passim* the horns are puny, the bass drum and tubas too robust.

The first tuba drags at [57], and at two before [59] the dynamics are uncertain. The section from [61] to [62] is strangely, inappropriately lyrical in this perfor-mance, but the trombone trills before [64] are satisfying (the Russians used valved instruments), and *ditto* the animal ruttishness of the tubas at [66]. Unfortunately, the rhythm is soggy.

6   Procession of the Sage

The trumpets at [70]–[71] stand out a decibel or so *au-dessus de la* (and I do mean) *mêlée.*

The oboes are too close to the microphone at [68], hence the center of the stage is taken by a detail. The rhythmic polyphony and the orchestral balances at [70]–[71] are marvelously clear.

The polyphony at [70] is clear enough, but the balances are much better in the Boulez recording.

7   The Sage

The string chord is not balanced, the higher instruments being too close to the microphone.

This is more than twice too fast: if there were an Olympic Game for speedy conducting . . . No, I had not heard the head-chopping music in *Salome* when this passage was written.

The tempo is correct but the string chord does not balance; I would write it with a *szforzando* now.

8   Dance of the Earth

The gratuitous *accelerando* weakens the build-up *in* the music, and the final chord is a shambles.

The bass clarinet is too directly "on the mike" at [75], and at [78] the basses and tubas are too far "off." It may be dangerous to say so, but a faster tempo than the metronomic 168 would not be amiss; it is a *prestissimo* dance, after all, not an *allegro.* Bernstein's tempo for this movement is correct.

Of the three recordings this is the best and most exciting tempo, and the *Hauptstimme* at [75] is, as it should be, in the violas. Thanks to articulation, the strings are clearer than in the other two performances.

9   Introduction

I seem to hear a cricket at the beginning; added natural atmosphere? Are

This is too hurried, and the second trumpet after [84] is too discreet. The

This is the best string balance for the section beginning at [84], and thoughts of coming estivations responsible for the sleepy tempo? The basses are weaker than the other strings at [84], and at [85] the *piano* of the horns is a *forte* compared to the *piano* of the trumpets at [86]. The changes of tempo at [89], [90] . . .

solo cellist swoops before [91] as though he were in sympathy with Saint-Saëns.

the best balance of the two trumpets, but tatter-demalion cello entrances mangle the passage at [85].

10   Mystic Circles of the Young Girls

. . . and [91] are slight in this performance, if they exist at all. The balance at [99] and [100] is perfect, but the level is too loud; the conductor is probably the victim of the recording engineer who, ideally, should be his *alter ego*. The tempo is shaky at the beginning of the second measure of [103].

The addition of a *ritardando* before [97] destroys the silent pulsation with which section [97] begins. The horn balance at [99] is poor, and the *fermata* before [101] is not well measured, but a more important fault is that the *accelerando* at [102] should lead up to the second measure of [103], instead of, as here, overshooting it and then being forced to skid back to a slower tempo!

The tempo is too hurried at [97]. The premature sally by the first cello at [100] shows how little known this music still is in the Soviet Union; in fact the present recording preserves the second performance by a Muscovite orchestra in fifty years. The *accelerando* at [102] is well managed and so is the orchestral hemorrhage at [103].

11   Glorification of the Chosen One

The tempo is good, but the notes should be needle-sharp. The *molto allargando* before [117] is played incorrectly as five even beats.

The Karajan performance is steadier, and the rhythm is askew here at one measure before [118], where a singultus occurs and offbeats become onbeats.

The tempo is *giusto*.

12   Evocation of the Ancestors

This is too slow! The pulsation should be the same as in the preceding

The tempo is perfect and so is the articulation . . .

The "E" in the basses being indistinct, and not only here but as a rule, piece, the old eighths equaling the new quarters like interlocking wheels.

I amended the part for this performance, making a triplet of the F sharp (up bow), E (down bow), D sharp. In the future I would have the timpani play only the first note in each group. But the result of these changes in *this* performance is an unwarranted and unfortunate loss of speed.

13   Ritual Action of the Ancestors

Whether metronomically correct or not, this *tempo di hootchy-kootchy* is too slow, and at [138] the music is duller than Disney's dying dinosaurs. At [136], second measure, the notes of the triplet must be separated, not glued together. At [139] the bass trumpet is too feeble, the English horn too powerful. At [140] the clarinet intonation is bad. The *rubato* three measures before [142] is unnecessary and debilitating.

. . . but *this* is too fast, and the onbeats of the *ostinato* are too loud, especially in the first horn and first violins. The trumpets begin so indecisively at [132] and are so slow to screw up confidence that they seem uncertain of being in the right place. I do not like this passage played *legato*, incidentally, even though it is printed that way.

I hear peculiar percussion "happenings" at [131]; someone drop something? someone rehearsing another piece? The trumpet articulation is commendable at [132], but at [134] the trumpets and trombones are too loud for the horns. The balance between the bass trumpet and the flute-in-G is good; this little dialogue, together with the clarinet melismata that follow, is the best music in the movement, incidentally; the rest of it, long since become a model for film safari music, has worn least well in the score. It would be comforting to think that the fault is its easy imitability.

14   Sacrificial Dance

The sluggish tempo gives the *coup de grâce*

The tempo is fast but good at the beginning.

The timpanist miscounts somewhere near [148]

to whatever tension has survived to this point. At [189] the balance is awry, the first trumpet, among other offenders, being too loud for the trumpet in D.

Then at [157] and [159] it seems unsuitably fast, and the tension is dissipated by it as much as it is by Karajan's slow tempo. Incidentally, neither performance pays the slightest regard to the *ictus accent*

$$\left|\begin{smallmatrix}2\\8\end{smallmatrix}\; \gamma\; \overset{>}{\flat}\, \flat\, \flat \right|$$

The *accelerando* begins too soon at [165], the tempo drags at three before [190], and the orchestra is not always together, as for example at two before [154].

and completes this section ahead and independently of the orchestra, a type of mistake that again indicates the unfamiliarity of the score to Soviet musicians. The tempo is good, and in spite of messiness the adrenal excitement is much greater than in the other recordings. The second measure of [197], the pivot to the last section and the change in the rhyme, *does* feel like the turning point in this performance.

RÉSUMÉ: The recording is generally good, the performance generally odd, though polished in its own way—in fact, too polished, a pet savage rather than a real one. The *sostenuto* style is a principal fault; the note-lengths are virtually the same here as they would be in Wagner or Brahms, which dampens the energy of the music and leaves what rhythmic enunciation there is sounding labored. But perhaps I should have begun by saying that the music is alien to the culture of its performers. Schoenberg recognized it as an assault on the Central European tradition, saying that it made him think of "those

RÉSUMÉ: First, the recording. The vast dynamic range of *The Rite* is emasculated to standard recording *mezzoforte* which, next to the wrapping of every sound in echo-chamber flannel, is one of the most irritating misrepresentations of the recording industry. Noise itself is "phatic speech," and volume is an element, and while the mediumizing of sound levels does only negligible damage to some music, it deprives *The Rite* of one of its dimensions; which is partly why a live performance is a shock even now to anyone who has learned the work from recordings. Second, the performance. It is

RÉSUMÉ: As this is the mere tape of a concert, neither performance nor engineering can stand comparison to the two edited recordings. But whereas the music sounds French in the French recording, and German in the German, the Russians make it sound Russian, which is just right. (I have no space to explain what I mean by these nationalizations in musical terms.) Then, too, if *The Rite* is new to the Russian orchestra, it must have sounded like the battle cry of the sans-culottes to the conservative Socialist audience. This, at any rate, helps to charge the atmosphere, more at least than the smog-charged savage black potentates who wear only a cravat and a top hat." (When told, in 1925, that I had declared his "twelve-tone system" to be a dead end—a *Sackgasse*—he answered with the pun: *"Es gibt keine sackere Gasse als 'Sacre.'"*) But I doubt whether *The Rite* can be performed satisfactorily in terms of Herr von Karajan's traditions. I do not mean to imply that he is out of his depths, however, but rather that he is in my shallows—or simple concretions and reifications. There are simply no regions for soul-searching in *The Rite of Spring*.

less good than I had hoped, standards for Maître Boulez being high. One would suppose the music to be his *entrée* too, his very lack of Herr von Karajan's *Kultur* being a natural advantage here. Apart from sloppinesses—surprising but of no importance—there are some very bad *tempi*. The articulation is generally excellent, and a good antidote to the D.G.G. performance.

atmospheres of our own big cities, where *The Rite* has become a conductor's showpiece and where, with luck, it receives one rehearsal.

None of the three performances is good enough to be preserved.

I.S.

A Realm of Truth [1]

M r. Kerman is a high-minded guide. I recommend him to high-minded readers, as well as to credit-minded students in need of a crib—if in these days of student power anyone still is. I also urge musicians to try the book, especially those who despise ancillas and tend to shirk harmonic algebra and the other relationships Mr. Kerman details. But general readers

[1] *The Beethoven Quartets* by Joseph Kerman (New York: Alfred A. Knopf; 1967). Review published in *The New York Review of Books*, September 26, 1968.

should try it, too. They will complain of key naming and harmonic path mapping. Yet Mr. Kerman never loses sight of the grand design of each quartet, and he can still be followed at that elevation by sidestepping the thickets of technical exposition. Music is the subject of the book, in any case, not Beethoven's illustrations of the author's critical principles, and not functional analysis or the other brands that prowl about nowadays like solutions in search of problems.

The discussion of the late quartets, to which I must confine my own remarks, is piecemealed under the headings "Voice," "Contrast," "Fugue," "Dissociation and Integration." The diversity of stances is useful in dealing with Beethoven's own multifariousness, but unhelpful to those who would prefer to have the whole dossier on each quartet in one place, and who imagine that they are less concerned with group characteristics than individuating ones. The book is rich in insights, nevertheless, no matter how they are subsumed. Mr. Kerman has an acute grasp of the powers of Beethoven's tonality instrument; of, for example, the focal means with which he creates both anticipation—making distant destinations loom— and surprise. Nor is Mr. Kerman's study of the other aspects of the quartets, and of Beethoven in general, less perspicacious. Valuable observations on such matters as the proprieties of the genres, and the rarity of relationships based on the augmented triad, are found on nearly every page.

Earlier criticism is dealt with, but little of it seems to have been intelligent enough to cause irremediable mischief. (I would have made shorter shrift of it myself, and I do not see why Daniel Gregory Mason should matter so much, or at all.) I admire Mr. Kerman's . . . well, bravery—was stopped in my tracks in fact by his demonstration of how the "prolix" first theme in the finale of the Quartet in E-flat might have been trimmed. I admire his writing, too, if not such favored locutions as "contrasty," and "doublet" (my mind insists on going to "garment" first). Slips are so rare that when he does fall ("One almost thinks of the *Heiliger Dankgesang*": one cannot *almost* think of that), the reason can only be that he is so highly polished. His arguments are the crucial ones, and they are clearly and cogently propounded. They are arguments, after all, about the highest values in the art.

❊ ❊ ❊

Restriction to the late quartets—and in them to some points in which I find myself most out of step with the consensus—is unfair to the three masterpieces composed for the Russian ambassador in Vienna, Count Razumovsky. (It is unfair as well to *La Malinconia*, that trial balloon not only for later Beethoven but also for the Wagner of the first act of *Die Walküre*; the interim quartets, however, are not to my mind evenly sustained.) If the "Razumovskys" had been the end of the line, we would exhibit them as the *ne plus ultra* of the literature, and no doubt put a futuristic interpretation on such passages as the beginning of the Quartet in C-Major, discovering in its breathbating, left-field harmonic movement the very fever of the future.

As it is, the "Razumovskys" hold their own, partly—*only* partly—because they do not compete with the late batch, are in fact so different as to offer few comparisons. No music more abounds in high spirits (the operatic finale of the same quartet) and elegance (the tune with the skipping appoggiatura in the *Andante*). But these are hardly the first qualities to come to mind in connection with the late quartets; rather, by "Razumovsky" standards, the anomalies and unevennesses, just as, with the view the other way around, the "Razumovskys" inevitably remind the listener of the developments in depth and compression, in the conversion of the form to new expressive ends, in stylistic refinements, that lay ahead. But comparisons are odious. We cannot make love to the future, or listen to the "Razumovsky" adagios with the thought that the later quartets contain even "better" music.

Razumovsky himself deserves a word. (More than that, in this election season: a twenty-one gun salute, say, and preferably in time to drown out yet another reverberation of paralyzing platitudes from those unspeakable nominating morons, whose "hoopla" in Miami included a "rendition" of the "Moonlight" Sonata on fifty-gallon oil drums.) His duties representing the Russian Empire to the Austrian Empire in that year of Austerlitz must have been as demanding as those of Comrades Gromyko, Dobrynin, and others representing Soviet Imperialism to American Imperialism. Count Razumovsky not only commissioned these quartets, however, but also acquired and kept the nimbleness of fingers and mind to be able to play one of the violins in them. I wonder how many ambassadors, political incumbents, spokesmen for the Ministries of Truth, or other high officials of the Great Powers today would even recognize them.

※ ※ ※

"Quartets are in demand everywhere; it really seems that our age is taking a step forward."   BEETHOVEN, April 1826

The string quartet was the most lucid conveyor of musical ideas ever fashioned, and the most singing—*i.e.*, human—of instrumental means; or, rather, if it was not that natively and necessarily, Beethoven made it so. As for inborn powers, it could register a faster rate of harmonic change than the not yet fully chromatic orchestra of Beethoven's time, which was further impeded by weight problems and balance problems. It is a more intimate medium, furthermore, partly by the same tokens; and a more pleasing one, long-term, as color: to me at any rate, and in my case partly because I am least conscious of the color element in it. Its sustaining powers are greater than those of wind-instrument ensembles, and its ranges of speeds and of degrees of soft volumes are wider. Compared with the piano, it has advantages in polyphonic delineation and in the greater variety of dynamic articulation and nuance.

E-flat Major

"He heard nothing . . . but his eyes followed the bows, and from that he was able to judge the smallest fluctuations in tempo and rhythm."   J. BÖHM, March 1825

The E-flat and the larger and more innovatory C-sharp Minor are the most unified, consistent, satisfying of the late quartets. But apart from success, the parallels—"morphological" and "architectural" similarities in the variation movements, mainly—seem to me factitious. What the two quartets do share, incontrovertibly, is an influence on Wagner. "Who comes after him will not continue him, but must begin anew, for he who went before left off only where art leaves off." Thus, Grillparzer's oration for Beethoven's funeral, and if the poet seems to have been writing with Wagner in mind, so does Beethoven himself in the *adagio molto espressivo* variation in this Quartet in E-flat. It is clear that the music's message to Wagner, at any rate, was *"Bonjour, 'Tristan.'"*

The *pizzicato* figure at the beginning of the *Scherzando* movement derives from the preceding movement (at ms. 120, and, with *arco* articulation, at ms. 95); which may not be "hard" news, exactly, but is an interesting connection all the same because aurally obvious even with the interval inverted. A similar link, no less apparent to the ear, is the recurrence of that feature of the *Scherzando*, the accented second beat (and silent first and third beats), in the last measures of the finale.

I prefer this finale, incidentally, to any other in the quartets, *all* of it, too, the blustery, orchestral second theme no less than the coda, with its miraculous change of mood and meter. But, then, I am inclined to resist gypsy and Hungarian finales, even by Beethoven, and the ending of the Quartet in C-sharp Minor is a Magyar uprising.

A-Minor

Beethoven describes himself in the epigraph to the third movement as "one recovered" (*eines Genesenen*), but the continuing trauma of the illness is more apparent in the music. "Hysterical," Mr. Kerman's word for the violin outburst with which the *allegro* begins, applies as well, I think, to the oscillations of mood throughout the quartet.

Whereas the first movement is slow in starting, and patchy and spasmodic much of the way, the second fails to stop in time; or seems to, probably because the subject matter is not grippingly interesting in the first place, and for a moment (ms. 63–68) is actually dull. But the serenity of the trio presages the movement by which—or by part of which: the hymn in white-key counterpoint if not the interspersions of minuet [2]—the quartet is remembered. Two slices of "minuet" and three of hymn pile up like a five-decker Dagwood sandwich, except that the hymn decks and "minuet" decks fail to integrate, and even to react on each other. In consequence, the listener forgets the "minuet," and therefore that Beethoven ever did feel any "new strength."

The last movement is very odd: a march that might have

[2] As the 3/8 is played on my recording, a performance otherwise notable for a great deal of Xenakis-like sliding about, presumably under the stress of emotion, an inability to count from one to two steadily, and to produce two consecutively in-tune notes. Schnabel's dictum, "Great music is better than it can be performed," has been taken too complacently.

been composed thirty years earlier and shelved; a bombastic recitative incorporating a version of the violin paroxysm from the first movement; a dance whose frenetic later adventures are unforeseen in its beginning as a *Valse noble et sentimentale.*

B-flat Major

This is the most radical of the quartets; most modern, too, in the local sense: the written-out violin glissando in the *presto,* for example, would pass undetected as a contribution by Beethoven in a collage of last week's premières. But nearly everything about the quartet is controversial, I discover, including my assumption that the wide assortment of the pieces indicates a desire to enlarge the form and enrich the variety of the contents: which seems obvious if for no other reason than that an expanded form is again pursued in the next quartet, but realized through continuity rather than variety.

The substance of the first movement is rich, but the exposition vacillates. At moments, such as the faltering between ms. 192 and ms. 197, and the premature return of the D-flat episode in the recapitulation—*I* am not ready to welcome it back, at any rate—it does not altogether cohere. But to some extent the open stretch of allegro at the beginning of the development section saves the movement. A mitigated disaster, then.

Reviewing the *Cavatina,* Mr. Kerman rightly takes to task a remark from an I-had-hoped long-forgotten anthology of my own *ex cathedra* utterances. But I do not think—it is part of his argument—that the love and care which Beethoven put into the piece (never a dry eye later at the thought of it) and the evidence in it of emotional scar tissue are entitled to any allowance on the receiving end. Elsewhere Mr. Kerman concedes the impossibility of harnessing technical analyses to aesthetic results, and at the end of his study eloquently questions the efficacy of what in fact he has done so very well. But neither is there any ratio between the amount of labor and the value of the result; which is why the labor is strictly the artist's affair. Genius strikes where it will, in any case, even Beethoven's.

To my mind it did not strike very deeply in the *Cavatina* apart from the *"beklemmt"* episode. (Which does not mean that I am right and Mr. Kerman wrong. But whether or not I am "over-reacting" to Mr. Kerman, I am, as a composer myself, unavoidably doing so to Beethoven.) I do not find its melodic-harmonic substance especially distinguished, and the treatment attenuates it. The piece is handicapped in the first place, however, by constituting a too-extreme contrast to the preceding *Andante*. If the *Cavatina* is the most tormented movement in the late quartets, then the *Andante* must be one of the most insouciant (in the manner of the *Allegretto* of the Eighth Symphony, as Mr. Kerman notes of the ending, and I would add of ms. 18–19 as well). But while the *Andante* seems to skim over the surface of the composer's "personal emotions" as lightly as a hydrofoil—in comparison, that is, to the depth plunge of the *Cavatina*—its musical emotion, whatever the cost to him and his later feelings about it, is the less shallow of the two movements.

The Great Fugue

*"And why didn't they encore the Fugue? That alone should
have been repeated! Cattle! Asses!"* BEETHOVEN, March 1826

The Great Fugue enlarges the meaning of Beethoven more than any other work (which does not mean that I regard it as a separate piece rather than a quartet movement). It breaks all of our measurements, too, human no less than musical, especially the sudden, sustained, scarcely believable energy, as if from a dose of musical Platformate. We can know the other quartets, even to faulting them, wanting what we love to be what *we* want it to be. But the Fugue is not knowable in the same way. Prejudices as to dimensions and elements must be overcome. When they have been, if they can be, we discover that no chain of expectations is built up in us, that the music defies familiarity by being new and different every time.

Whether the substantive difficulties are attributable more to isolation—the Fugue lacks both ancestors and inheritors—or the other way around, is an imponderable; so is the question whether the possibility of the masterpiece is a consequence of historical intersections, or whether the intersections are retroactively brought about by the event of the masterpiece. So far as "stylistic environments" are concerned, in any case, and works of art as "personification of their time," parts of the Fugue might have been incubated in a space satellite. As for the absence of an influence of its own, this may be simply a case of no one being able to "join it," let alone "beat it." But if the music *had* entered the consciousness of its time, Modern Music would have lost some of its sting at a much earlier date, and where would we be now? (Where are we?)

The Fugue still has a bad press, is still reputed to be abstruse, intractable, dissonant, relentlessly loud; which proves how little known it is. Nor has criticism, deprived of comparisons, its main tool apart from the knife, won it new love; nor while picking it apart noticed the range in it, the annexation of territory reserved for Debussy (from ms. 581), for instance, and the playful delaying of the cadence at the end of the G-flat section.[3] But the critic must feel the ineluctability of

---

[3] As for the octaves immediately before, I wonder if the strategic effect of the same device in Bach's two-voice E-Minor Fugue [which Stravinsky orchestrated on April 3, 1969—R.C.] had lodged in Beethoven's imagination at some earlier time.

new measurements and is at best only guessing at something the artist knows.

The *Overtura*, Mr. Kerman says, "hurls all the thematic versions at the listener's head like a handful of rocks." The Davidic image seems to betray persecution feelings about the music, however, the more so as the versions marked *piano* and *pianissimo* are outstandingly non-lithic. (Hawkish similes are best suited to the first fugue subject, I think; in fact I was about to compare it to an ICBM, as an example of musical escalation from the "Mannheim Rocket" in the Sonata, Opus 2.) If this is actually the case, the more remarkable Mr. Kerman's understanding of it, and of the main issue, which is the switch in focus from contrapuntal devices to thematic transformation.

The importance of design in this new perspective is apparent in the *Overtura*, a thematic index identifying the different versions of the subject as well as prognosticating and priming the larger components of the form. Each thematic version is endowed with distinctive secondary attributes (counting pitch and rhythm as primary): a trill and appoggiatura, for instance, in the version destined for the most complex treatment, and a slow tempo and soft dynamic in the version predicting an episode in the same speed and volume. These secondary characteristics constitute an auxiliary set of referents with which to identify thematic material in remote transformations, as well as to construct alternative views: silhouettes, for example, on the analogy that the full face is revealed only in the pitches; and fragmentary contrapuntal refractions, as in the double mirror, rhythmically speaking, with which the A-flat fugue begins.

The rhythmic aspect of the Fugue is the most radical, but the least isolable: the rhythmic units and patterns are so consistently identified with the thematic versions, in fact, that the barely numerate composer (he could not multiply) might

have been using what is now called (by mathematical composers who cannot write Great Fugues) a parameter of
rhythmic entities. The vocabulary itself is new, formed in
part by an unprecedented use of syncopation, by a new degree
of subdivision,[4] and by irregular durations. But here, above
all in the A-flat fugue that is the climax of this giant creation,
Beethoven is exploring a region beyond the other late quartets.
Who, being taken there today, can imagine that he would
have reacted less dumbly himself, in 1826, than the "cattle"
and the "asses"?

C-sharp Minor

"Thank God there is less lack of fancy than ever before."
BEETHOVEN, summer 1826

Everything in this masterpiece is perfect, inevitable, inalter-
able. It is beyond the impudence of praise, too (partly because
of difficulties with the vocabulary in that service), if not
quite beyond criticism, which can only be overstated and is
destined to disappear in context. Thus the *Presto* could con-
ceivably be considered repetitious, by itself, while the objection is obviously untrue of the movement in its place in the
quartet, where less would not be more and abridgment is
unthinkable anyway. Thus, too, the final *allegretto* variations,
which fittingly succeed music of the most exalted feeling and
ineffable radiance, could imaginably seem almost trivial "in
themselves." The *Presto* recalls the "Pastoral" Symphony
in the character of the second theme and its accompaniment, the limited harmonic plan, the echoed hallooings, the

---

[4] The tied-eighths-for-quarters notation "conveys the grasping urgency of
the theme," says Mr. Kerman, and so it does, at any rate to score readers,
but before doing that it conveys the imminence of rhythmic subdivision. It
may also indicate a change of bowing but with little or no separation.

silences like the pauses before the storm in the symphony.

To say that each quartet is distinguished by a quality of sonority is probably to say nothing more than that the quartets themselves are different; yet the luster of the instruments in these variations is unique. ("Singing masons building roofs of gold," says the Archbishop in *Henry V.*) One's "soul" actually seems to migrate during this music, in fact—to one's no small surprise, the earlier movements having formed and implanted this ill-defined zone by stealth. Nor is the ethereality shattered by the *pizzicati* in the 6/8 variation, even though this effect has now been associated with pirouetting hippopotamuses or other improbable acrobatics by other denizens of the Disney animated zoo.

The most affecting music of all, to me, is the beginning of the *andante moderato* variation. The mood is like no other ("impassive," one commentator called it, but he meant "impenetrable"), and the intensity, if it were to endure a measure longer, would be intolerable.

F-Major

"It will be the last and it has given me much trouble . . ." BEETHOVEN, October 1826

The weaknesses are obvious: the shortness of breath, the failure to push the argument, the stylistic jolt of the final movement and its musical-snuffbox tune; but the strengths outweigh and outnumber them. The quartet is said to be short on innovations, but the repeated figure in the *Vivace* is the newest and most astonishing idea Beethoven ever had. The modulations in the end movements are new and fresh, too, but also abrupt, some of them, as if the composer's restlessness had been translated to a dislike of being confined in any tonality for long. In defense of musical snuffboxes, moreover, it is at least arguable that the now-too-tinkly pretty effect of the *pizzicati* on the last page is really the fault of Tchaikovsky, who oversold it.

Beethoven described the slow movement in a preliminary stage as a *"süsser Ruhegesang oder Friedensgesang"*; but to me it is *Trauermusik*—not necessarily a contradiction. The second variation is a dirge, in any case, and the prescience of death in the elegiac fourth variation is unmistakable.

✻ ✻ ✻

These quartets are my highest articles of musical belief (which is a longer word for love, whatever else), as indispensable to the ways and meanings of art, as a musician of my era thinks of art and has tried to learn it, as temperature is to life. They are a triumph over temporality, too, possibly a longer-lasting one, as events are threatening to prove, than other triumphs in other arts, for at least they cannot be bombed, melted down, bulldozed by progress. This "immortality" in the music appears to have been recognized even by Beethoven's contemporaries. "He will live until the end of time," Grillparzer said, the words being read out in the Friedhof cemetery as the mortal part was lowered into the earth, taking with it the largest share anyone ever had of the power of musical creation itself. The poet then asked the departing mourners to "Remember this hour in times to come when you feel the overpowering might of his creations like an onrushing storm."

PART II

From the Diaries
of Robert Craft,
1948—1968

1948

March 31

Washington, D.C. Arriving at the Raleigh Hotel for my appointment with Stravinsky this morning, I find Auden pacing the lobby. "The night train from Pittsburgh was late," he says, "and the Stravs aren't receiving yet." In that case, I asked would he care for a second breakfast? But no, he wouldn't. "There are no hard rolls in America." He fidgets and chain-smokes instead, and lay-analyzes "the old boy, in whose case, obviously, the mother-figure is money." Suddenly remembering *The Rake's Progress*, he delves into a battered attaché case and brings forth the typescript wrapped in *The New York Times*. Counting on only a brief wait, perhaps, he opens the libretto to the final scene and hands it to me, saying, "This might interest you." Then while I read, he turns the *Times* to the obituary page, registering disappointment, and to the book page, emitting a groan, thereafter watching me at a tangent. I tell him that I think the Bedlam scene contains the most beautiful verse ever intended for an opera, and he reacts by granting me ten additional minutes for the remainder of the book, or approximately the time it would take *him* to read it. In fact I have hardly finished scene one when he jumps up exclaiming, "Surely the old boy must be ready by now," and fire-chases back to ring the apartment.

"The Lily Pons Suite," says the brass nameplate, but we are admitted by the tall, queenly beautiful Mrs. S., in blue turban and white piqué housecoat. Mr. S., in a *robe de boudoir*, waits behind her, and he continues to hide behind and to depend upon her throughout the meeting, like a small pet mouse with a large friendly cat. They greet me warmly, and smother Auden, whom they have not seen since the scenario-planning in Hollywood last November, with Russian-style kisses. But Auden, lovable, even kissable though he may be, is a Public School Englishman, plainly horrified by such open demonstrations of affection. He winces and quickly poses a number of deflecting questions about the S.'s' health, house, lovebirds, parrots, cats. Then, yes, too, dear me, we are forgetting the opera. And the manuscript is again delved for, and this time handed in like an exam returned by a schoolboy. Mr. S. receives it solemnly, even superstitiously, asking Mrs. S. ("Verusha" this time, at other times "Vierotchka") to bring whisky, which is not Auden's drink, but he takes it. Four tooth-glass tumblers are rapidly sunk in toasting to the opera, after which I feel less nervous, if also a little too well oiled. But why have I not been more nervous in the first place? Is it because Mr. S., from his music as well as from the rehearsals and concerts in which I have watched him, sometimes hitch-hiking to Washington, Philadelphia, and Boston to do so, seems like someone I know very well already?

Mr. S. talks about his new concerto for strings, the "Basiliensis," and his performance of it in Mexico City a few weeks ago. Whereas all exchanges with Mrs. S. are in Russian (a long one in which I think they are trying to decide what to do about me with regard to seating strategy at luncheon), the language of this narrative is an assortment of handy French, German, and English phrases; but his pursuit of verbal exactness and interruptions of himself to demand

English equivalents for foreign expressions can be exasperating. At one point he seeks edification on the difference between a cad and a bounder, words encountered in a detective story, but apart from the distinction that one of the terms applies chiefly to moral, the other chiefly to social, behavior, I do not catch Auden's would-have-been-immortal answer, being obliged in that instant to open the door for the waiter.

According to popular concepts of the changing evolutionary design of human physique, Mr. S. is something of a throwback. He is so extraordinary, physically, in any case, that nothing less than a life-size statue (not merely a head or bust), or scaled-to-life-size drawing (the seated portrait by Picasso is misleading), could convey his uniqueness: the pygmy height, short legs, fleshlessness, football player's shoulders, large hands and wide knuckles, tiny head and recessive frontal bone, sandy hair (black in photographs), smooth red neck, and high hair line. He is so absorbing to look at, in fact, that an effort is required to concentrate on what he says. And when that predicament has been overcome, a greater one arises in knowing how to respond. Many of his remarks are so sweeping, absolute, exclusive, as well as so exaggerated and *parti-pris*, that the listener is uncertain whether his leg is being pulled. Add to this the difficulty that agreement is obviously expected for no matter what he says, and that the composer in person frequently seems to be saying the opposite of the composer in his autobiography, at any rate so far as some of his colleagues are concerned. Mention of the *Symphonies of Wind Instruments*—my own forthcoming New York performance of this opus being the object of our business today—provokes a tirade against Ansermet and his recent broadcast of it with the NBC Symphony.

Still, respond one must. I do so easily to a joke about "Hollywood composers who farm out their orchestrations and whose scores should be marked 'coloring added' like the labels on food cans." But I have no idea how to react to a

verbal thumbsdown on the Beethoven Violin Concerto because, "That D sharp in the first movement is such an ugly
note"; or to a Nietzschean argument denying the German-ness
in German music, "Because, you see, Bach was a Saxon,
Beethoven was Flemish, Haydn was a Croat, Mozart was
Austrian, Mendelssohn was a Jew." I do not quarrel with
these demographic attributions, or propose other candidates,
but then neither does Auden, and he cannot have thought
them less preposterous than I do.

We pair off for a moment, Mr. S. and Auden to look at
the libretto, Mrs. S. and myself to talk about books. Her
English is as charming as everything else about her. "I tried
but could not read 'The Nak'd and Dead,' " she says (whereas
at table, later, she holds that "ba-ked potatoes are good in
America"). She says "here it's"—the logical reversal of "it's
here"—and fas-ten for fasten. Her accent, however, is more
French than Russian. "Tell me, please, what means 'doctrine'?" she says, but the word comes out so French-sounding
—"doctreene"—that I cannot help answering "a female doctor." Her long cilia flutter slowly, seductively, over her large
blue eyes as she asks whether I agree "that women are more
appreciative of flowers than men, and that intellectual men
hardly notice, and are rarely able to identify, any flowers with
the exception of carnations and roses? Wystan not only failed
to sniff our bouquets, but he actually deposited his coat on a
cluster of gardenias still lying in its box. 'Eager' loves flowers,"
she goes on, leaving me no time to consider the relationship of
floral indifference to male intellect, "and always has flowers
in his room while he works. He cuts and waters them himself,
too, and gardens every day if he has time." But "Eager's" delectation of the blossoms is less apparent than his compulsive
folding up and tidy tucking away of the wrapping paper and
ribbons.

Lunch is welcome more for the relief it brings from the

tonnage of Mr. S.'s tête-à-tête attention than gustatorily. But we get smashed. I do, anyway, and my head begins to turn like a pinwheel halfway through the third bottle of Bordeaux, at which time Auden, his intelligence unbowed, begins to chat about linguistic science as a key to thought structure, and about the "British nanny as the true source of all philosophy in the Empiric Isles." He devalues philosophy further with the statement that, "It can be no more than a game anyway, for St. Paul's reason that 'We are part of what we know.'" Besides this I recall only Mr. S.'s fuss about a wobble in the table, his annoyance with a butterfingered waiter, his obsession with scraping up crumbs, and his exculpatory rubbing out of two spots on the tablecloth (what is he apologizing for?). He also makes a marvelous remark to the effect that "music is the best means we have of digesting time." And he talks at some length about words, which involves a great deal of slow-fishing translation and of which, probably because of its non-logicality, I retain only the information that the Russian for "ladybug" is "God's little cow." After several demi-cups of *espresso* Mr. S. retires for a catnap, as he says, though Mrs. S. predicts it will last until dinner.

1949

February 4

New York. Dinner with the Evelyn Waughs, who come in evening dress—for a late party at the Astors, they explain—the glaring perfection of which seems to exaggerate the crumples in our own everydaytime togs. Mrs. W. is fair and lovely, Mr. W. pudgy, ruddy, smooth-skinned, ramrod. He offers favorable comment on the temperature of our hotel rooms (at the Ambassador), complaining that he is obliged to keep the windows of his own rooms (at the Plaza) all the way open or suffocate, a confession that may help to account for both his icy exterior and inner heat. I.S. replies in French, attempting to excuse the switch in language with a compliment on the French dialogue in *Scott-King's Modern Europe;* but Mr. W. cuts in, disclaiming conversational command of the tongue, and when Mrs. W. contradicts him—"That's silly, darling, your French is very good"—she is reprimanded in injured tones.

We mention Mr. W.'s lecture on *The Heart of the Matter* in Town Hall last week, the coolest performance of the sort I have ever seen, however much he disparages it. Unencumbered by a text or notes, the novelist was able to study the audience (he says), and even to turn the tables on it (I say), judging by the ruthlessly observed details in his descriptions of three people who walked out. But Mr. W. prefers to talk about the Undertaking Industry and the ban it has imposed against burying him should he, as the Industry must fervently hope, expire while in the United States. He is keenly interested in our own burial plans, too, and eager to know whether we—our *beaux restes*, that is—are destined for family vaults. But this down-to-earth talk makes I.S. very uneasy.

A crisis occurs when the W.'s refuse the S.'s' whisky and caviar, not because of the refusal, but because the S.'s unthinkingly exchange a few words in Russian, a pardonable recourse for them in many instances, but not now. The W.'s are not taken in by V.'s pretence of referring to the cigarettes she rummages for in her handbag, and they naturally, and correctly, deduce that the subject of the exchange is themselves. At long last I.S. proposes that we go to dinner, thus bringing the abstemious and uncomfortable half-hour to a close.

Mr. W.'s spirits take an upward turn during the freezing, and in his case, coatless, block-and-a-half walk to "Maria's"; and the sight of the Funeral Home at the corner of Lexington Avenue and 52nd Street restores his *joie de vivre* to the extent that for a moment we fear he may actually take leave of us and explore the Service Entrance. "Maria's," small, dark, crowded, is the wrong restaurant: the W.'s are too swank here. But the starchiness and defensive verbal sparring, that the I.S.'s think of as the normal English method of making acquaintance, vanish with the Valpolicella, which the temperature-sensitive Mr. W. mulls. It seems to me, too, that the eminent author is succumbing to V.'s charm; he has begun to behave gallantly to her, in any case, and even some of the suspicion in the glowering glances directed at intervals to I.S. has diminished.

With the fettucine, talk turns—no apparent connection—to

the Church. Here I.S. shines, showing himself to be at least as ultramontanist as Mr. W., as well read in Chesterton and Péguy, and as prone to believe in the miraculous emulsification of Saint Januarius's blood. I would deduce from the novelist's remarks that he supposes the composer to be one of Maritain's Jewish converts, which is a common and, so far as the Maritain influence is concerned, partly accurate supposition.

Another crisis looms after V. mentions the forthcoming New York première of her husband's *Mass*, and invites the W.'s to attend. Mrs. W. handles this, regretting that they have already "booked passage home," but lest the conversation continue in this dangerous direction, *her* husband adds, with a bluntness that seems to show that the threat of I.S.'s cacophonous art has been lacerating him all evening: "All music is positively painful to me." The statement can only be ignored, and V. does so, superbly, with a compliment to Mr. W. about *his* art, and a comparison between his *Decline and Fall* and Sade's *Justine*. When at length Mr. W. realizes that the S.'s have read everything he has written, a new character emerges in him, as magnanimous and amusing as the old one was unbending and priggishly precise. If he does not brook the literary talk of literary types, he certainly seems to enjoy it from outsiders like (though no one is quite like) the I.S.'s, and even from semi-insiders like (there are many like) me, for I admire Mr. W.'s fictions, too, and no longer object, as I once did, that chance and arbitrariness are too important in them.

We seek to draw him out on other writers, but are rewarded with only one acidulated reference to fellow lecture-touring compatriots and the commendation, in which the last two adjectives are rather wickedly emphasized, of Christopher Isherwood as "a good young American novelist."

The meal concluded, Mr. W. asks permission to smoke a

cigar. Choosing one from a case in his breast pocket, he holds it under his nose (where it looks like a grenadier's mustache), circumcises the sucking end with a small blade, passes a match flame under the other end as if he were candling a pony of precious cognac, avidly stokes and consumes it. Holy Smoke!

August 10

Hollywood. Lunch at the Farmer's Market with Christopher Isherwood and the Huxleys, the latter cooing at each other today like newlyweds, or oldlyweds making up after a spat. Owing to its extensive variety of salads, seeds (Aldous eats quantities of sunflower seeds for his eyes), nuts, health foods, exotic fruit (Milton: "The savoury pulp they chew, and in the rind"), the restaurant is a Huxleyan haunt. The other tables are held down mostly by drugstore cowboys, movie stars, Central European refugees, and—judging from awed glances in our direction—Aldine and Igorian disciples. All are vegetarians, for the nonce, and all nibble at their greens like pasturing cows.

Virginia Woolf's likening Isherwood to a jockey is perfect. Not the clothes, of course, though they are less conspicuously suited to Hollywood than those of Aldous or I.S. (both are sporting much too resonant neckwear, as if their sense of the dapper had run to seed at such a remove from the centers of discriminating haberdashery), but the stature, bantam weight, somewhat too short legs and disproportionately, even simianly long arms, a comparison forced on the attention because of their frequent employment for metrical purposes. But one easily sees Isherwood, or sees how Mrs. Woolf saw him, whether at the pari-mutuel window or the furlong post, as an ornament of the track and the turf.

His manner is casual, vagabondish, lovelorn. One does not readily imagine him in a fit of anger, or behaving precipitately, or enduring extended states of great commotion. At moments he might be thinking of things beyond and remote, from which the conversation brusquely summons him back to earth. But he is a listener and an observer—he has the observer's habit of staring—rather than a propounder and expatiator, and his trance-like eyes will see more deeply through, and record more essential matter about, us than this verbosity of mine is doing about him. At the same time, his sense of humor is very ready. He maintains a chronic or semipermanent smile (a network of small creases about the mouth), supplementing it with giggles and an occasional full-throttle laugh, during which the tongue lolls. (This happens as he tells a story of why he is no longer invited to Chaplin's: "Someone had said I had peed on the sofa there one night while plastered.") But he is not at ease in spite of drollery. Underneath —for he is as multilayered as a *mille* (which in practice is rarely more than a *huit* or a *dix*) *feuille*—are fears, the uppermost of which might well be of a musical conversation or high general conversation about The Arts. But I could be miles off. Perhaps he is merely suffering from the prohibition rule of the Farmer's Market, and in this case the contents of I.S.'s thermos bottles will come as an agreeable surprise.

Isherwood brings a greeting to All-deuce, as he pronounces it, from a Swami. The voice, both in pitch and volume, is somewhat too high, and the words are deliberated. Aldous, replying, digresses to make room for a ribald story, which Isherwood follows like an eager schoolboy, exclaiming "Oh boy!" once, and rubbing his knees in anticipation of the outcome. He also says "Heck!" and "By golly!"

How do the two men regard each other, apart from their

very evident mutual affection? Isherwood cannot match the softly orating Huxleyan delivery or the Huxleyan intellectual ammunition (a stunning aside on the "haeccities of the later Persian mystics," an apt quote from the *Biathanatos*, and some information about the amino acids and cellular differentiation), but, then, the younger man has made his name partly because of his wariness of fluency at supernal intellectual altitudes. Is he mildly baiting the sage, perhaps, gently tweaking his nose a bit by that overly credulous way of asking those further questions about the marvelous, the horrendous, the barely believable that loom so large in the older man's talk? Does he regard him as ever so slightly unbalanced from too much book learning? Not really deranged, like Don Quixote, of course, but a bit "off" nevertheless?

And am I wrong in detecting just the faintest tinge of doubt on the Huxley side as to the hundred-per-cent impregnability of the younger colleague's spiritual dedication and final severance from The World, and just the hint of a suspicion that one last unburned boat may still be hidden somewhere in the reeds? We suppose, in any case—it is the I.S.'s impression as well as my own—that the younger man is obliged to apply himself to those spiritual exercises which the older man masters merely by turning his mind to them. But while the Huxley universe is the larger of the two, the author of it does not sit more conspicuously in the center of it than the author of the Isherwood books does in the center of the Isherwood universe. Partly for this reason, it is more of an encounter to meet Isherwood than to meet Aldous, though another reason is simply that most of us are little more than enchanted audiences to Aldous, not because he wills it that way, but because we have no choice. Finally, whatever, if any, the truth of these speculations, how improbable a team the two of them make to represent Vedanta in the Wild West!

I.S., as I know him, is even less comfortable than Isherwood. He dislikes being outnumbered by Englishmen speaking their language, and these particular Englishmen probably seem to him too freely, richly verbal; in I.S.'s book the important things must never be, cannot be, said. But I.S. presents an almost exaggerated contrast in other ways as well: in, for instance, his deep diapason (*versus* their duet of flute-stops); in his love of concreteness (the Englishmen's talk about religion must seem abstract to him, but then he believes in the physical existence of the Devil, as at one time people believed in centaurs and mermaids); and in the autocracy and absoluteness of his views, though these can seem more extreme than they are because of his imperfect command of the fluty language's syntactic qualifying paraphernalia.

I would exchange some, but less than half, of my kingdom for a peek at the picture these two observers draw of I.S. Will they discover that the barricade of epigrams, paradoxes, *bon mots*, conceals nothing at all in their line, the line of "intellect"? Or will they conclude that the treasures are being kept to the deeps out of reticence, to be surfaced again on other, more favored days? Whatever the answer, and both conclusions would be wrong, the polite side of I.S., that Bellona's armor of will in the man and of style in the music ("Music may symbolize, but it cannot express"), is the only side anyone except V. ever sees.

Why, then, have so many people mistaken I.S. for an "intellectual"? Primarily, I think, because it was his own preferred image of himself. He is vain of his "factual knowledge," and would like to be regarded as a *summa* of erudition, the wielder of the ultimate gavel of sophisticated judgment. Nor will he tolerate the application of such terms as instinct and genius in regard to himself, pretending instead that "brains" and technique, meaning the mastery of means and the perfection of the ear, constitute the composer's full equipment. "Emotions," I hardly need add, are scarcely allowed to be an ingredient. Moreover, he seems to think of the affective functions as physiologically zoned, like the separation of emotion and intelligence in Comte's *tableau cérébral.*

Little that it may matter, I.S.'s intellectual world apart from music has been formed to an unusual extent by his intimates. He is radically susceptible to personal influence, in fact, which I say because I can see reactive effects I myself have had on him. (V. has said that I am the only friend in his adult life to have disagreed with him directly and to have survived, which is a dubious distinction both as to conduct and as to consequence.) For my own part, and though it hardly requires saying, I entertain few if any fixed views capable of withstanding "rigorous intellectual investigation" (I am a "feeler" rather than a "thinker," myself), and I certainly want no responsibility for any of them, musical or otherwise, settling on such a man. But the point is I.S.'s susceptibility, not *whose* views.

The chief influences were Diaghilev (V. cites certain aesthetic attitudes as virtually parroted from him, and she insists that "before age and America changed Stravinsky's character, he opened his heart only to Diaghilev, and Diaghilev's criticisms were the only ones he ever heeded"); Arthur Lourié (proselytizing for Maritain); Suvchinsky (a philosophy compiled from Herzen, Rozanov, Shestov, Berdyaev); C. F. Ramuz and C. A. Cingria (a *homo faber* philosophy and the ideal of the village virtues, meaning the moral superiority of simple things: *les vins honnêtes,* for instance, which unfortunately often means Grade B as well). Certainly these men, and the few others who knew I.S. intimately, must have realized that, uncanny as his artistic intelligence is, and acute and varied as are the palettes of his sense perceptions, his critical range outside of music is peculiarly limited. What he offers are judgments without trials in a no-man's-land of likes and dislikes, and at a time when no-man's-lands quickly become so much real estate crossed by so many beaten paths, the hazard to himself hardly requires spelling out. Taste, as we grow older, may easily become a narrowing tyranny.

I would like to have put many questions to these illustrious predecessors, of course, but must put some prior ones to myself. What, for example, of Chamfort's warning that, "A philosopher attached to the train of a great man finds it necessary to conceal his true feelings"?

1951

February 28

Miami to Havana, in a Cuban airplane. From the air, lower Florida is a brocade of swampy islands, sheened pools, and a rim of indigo sea. The colors of the Caribbean shimmer like shot silk, and the sand and coral floors sloping away from the Keys seem to be hardly more than a thin pane of aquamarine glass from the world of air. The Keys near Key West, which resembles a fortress on an old map, are shaped like the skeleton tail of an ice-age mammoth. At the Havana airport, our stewardess, a dumb soubrette with retroussé nose, announces that "This is Cuba." I.S., to me: "It better be."

The Customs officers bring us frozen daiquiris, which is nice except that they lose our luggage meanwhile. Havana is an odorous city, preponderantly of cooking oil and coffee, the latter almost thick enough, it seems, to filter out of the air. We go directly to a press conference in the bar of the Hotel Nacional where we are greeted with more daiquiris and *entusiasmo*. Lunch at La Zaragozaña (two lisps) follows, in an atmosphere of Habana Habana smoke; and a visit to Wilfredo Lam, who gives us a private exposition of his paintings, accompanying it with a great deal of talk about his gods, Stravinsky and Picasso.

The hacienda of Fifi Tarafa, where we go for dinner—a carafe of daiquiris this time—contains photographs of, and many recordings by, *her* god, Toscanini. It could be partly for this reason that I.S. elects to sit in the patio, which is paved with eighteenth-century terra cotta beer bottles (bottoms up) and which looks toward a garden with a statue of Benjamin Franklin. I.S. confides to me that he is impatient to go home and finish the *Rake*.[1]

August 20

Naples. The boat to Ischia, an absurdly class-segregated pocket steamer, is crowded and excruciatingly smelly; I am obliged to stand all the way to Casamicciola, where I finally find a seat next to a man who is reading Goldoni and apparently trying to memorize a passage he thinks extremely funny. At Forio I transfer to a scavenger-like trawler and am rowed to shore.

Wystan meets me at the pier, barefoot and with "the bottoms of his trousers rolled," and he carries my bag (the world's most intellectual portering service) through the toy-like town to his house on the Via Santa Lucia. At street level this is an empty stable and carriage room, but the upstairs rooms are ample, bright, and immaculate except for the burnt offerings in unemptied ashtrays, which might well represent a protest against the sterility of American cleanliness. Americans are not responsible, in any case, but a handsome Neapolitan Ganymede with a manner like his not-quite-believable name,

---

[1] The *Epilogue* was completed on April 7. A note in my diary reminds me that we played it together, four-hands, that evening. The *Prelude* was composed three days later.

Giocondo. While Giocondo spreads the lunch, we move to a patio, the domain of a scruffy cat and a dog, Moshé, for whom Wystan throws a ball, taking in the eager retriever again and again with the same feint, but once cuffing the poor cur for barking, which alters the quality of the noise to something resembling that of a screech owl.

Giocondo seems to understand little of Wystan's Italian; it must be a relief to him, and certainly is so to me, when the poet resumes the language of his muse. What, he asks, will become of I.S.'s promised Ischian visit? I say that it can take place only when the doctors allow and when I.S. is prepared to brave the gantlet of journalists now standing round-the-clock guard in the hotel lobby. "Oh," says Wystan, "but the way to rid oneself of journalists in Italy is to pretend to believe in the Church. They will look at you, at that, as if you were wearing lawn sleeves, and scatter as if you had brought news of the plague." In this instant a courier arrives with another form of news, in an express letter which Wystan passes to me, asking for a précis, without so much as glancing at it. It is an invitation from the Intendant of La Scala to attend the *Rake* in Venice at La Scala's expense, and Wystan is unable to conceal his pleasure.

Conversation automatically turning to the *Rake*, Wystan repeats his story about Benjamin Britten liking the opera very much, "Everything but the music" (a story I.S. did not find in the least amusing). But Wystan is worried about the score, I think because of some of the obvious resemblances, as for example between the first Bedlam aria and an aria in *Semele;* between the *fandango* in the graveyard scene and, well, a *fandango;* and between "Love that too quickly betrays," "Dear Father Truelove," and the whores' chorus, and three pieces in *Così:* "*Un aura amorosa*," "*Vorrei dir*," and "*Di scrivermi ogni giorno.*" In short, what if the Great Auk (which had white spots around the eyes and was called pengwyn by the Newfoundland Indians) proves to be a dodo in the colloquial sense?

We walk to a beach in the afternoon, Wystan at high speed (he is now wearing Plimsolls), in spite of the heat, and, himself excepted, universal indolence; but the water is bathtub warm, and only Moshé, still starting at every false throw, is aquatically inclined. On the return to Forio we meet Chester Kallman, himself just back from a visit to another part of the island. Wystan is always happier in tandem with Chester, and the best of his former good spirits now seem like doldrums in comparison. He dotes on the younger poet in fact, listening admiringly to his talk and even calling attention to jeweled bits of it, or supplying helpful interpretations for rougher gems, though as a rule if Chester goes to the kitchen for a moment, Wystan says of him that "He is a very good poet and a far cleverer person than I am." Whatever the truth of these assessments, Chester most certainly *is* a very good cook. By some oversight, however, tonight's spinach has not been washed, and after what sounds like a painfully gritty bite, Wystan reports a considerable presence of sand; but then, lest we think him persnickety, he quickly adds that he doesn't in the least mind, and even manages to suggest that he has become quite fond of it.

His talk, otherwise, flows with generalizations, not all of them a hundred per cent self-evident at first flash. "Jews are more complicated than Gentiles," he says, which seems a vulnerable thesis under the circumstances. His Manichean mind is almost continually engaged with polarizing moral distinctions, but this sorting out of the Good and the Evil is conducted like a game, and is without the assumption of any rectitude on his own part. The language is oddly diocesan and Sunday School, as for example when, with vigorous rotary movements of his right hand and his always uptilted head held still farther back, he declares himself to be "very cross with

Stalin" because the monster has been "naughty." (Stalin's icons flourish on Forio's walls side by side with those of the Virgin Madonna.)

At *passeggiata* time, we go to a café in the piazza. There the librettists repeatedly raise their glasses to the *Rake* première—*"Prosit!"* from Wystan, whose natural foreign language even in Ischia is German. But the music the great man sings on the return to the Via Santa Lucia is from Fricka's filibuster in *Die Walküre*. It sounds more than a little strange in this deserted (the whole town has gone to bed by ten o'clock) Mascagni scenery.

August 21

At six A.M., Wystan, discalced in spite of the cold flagstones, escorts me to a bus which meets the Naples boat at Lacco-ameno; and only just meets it, for we stop at every turn to collect yet more passengers and tie still more bundles and cardboard suitcases to the roof. The boat being overcrowded as well, I debark at Pozzuoli and return to Naples by taxi. The driver is a testy type, very free with oaths. His favorites are, at high speed, *"Cretino!"* and, at low speed, *"Mezzo-culili-ello!"* (half-assed), the latter being directed largely to inattentive pedestrians and animals: once we nearly collide with a vegetable cart hauled by a poor old Rosinante.

As I reach the hotel, Dottore Musella is on his rounds and just pronouncing I.S. cured of his pneumonia, but confining him to bed for the balance of the week and forbidding the Ischian trip. (I.S., very thin and aquiline, knees hunched to chin and a pack of hot compresses on his crown, looks remarkably like an eagle.) Dottore Musella, like many of I.S.'s physicians around the world, is eager to chat with his patient about the arts, but when he brings up the name of Eleonora Duse, V. does the talking, describing a performance of *A Doll's House* that she saw in Moscow as a child, and in which Duse played Nora in Italian "supported by" an otherwise Russian-speaking cast.

When the Dottore departs, V. attempts to dissuade I.S. from conducting *The Rake* even if he has fully recovered his strength, attributing his desire to conduct it in the first place mainly to vanity. In an access of pique, I.S. answers that he *is* a performer, and hence an actor, but *not* a vain one. "Acting," he continues, "is an important element in my make-up. My father was renowned for his dramatic talent more than for his voice," he says, "and furthermore, I *like* to perform."

After this burst of off-telling, I accompany V. to the *farmacia* to fetch I.S.'s medicines. We join a queue of American tourists there, all of them purchasing paregoric and all looking intensely uncomfortable as V., in her turn, asks for milk of magnesia.

September 5

Venice. Wystan, finding his La Scala-financed accommodations at the Bauer to be bathless and viewless, flees to the I.S.'s over-upholstered and luxuriously uncomfortable Royal Suite and bursts into tears. V. then calls the *"Direzione,"* explaining that not only is Maestro Auden the co-author of the *Carriere della Libertina* but "a kind of Guglielmo Shakespeare who has been received at Buckingham Palace by the King." A better room is promptly found, of course, but Wystan's tears, exposing so much frustration and wounded pride, have watered us all a bit, not because he is beyond the most appropriate age for them, but because of his vastly superior mind.

1 9 5 2

May 10

Paris. The people with whom we dine at noon devote the greater part of their conversation to gossip about the people with whom we dine in the evening, and *vice versa;* which is uncomfortable because, as I.S. says, "People who talk this way *to* you will talk the same way *about* you. 'The Judgment of Paris' is not a pretty picture, but you can learn from it that hate and greed make the world go round."

In the evening we go to the Deux Magots with Balthus, who is slim, pale, handsome, bittersweet, dandyish, and femininely conscious about his clothes, which are apparently meant to identify him as a Hebridean laird or, at any rate, to conceal that he could have anything to do with paint. He will say nothing about art, in any case, except to vent some scorn on the latest daubs of Chagall, whereas it is difficult to steer him away from music, Schubert's above all. Conversation centers on the Reverend James McLane, pioneer Balthus collector and Los Angeles friend of I.S.; in fact, I.S. is soon performing missionary and ambassadorial roles for artist and buyer alike, the painter being as curious about his clergyman admirer as the reverse; but the first question in the minds of both undoubtedly concerns the erotic sensibilia of the other, and that question Balthus broaches only very indirectly.

What about Balthus's portrait of Eros? Do his mirror-fixated and open-legged pubescent girls represent joyful innocence, as Camus and Artaud think, or project a Lesbian appetite (a storm behind the dyke), as I think, for it seems to me that the girls openly dream of being fingered by an older woman—which actually happens in *The Guitar Lesson*—and that all of them are either flushed with desire or pale with satisfaction (or is it the other way around?). They are definitely not little girls to please little boys, in any case or, for that matter, big ones: those barely-budding bosoms and itchily self-conscious pudenda, those girl-bodies with acromegalic boys' heads, those stubby legs—edematous calves, puppy-fat ankles, teeny feet—are a long way, at any rate, from *my* visions of the voluptuous.

But I fail to glean any insight from the man concerning the other oddities of his artistic eidos. Why, for example, indisputable master of his technique that he is, does he seem at times hardly to know how to draw? And why, apart from the juvenile would-be-delinquents, is his work in no way concerned with the contemporary? In fact, a list of influences on it would read like a catalog of loans from the Louvre: Piero, Carpaccio, Caravaggio, Velázquez (the dwarfs, duennas, mirrors, cats, goldfish bowls), the French seventeenth century, and Courbet, Corot, David, Ingres, Seurat, Cézanne. Whatever the answers, Balthus is peerless among living portraitists—his "Miro" and his "Derain"—and the same could be said, in their genre, of his landscapes, especially those with trees in the early Mondrian manner. He stands no less alone in another dimension, too, namely, the representation of Evil. I am thinking of *La Chambre*, in which, surely, the sexually ambivalent Satanic dwarf-witch cannot be ignored, the picture meaning more than, as I.S. would have it, spatial architecture and *chiaroscuro*.

May 19

We reach wild and holy Rocamadour in mid-afternoon, and immediately begin the ascent of the great crag, at first *via* one hundred and forty-three stone stairs worn and grooved by the knees of a millennium of expiators, including those of Thomas à Becket's assassin, Henry II. A chapel clings like a clematis to the precipice. Inside are the bones of St. Amadour and the shrine of a Black Virgin, a worm-perforated doll with crown and streaming tulle, but a hypnotizing totem, too, its eyes abjuring the world, fixing to a point beyond, and its smile radiating a higher, gnostic wisdom. The attribution of miraculous powers to the carving would not have been surprising a few centuries ago, and is in fact not very surprising now, as a party of pilgrims, some prostrate, some piously telling their beads, attests.

The cliff is scaled by another route as well, a Stations of the Cross, and it is by this path, leaving the chapel, that we continue the climb. At each Station's stop is an ancient stone bench in which we discover wavy trilobite imprints, and we wonder whether the medieval masons chose the stones because of the fossil patterns, and if so what did they suppose them to be?—as, for example, Xenophanes predicated his cyclical theory of geological history from fossil imprints of fish in the marble quarries at Syracuse.

The view from the summit is worth the exertions to obtain it, in spite of the souvenir touters. We return to Rocamadour village on an automobile road leading to the principal, twelfth-century gate. It is late afternoon now, the cliff is in shadow, and the chimneys of the windowless and tomb-like stone dwellings have begun to emit smoke—a macabre effect, in the absence of other signs of life. The claim of the *Guide Bleu* that these edifices have never been restored is too obviously true; it is more difficult to believe that people still inhabit them.

Our hotel, the Notre Dame de Rocamadour, has not been disturbed by post-medieval developments in plumbing, but the restaurant is of reasonably recent date, and is highly recommended for truffles. We dine on the terrace, not wishing to disappoint the waiter, who has attached some Chinese lanterns to our table. From there we watch the townswomen spreading laundry on the nearby banks of the Alzou; the smack of wet clothes on stone flip-flaps through the valley long after dark. Dinner consists of a *paté maison*, which is a meal in itself, an omelet, roast veal, all *truffé*.

May 20

Cave entrances, some of them partly or wholly boarded-up, are in view from time to time during the forty-mile ride to Lascaux, and many of the names on the route signs—Les Eyzies, and Les Combarelles, and Font-de-Gaume, famous for its paintings of mastodons—are renowned in archeology. (I might add that the road itself competes with these main attractions of the region by plunging our 1932 Studebaker, the best rentable automobile in Souillac, to its fenders in holes.) But the name Lascaux does not appear until Montignac-sur-Vézère, the town nearest to that most celebrated of the Magdalenian painted caves. A mile or two beyond Montignac, and up a hill, we come to a clearing from which a footpath leads through pine woods to the entrance. There, posted to a tree, is a hospital-type notice of visiting days and hours. As there are few enough of either, we are left wondering why this possibly ruinous information was not available in Paris, and at our luck in coinciding with one of the rare times of admission.

The guide is one of the cave's discoverers, a former member of the group of schoolboys who stumbled on it twelve years ago searching for a ball that had disappeared in a golf-size hole; after probing with sticks, and eventually digging their way in, these youths were the first to see the great buried Sistine chapel of Stone Age art. In fact, the true entrance has never been found, probably having been closed as a result of volcanic faulting, and the one we use, an air lock with double sets of iron doors, was only recently installed.

Seepage from overhead rocks has flooded the ground beyond as well as before the first door, but on choice I prefer the clamminess, and the creepy-crawlies which this brings on in me to the twinges of claustrophobia afflicting me as soon as we pass from the air-lock propylaea to the cave proper. These sensations are dispelled or forgotten, however, when our eyes have adjusted to the dim glow of a dozen feeble footlights—eerie because they suggest the troglodytic artists' grease lamps—and when, with the supplement of the guide's electric torch, we begin to distinguish vivid red and yellow patches and glistening black lines on the walls and ceilings ahead and overhead.

When my eyes form a system of these lines and colors into a bull, I suspect an ocular trick. Then the beauty and power of the animal, and the rhythm of it on the rough surface, begin to exert a spell, and an awe comes over me such as no terranean temple has ever inspired, the stronger, no doubt, because Stone Age Man, when I have thought of him at all, has heretofore provoked only a vague loathing. But I think that no spectator could fail to be humbled before the spectacle of so much resplendent life—that is, after an instant of incredulity attributable to the immeasurable and incomprehensible gulf of so many thousands of years.

The cave is tooth-like, not only in that the two principal chambers branch from the main rotunda like dental roots, but also because the right root contains a cavity boring into the earthen gums to a depth of about eight feet. The cave's unique representation of a human being is found in this cavity, and our visit there is the turning point in the trip, for our experience before seeing it is primarily aesthetic, whereas afterward we are concerned with meaning. The human figure is schematically scratched, like a stick man. It is bird-headed, as well, and its other most conspicuous feature is its half-erect and distended—with a Horim?—sex. Whatever the figure represents, shaman, hunter, god, the contrast between the naturalistically perfect depictions of animals and the crudeness of this pictograph implies a complex relationship of human being and beast involving a system of natural gods and divine attributes (zoomorphism); and of ritual and sympathetic magic, for a matching bird-headed wand is etched near the birdman, as are a club and an arrow. In short, we are confronted with symbols and the symbol-making power, hence with evidence for the existence of a dualistic belief system some two to three hundred centuries ago.

Still, this discovery of a metaphysical cave man is not more impressive than the discovery of the refinement of his artistic technique and delicacy of artistic feeling. He must have lived very like the beasts he killed, after all, yet, even by academic standards, his art is the least primitive imaginable. The purity of the artists' emotion, partly because of which the animals are as real as yesterday and almost breathingly alive, is matched by a mastery of proportion, a power of line, an intelligence in abbreviation, all as canny, it seems to me, as the pictorial creations of any historical period since.

To acquaint us at the start of the tour with the astonishing profusion of the paintings, the guide plays his torch panoramically over all of the decorated surfaces of the oval-shaped main room. The superimposition of animal on animal, presumably by successive generations of artists, is bewildering at first, nevertheless the form of whichever individual outline the eye seeks to trace stands out clearly. This, I think—as if I could "think" anything about the state of consciousness of a prelogical mind thirty millennia ago—is because each artist must have formed his own view of a painted area, and composed his own picture according to his own new and different scale. In every case the contours and surface qualities of the calcite walls seem to be determining factors in the composition. Thus the line of a vertebra will overlap or run congruently with a crack in the rock, and an eye-socket prove to be a natural hole or indentation, from which *locus* the entire animal has been designed. No animal has been set in a rectangular field, and none seems to have been composed to any sight line, or Beholder's Eye, other than the artist's, which is a reminder that in spite of all the framed squares of paint in square rooms throughout the world, neither nature nor the human eye is box-shaped.

By similar tokens, photographs and drawings are no preparation for the 3-D effects of the convexities and concavities of the surfaces, and all photographs have positively misled us in matters of color and scale, the sizes of the animals being so various, and the colors—one expects to see faint, flaked lines, scarcely visible in the dark, and forms at least as faded as Uccello's Noah frescoes—so brilliant. In fact, the reds, yellows, and the blacks glisten as if they had been newly varnished and not yet had time to dry; the *Last Supper* is in far worse condition. This vividness and extraordinary state of preservation—which were part of the reason for that initial moment of disbelief—is explained to us as merely good geological luck. The cave must have been sealed like a jar for most of its estimated twenty to thirty thousand decorated years.

The right wall of the right root is traced with engravings from the main room to the crypt of the bird-headed man.

Beyond that the bulging and hollowing—and surprisingly, to us, never artificially smoothed or flattened—surface is covered with horses and bovids, after which the chamber coils navel-like into the earth. And the left root funnels away even more suddenly and deeply and is even more richly embellished. Arrows are more numerously depicted here than elsewhere in the cave, too, both *in* their ungulate targets and on the ground; if it *is* the ground: the viewer's perspectivism limits *him.*

Our inspection terminates when the guide reminds us that because of the small ration of air, visits are limited to an hour. A longer term would corrupt the paintings, but it would also provoke visual indigestion, at any rate in me, for outside again, in the morning sun, I attribute my own sense of suffo-cation and intoxication less to the cave's anemic air than to the teeming chthonian life. The silence of the cave continues to reverberate, too, and I seem to suffer from a kind of aerio, or rather, tempero embolism, for want of a time decompressor or Wellsian time machine to throw me back into the present.

We climb the hill above the cave and emerge from the woods into a field of cornflowers and wild poppies. But the cave continues to haunt us there, and it will continue to haunt me in some degree all my life.

December 26

New York. A Christmas dinner at Auden's. He kisses us as we enter, the prerogative being granted by a sprig of mistletoe dangling over the barricade of book-filled crates by the door (which does not shut tightly and exposes the residence to

footpads). Shuffling about in *pantoufles* (bunion-accommo-
dating babouches, actually), he distributes a pile of very
fetchingly wrapped and ribboned Christmas presents: for me
a copy of his essay on Sydney Smith, *Portrait of a Whig,* and
his new poem, *The Woods.*

The apartment is imaginatively decorated for the yuletide,
with empty bottles, used martini glasses, books, papers, gramo-
phone records, all realistically strewn about to create a marvelously life-like impression of randomness. And the decorators
have achieved other, subtle touches of picturesqueness as well,
such as, in lieu of frankincense, filling the flat with stale,
boozy air. We compete for the most recently occupied, and
hence, dusted, chairs—the furniture looks as if it had been
purchased with Green Stamps—then choose drinks, tipping
out cigarette butts and ashes, dregs of earlier drinks, and other
detritus from the glasses in which they seem most likely to
be served. But, shortly before dinner, the fine line between
décor and reality momentarily confuses V. Visiting the lavatory and finding shaving utensils and other matter in the sink,
a glass containing a set of snappers (store teeth), a mirror in
which it would be impossible even to *recognize* oneself, a
towel that would oblige the user to start over again, and a
basin of dirty fluid on the floor, she unthinkingly empties the
basin and fills it with fresh water. Not until dessert time do we
discover, with mixed emotions, that she has flushed out
Chester's chocolate pudding.

Wystan diverts us at dinner with stories about a mouse
who shares the flat (born and brewed there no doubt), and
of whom he claims to have become very fond. "There are
usually scraps enough lying about for the poor dear to eat,"
he says, inviting speculation about the other livestock that
may be boarding there. And not just lying about, either: the
plates and silverware are greasy and, such is the dishwasher's
myopia, not entirely free of hardened remnants of previous

meals. The dinner—smoked clams, steak, potatoes with dill —is excellent, and Wystan tucks in as Oliver Twist might have done, which helps to explain the appearance of a marsupial-like paunch; before long his plate looks as if it had been attacked by locusts. Five bottles of Pommard, from a case deposited on the floor at the end of the table, are drained as well, but whereas I am heavy-lidded afterward, Wystan is a searchlight of intelligence, and without once putting on his mortarboard. In fact the Christmas merriment is ruffled only by a telephone call from a female admirer (the same who followed him to Venice at the time of the *Rake,* and from whom, like Casanova but for the opposite reason, he was forever escaping, jumping into passing gondolas, and once almost taking a header into a canal).

After dinner he plays recordings of bits of *Dido, Nabucco,* and *Die Walküre.* I.S. knows he is being courted with the Wagner, but he is not in a compliant mood, and after about twenty minutes of squirming, puts it down as "improvisation," which visibly disappoints Wystan.

December 27

A visit from Wystan, with Edith and Osbert Sitwell. "Now remember," says Wystan, briefing us an hour before, "Edith drinks like a fish." On this recommendation V. places a standing order for double martinis and double Scotches to be sent up at regular intervals. But the poetess merely sips her concoction, and her brother's hands shake so uncontrollably that they would be unable to hold anything; in fact he sits on them during most of the meeting. The toping is done entirely by I.S. and Wystan himself, who between them siphon off the contents of a full tray.

Dr. Edith's accoutrements include a Persian-lamb coat, thick tubular gold bracelets, a rosewood walking stick, a strong dose of unidentified scent. But after a first glance our attention never leaves her head. It is swathed in black silk (denying verification to Wystan's contention that she is "as bald as a coot") which, in conjunction with her most estimable nose, evokes a likeness, in profile, to a pileated woodpecker. The spectral, Blanc de Chine face might have come from a tapestry, or beneath the swirling *lettrine* of an illuminated manuscript. Yet the eyes are her most remarkable feature. They are heavily underpenciled with blue, like the woad-dye of a Briton warrior, and they squint as narrowly as the eye slits in a helmet.

Dr. Edith enters the room peeling long black gloves and remarking that once a gorilla in the Ringling Circus at Sarasota watched her do this, then tried to do the same with his hands, failing in which he kissed hers—an homage that appears neither to have surprised nor frightened her, whereas she reports the animal's trainer to be in hospital still recuperating from the shock. And who, having met this intimidating woman, would presume to doubt the story?

Turning the talk to Hollywood, Dr. Edith asks I.S. for his opinion of "the extent to which Aldous really believes in *Tantra*." But whatever I.S.'s estimate of Aldous's beliefs (which he undoubtedly regards as strictly Aldous's affair), his mind turns like a compass needle to the center of his own: "Sacrifice is the basis of religion, and sleeping on beds of nails and living on diets of grass are not sacrifices but experiments." Later in the evening, nevertheless, he resolves to "bone up on the Upanishads."

Shortly after the departure of this literary royalty, Mrs. George Orwell, our upstairs neighbor at the Gladstone, tells us she had been giving a party in her rooms at the same time as ours, but that bar service was very slow. "When I complained to the waiter, he advised me to 'Do like those Russians on the seventh floor, lady, order doubles.'"

1953

January 21

Dinner at "Maria's" with Auden. He is whey-faced, much shaken by the latest trials with his female admirer, who has finally had to be taken to the coop. "She was ringing up every few minutes, hammering at the door in the middle of the night, even bribing the manager of the building to be let into my apartment, though once inside she did no more than take the measurements of my old suit in order to buy me a new one. Finally she began to shout in public that we had had intercourse together, though God knows, and she herself *in petto*, that I had met her only once, at the request of *her* psychiatrist. Still, it is unpleasant to commit someone: the ambulance, the men in white coats, the strait jacket, that sort of thing."

He talks about the Yale Younger Poets series, and his job of introducing a sheaf of poems by the winnowed final candidate. "Everyone is writing fragments now, but I continue to look for good whole lines, and 'originality' and 'striking images' are the very last ingredients I could care about." He then discourses on whisky-cultures *versus* wine-cultures, dividing all Europe by this measurement, as Feuerbach divided it into bean-eating cultures and potato-eating cultures. Finally, he expatiates on the texts in I.S.'s *Cantata*, explaining that "the Whinny-Muir is the gorse moor where souls are ceaselessly nettled, a familiar landscape of the time," and that "the Brig o'dred is the narrow bridge to Purgatory from which the wicked topple into Hell." I.S. says that he had not thought of the *Lyke-Wake Dirge* as Scotch, but it seems to me that the accompaniment has a Scotch drone.

We go to *Pal Joey* after dinner, but Wystan hates it, and the bawdiness shocks him. In one number the chorus girls bump their bare bottoms audiencewards, revealing bouquets of violets fixed in the cleft like tail feathers, and at this he dashes from the theater and does not reappear.

1956

July 10

Aboard the S.S. *Vulcania*, somewhere in the southern Adriatic. Awakened by the periodic moan of the ship's fog signals, I go to my porthole, but the sea itself is invisible, and the pulse of our engines is so feeble that we can hardly be moving at all. Later in the morning a trajectory of clear atmosphere exposes a wall of blue mountains, then Cephalonia and Zante appear, but still in dense vapors, like fragile objects wrapped for shipment.

At Patras we wait several miles offshore for a welcoming deputation, but when at last it arrives, no doubt having been difficult to convoke, hospitality proves to be a lesser article of its business than propaganda. I.S. is asked to make a statement protesting British atrocities in Cyprus, but he parries the request by condemning all atrocities everywhere and at any time. Finally stamped and ticketed for landing, we go to a sponson amidships and transfer from there to a pinnace whose leathery old Charon guides the rudder handle with his bare feet and acknowledges his gadfly passengers only by several contemptuous expectorations in their (our) direction.

The walls of the customs shed display many photographs

of the Cyprus atrocities, but the point of those showing soldiers frisking priests is confusing, clerical transvestism suggesting that the real complaint may be indecent assault. Prodigal sons back home from the Bronx or Chicago are evidently not trusted in the always highly corruptible Customs Service, hence none of the officials who mill us through the turnstiles of questions, documents, inspections, speaks a word of any language but Greek. Add to this the confounding by a declaration form that requires wildly disparate commodities to be counted under one heading. Thus a tourist with a camera, a watch, a fur coat, and one hundred cigarettes would declare a total of 103.

We are rescued from this pandemonium by the dust-raising arrival of a taxi, whose driver's cap advertises our hotel, the Cecil. The man's authoritative manner in dealing with the officials, and in paying one or two of a suddenly formed regiment of porters, might otherwise have identified him as the satrap of the province, or at least the mayor or chief of police. That this timely, mettlesome person *is* something more than he seems we discover on reaching the Cecil. There, removing the cap and exchanging his civies for a uniform with aiguillettes, he becomes, in rapid succession, the registering clerk, waiter, unique supplier of room service, sole operator of a reluctant and extremely tremulous lift. He is in fact the only staff, as we learn eventually, but now, entering a lobby crowded with other guests clamoring for his miscellaneous functions, we do not yet realize that they could have been clamoring during the entire boat-meeting expedition.

Patras is a miserable city, a threat to our preconceptions that several rounds of mastikas—Greek "redeye"—do not offset. At twilight we go to a restaurant on the Gulf shore, on a road whose other traffic consists mainly of overcrowded buses, women with head bundles, and bearded and stovepipe-hatted priests, some of them skillfully managing bicycles in spite of their skirts. We sit at the water's edge, facing the mountains of Aetolia, with Calydon behind and Missolonghi to the west. But the view is better than the alimentation, excepting the olives and a non-resinated though thick-as-malmsey Achaian wine; to me, anyway, but the very thought of calamari, like the thought of haggis and chitterlings, is enough to sustain a fast, in my case, whereas I.S. eats so many of them that he complains later of having "swallowed too many spiders."

At nightfall, lights begin to flicker like fireflies on the opposite shore, marking, we suppose, a heretofore invisible city, until they move into the Gulf and are identified as fishing boats. In fact the moth-like dazzling of susceptible fish (and the knocking of them, when dazzled, with knobkerries) is a method of angling described by ancient writers—"the fire-producing stone of night-rowers" is in fact Satyrius's somewhat periphrastic definition of flint—with the difference now that pine torches have been replaced by electric and kerosene lanterns. Our pleasure in this spectacle is soon interrupted, however, by a parcel of tourists dumped from a bus to a nearby table for an al fresco banquet. We retreat to a café in Patras and there embalm ourselves with more mastikas, though even one can make it difficult to tell whether the starry firmament is inside or out.

July 11

The view from my window at 6 A.M. is a Chirico: a deserted square and an empty railway station, with a large new clock over the entrance dividing the void into hours and fractions of hours. Directly below me, men are drinking coffee at sidewalk tables, reading newspapers, extending their feet to shoe polishers. Beyond the station, fishermen are tying up at the docks, and the Ionian Sea is already blazing with the morning sun.

Our bills paid, we pack into a "limousine." It is driven by Mr. Spyrakis, an expert chauffeur, "nimble planner," informed *cicerone* (like Mr. Eugenides, he speaks demotic French), and able exchequer, whose perquisites are justly proportioned, or so his manner, if not invariably that of the recipients, implies. In fact Mr. Spyrakis's only evident failing is a national one, the too-frequent use of his automobile's too-resonant horn. He takes us east of Patras to a ferry slip, which is the reason for our early rising: crossings are infrequent, and, after the first one, unscheduled. The vessel, a war-surplus LST, does not inspire confidence, but we embark along with some dilapidated donkey wagons, a tribe of goats, and the pedestrian *polloi*, among whom an unshod and ragged boy attempts to dispose of a trayload of preposterously stale-looking cakes. The ferry plies between the castles of Morea and Roumeli, twin Venetian forts on facing promontories.

The north-shore road is obstructed near the outset by a gypsy caravan in process of leaving a squalid roadside bivouac. The men are corralling donkeys, dogs, goats, and chickens, while the women, swathed in blankets and wearing headgear like the peasant women in *Les Très Riches Heures du Duc de Berry*, wait by the wagons in a one-hundred-degree sun. The I.S.'s are as much impressed by this encounter as I myself, a one-time addict of George Borrow, am disappointed. They still half believe in gypsy kidnapping, gypsy sorcery, and such other arrant superstitions as the gypsy power to charm away warts. Once in the rue Passy a gypsy called to V. in Russian(!), saying, "Come here and I will tell you interesting things about your future." And V. regularly consults a gypsy palmist in Los Angeles, a seer and clairvoyant discovered and patronized by the Huxleys; I.S. has also been influenced by the prophecies of this Azucena, in spite of his protestations that any knowledge of the future would make the present unbearable.

Lepanto, the first city on our route, has suffered little or no reconstruction since the battle of that name—which occurred south of Oxia, fifty miles to the west. It is a pile of crumbling fortifications, a description that includes the harbor's lobster-shaped sea walls and sea gate. After Lepanto, the road climbs steeply, and it climbs and descends sheerly and precipitously all the way to Delphi. It is narrow, bumpy, and unpaved as well, and a thick dust cloud trails the car. Two stretches have been bedded with crushed rock, but these are the most dangerous of all; we slide and stick fast in one of them and are obliged to brave a sheep dog and apply to a herdsman for help. During the entire seven-hour drive we see no other automobile, or in fact any vehicles other than the mules and old women who are evidently responsible for all transportation of freight on the road.

The ground is mostly barren in spite of the shaping and reshaping of terraces on every arable slope and the gathering and regathering of rocks into fences. We see only one remnant of an older civilization, a thin-waisted Byzantine arc-bridge spanning a gorge. Nearby, a squad of women is pounding stones to gravel; their faces are partly veiled, not for protection, but orientally, the eyes still being exposed to flying chips of stone. About three hours from Lepanto, in a mountain village still choked with rubble from the war, we stop at a locanda, and drink ouzos chased by cold spring water and eat rahat loukoum. At another table are three men dolled up in highlanders' tasseled caps, fustanella, tufted slippers, handlebar mustaches. They look like ex-brigands, in spite of the costume, and if I were to see their grizzled faces peering through my window at home, I would call the police, or take a pill, or say a prayer, or become a teetotaler. But they take only lateral and begrudging notice of us, their interest being directed entirely to Mr. Spyrakis's "limousine."

The road climbs again afterward to a point from which the Gulf is in view nearly as far back as Patras, so short a distance away, crow-wise, compared with all the colonic miles of the road. From here to Amfissa the landscape is less bleak, and the sempiternal olive trees are relieved by eucalyptus and pepper, and oleander and thistle, now in bloom. The inhabitants are less savagely aloof, too, and everyone from toothing toddlers to edentate beldams screams at us for cigarettes.

The hotel at Delphi is unfinished, and our balcony, overlooking the valley of the Pleistos River, has not yet been enclosed. The sun being too strong for ruin climbing, we venture out only at six o'clock, but the heat is still fierce then, and only the Phaedriades are in shadow. The ruins—broken columns, shattered walls, crippled temples and treasuries—are disappointing, nor does the superstitious, opportunistic, and cruel religion to which they are monuments inspire my awe. The oracle flattered the favored, told the powerful what they wanted to hear, and sold the equivalent of stock-market tips to big investors.[1]

July 12

To Athens, *via* Hosios Loukas, Levadia, Thebes. I.S., very grouchy because of the intense heat, dismisses the contents of the Delphi museum as "breakage." As the sun mounts and we

[1] See H. W. Parke's *Greek Oracles* (Hutchinson University Library, 1968) for an answer to this impudence. (R.C.)

descend into ever hotter valleys, he tries to protect his head by knotting the corners of a handkerchief and wearing it like an English housemaid's bonnet. An hour or thereabouts beyond Parnassus, when the stone huts of the shepherds have been succeeded by thatched roofs and wood, we come to a view, from a great height, of the Triodos, the intersection of the Delphi–Thebes and Daulis–Ambrysus roads. I.S. denies that he had pictured this landscape scenically while composing his *"trivium"* music, but says he would have supposed the area to be very small, whereas in these wide and now aforested slopes, Laius and his unrecognized son would hardly have noticed each other, let alone contested each other's passage. Suddenly a blast explosion fills the road fifty yards ahead with a fountain of rocks and earth and nearly jolts us over the unrailed ledge. When the debris has safely settled, a workman jumps down from a dugout in the hillside above, signaling us to stop (long since done) and warning Mr. Spyrakis—so I interpret his gesturing toward the abyss—that we could have been killed. And what if our departure this morning had been slightly less unpunctual?

The road to Hosios Loukas is bumpier, and the towns are more harshly destitute than any we have seen. Except for a few old women hoeing in the fields ("Ancient women/ Gathering fuel in vacant lots"), the country is nearly deserted, a circumstance Mr. Spyrakis explains in a horrifying account of the wartime murder of the entire male population in retaliation for the shooting of the *Gauleiter*. At Hosios Loukas we stop by an outdoor restaurant, but the thought of the murdered villagers has killed our appetites. As for Luke-the-Stiriote's churches, the walls and ceilings are cracked and bruised, while the dome frescoes are disturbingly new, spoiled by too much restoration. The monastery buildings are synthetic, compounded of segments of Roman and Byzantine walls and modern bricks and cement, and their most attractive feature, the stone-shingled roof with a round, whitewashed chimney, is indigenous to practically every edifice, sacred and secular, of the region.

The Athens road descends spirally, but whereas the countryside prospers with each downward loop, so does the heat. At Levadia, abode of the Oracle of Triphonius, we dip our arms in the icy spring waters and wade until we turn blue, which makes the heat blister, afterward; we are hardly able to turn our heads in the directions of Thermopylae, Thebes, and Marathon. But the latter holds at least the promise of a breeze: "The mountain looks on Marathon and Marathon looks on the sea," and compared with the mountain towns, Thebes, of which the ancient remains could be carted off in a few trucks, has an almost hopeful look. Refreshed, finally, by the pine forests of Attica and the sea air at Eleusis, we enter Athens from above, Mount Lycabettus coming into view first, then the Parthenon and the sprawling dusty-white city beneath. Our hotel, formerly the Grande Bretagne, is now simply the Grande, and the Byron statue across the street has been draped with a sign: "Aren't you ashamed to be an Englishman?"

July 13

In a shore restaurant several miles of dowdy cottages south of Athens, we choose our fish from a display laid out on morgue-like slabs in the bead-curtained kitchen, as if their aesthetic attractions were a clue to their culinary ones. In addition to the fin fish, there are tubs of cuttle fish and calamari. William James: "Such flexible intensity of life, in a form so inaccessible to our sympathy."

Back in Athens, we trudge steep paths and climb tall steps to the Acropolis, where sunburned and perspiring Teutons (dirndls, *Lederhosen*) are photographing each other and reading aloud to each other from Baedekers. The interior of the Parthenon is whiter, less wheat-colored than I expect, having been told as a child that it is beige.

July 16

Mycenae. Excavations are in progress outside the walls, but we are alone in the citadel, except for ghosts: "This house, if it had a voice . . ." The ascent is arduous, and the path is a cauldron except at the summit, under Prophet Elias Mountain, which is cooled by winds from Argos, and which looks over slopes of olive and cypress to Tiryns and Arcadia. Agamemnon's Tomb, below the citadel, is hive-shaped, but the stonework, unseen under bronze, gold, and jeweled lading in the time of the incumbent, is as smoothly chamfered as an Inca wall. The actual tomb was in a second room joined to the first like a Siamese twin, but with no outside entrance of its own, and hence totally dark. Mr. Spyrakis sets fire to a newspaper and thrusts it through the jointure, not for our view, he says, but to expose possible reptiles, explaining that a woman was snakebitten here only a few days ago. However fitting a retribution for a despoiler of Agamemnon's grave, the story rapidly terminates my own explorations of the site.

The bee farms and pine woods of Epidaurus are perfect relief, and the amphitheater is agreeably human-sized, after all the photographs that try to make it look like Hollywood Bowl. By the time we reach Nauplia the mountains are purple and the bay is rippling with boats. We climb Palomedes Rock, but the Lions of St. Mark on the walls there seem a glib emblem after the great lion gate at Mycenae. After dark the quay becomes a corso for the whole population, ourselves included, until some small boys ferret us out shouting "Stick-em-up!" and "Bang-bang!" followed by torrents of Greek the cowboys in our films do not know.

July 17

The mountains are brown and barren again as we drive to Nemea in the morning. Green and mountain-girdled, with its temple of Zeus tumbled in a deep field and its cave of Hercules-and-the-lion—a cave for Zarathustra or Jerome in other mythologies—Nemea hereafter will be my vision of the Valley of the Blest.

July 18

Sunion. Here on the windy cape where Daedalus begat Icarus is the Greece of my prejudices and, which is the same thing, child-picturebook imagination. The Temple of Poseidon is incontestably white, comparatively intact—although the surfaces are thickly carved with visitors' names and dates, including many early Bostonians'—and it overlooks blue seas.

November 4

Paris. A gray Sunday. It is stamp-exchange and purchase day, and the sidewalk across the street from my room on the Rond Point is filled with huddles of philatelists. In my room, too, I get all the applause, boos, stomps, shouts of *"Oui!"* and *"Non!"* from children watching *guignol* in the park.

Boulez comes at noon, bringing his *Marteau* recording, and we eat downstairs at the Berkeley. He is balder, shorter, stockier, more solid in the solar plexus than I remember, but as lithe and springy as a boxer. Quick, precise, very sure of himself (as if he were carrying infallible plans of conquest in his pocket, Parisians say), he seems to me a mental creature primarily, in contrast to I.S., who is a physical creature first, a rare escapee from "that violent severance from man's animal past" which bothered Nietzsche; in I.S., physical appetites and body gestures are apparent long before the mind comes out of hiding, which is partly why the self-identification and the personality of the physical gestures in the music are so immediate. Or, to put it differently, I.S.'s abstract thought, for which he has a high capacity no matter how contemptuously he regards it, is never disassociated (pre-scinded) from physical instinct, whereas Boulez's physical instincts are both more subtle and more neuter. Boulez is charming, even-keeled, laugh-prone, unfaltering, unneurotic —in spite of a rapid nervous blink—enviably intelligent. The thought occurs to me—perhaps because he talks about *Un coup de dès* ("Writers are in a worse way than composers, Mallarmé and Joyce already having done it all")—that with an eyeshade he would look like a croupier.

We speak our own languages, the arbitrary assignation of gender to every noun in his constituting an insurmountable obstacle for me, to say nothing of such pronunciation problems as the proper palatalizing of the cacuminals. We seem about equally able to follow each other, too, except that the wines, which do not faze him, both excite and fuddle me.

His musical opinions having preceded him, we talk about my performance of *Polyphonie X* in Los Angeles four years ago; and we talk about his background. He claims to be immune from religious feeling, saying that the Church never meant anything to him even in his earliest childhood, which tallies with the avowal that he has always been more interested in Oriental than in Latin cultures, this to the point of an aversion for most things Italian except food.

Finishing our own food, we go to a street near the Place de la Bastille and, in an apartment building next to a house where Cézanne lived as a young man, climb four flights of stone stairs and two of wood to Boulez's garret. Every object and utility in this tiny lair conforms to the size of his script and musical detail: the small bed, desk, reproduction of Klee's portrait of I.S., *salamandre*, upright piano—on which he improvises a funny Brahmsian accompaniment to the beginning of the second movement of Schoenberg's Violin Concerto. His own manuscripts are rolled like diplomas, and piled on the floor like logs.

November 7

Dinner with Boulez and Suvchinsky in a restaurant two Métro stops before the Pont de Neuilly: turbot and Sancerre; gigot and Richebourg; gâteau St.-Honoré and raspberry liqueur. Suvchinsky's hair is wintery, his handshake, in which the last two fingers do not engage, is limp, and his nearly albino complexion is mottled with patches of marchpane and pink as if from some tropical disease. But these aspects are belying, for he is also big-boned and *"robuste"* (a favorite word, in fact near the top of the list after *"con"* and *"salaud"*), has a trencherman's appetite, and speaks in a powerful (a Boanerges's), though also a musical (a *viola pomposa*), voice. As if in compensation for the unhearty handshake, he crushes me with Russian bear hugs and double-cheeked Russian-style kisses.

In spite of forty years in Paris and Parisian habits of criticism formed even before that—he is a student of the new semiology as well as of linguistic analysis à la Roman Jakobson —Suvchinsky is more Russian- than French-minded. In fact, he reminds me in many ways of I.S., is in truth more like I.S. than anyone else I have ever known. This Russian-ness—as I have come to think of it, for of course the qualities I have in mind are personal and individual first, and Russian second, if at all—is characterized by an openness and volubility, as well as by a warmth and generosity formerly combined in the loaded word "aristocratic."

Suvchinsky is renowned for his talent in discovering talent, and his selfless efforts to enlist support for it, efforts entailing special difficulties in his case because he himself is penniless and proud. He has been the friend, champion, and unsparing critic of both I.S. and Boulez. His talk tonight is entirely centered on I.S., the fact of whose confinement in the Rote Kreuz Krankenhaus in Munich neither softens any of Suvchinsky's asperities or pulls any of his critical punches. I.S. and Suvchinsky, intimates between the wars, have not met since 1939 because of Suvchinsky's alleged (correctly, as the conversation proves) derogation of I.S.'s American-period so-called neo-classic music. When I first met Suvchinsky, at a performance of *Erwartung* in Paris in 1952, I.S. received my report of the encounter in silence.

Suvchinsky leads off with questions about the Stravinsky children. He is very fond of them, obviously, and warmly sympathetic to the problems of life with a father who is a tyrant of genius. He contends that "the ambidexterity of Théodore and Milène is an inverted, or leftover, manifestation of their father's gifts; the cerebral zones themselves may even be transposed; after all, the speech control of right-handed people is located in the left cerebral hemisphere, and handedness is connected with speech, as any observer of the confusion in speech and thought in ambidextrous children will tell you. In all fairness, though, simply to know that one had *those* genes is a burden."

He then advances the theory that money is the root of all compromise in Stravinsky's case. "Money was always too important to him. The lure of it led him away from composition and into conducting, and the parting with it gave him so much pain that he would pay the smallest tradesman's bill as if he were being hijacked."

"But can you tell me what happened to Stravinsky after *Les Noces*, the descent into *Mavra*, the Pergolesi *rifacimenti*, the Tchaikovsky anthology, the titivated echoes of operetta composers in *Jeu de Cartes* and the other *gaietés parisiennes?* Surely some explanation deeper than money is behind such a '*bizarre metamorphose*'? Wasn't the real trouble that he did not understand the general ideas (in Taine's sense) of his time? The general ideas were Schoenberg's ideas, and it was Stravinsky, whatever he says now, who turned the younger generation against Schoenberg. Only the other day, Poulenc, describing the extent to which he and his group were dominated by Stravinsky, told me that the mere suggestion by any of them that Schoenberg or Berg might be worth investigating would automatically have made them traitors in Stravinsky's eyes. 'At that time Stravinsky was dismissing *Wozzeck*, which he had not heard, as *une musique boche*, and Mahler, of whom he knew nothing, as Malheur.' "

I put in my own oar here and protest that if Poulenc's version is true, he was at least as much at fault as I.S. and should not try to hang the blame on the older man. And I add that as Poulenc now goes about belittling I.S. as too old for the new hats he tries on in the *Canticum sacrum*, the French composer shouldn't mind being told that those new hats are part of the reason why I.S. is I.S. and Poulenc is only Poulenc. My interruption does not divert the arraignment, however, and Suvchinsky's engrossing analysis continues with the indictment that "Stravinsky is incapable of sustaining a reasoned and developed argument, never getting beyond doctrinaire aestheties, *le goût, plaisanteries,* and paradoxes: how he loves intellectual paradoxes!" This tempts me to interject that I would have thought *Les Noces* a highly reasoned and developed argument, but Suvchinsky would not agree, for what he means are certain habits of verbal discourse more cultivated among professors than among creative artists.

He goes on to say that "Arthur Lourié, Olga Sudeikine's lover, was closer to Stravinsky in the Twenties and Thirties than anyone else. In fact, Lourié's ascendancy between 1920 and 1926 was nearly complete and nearly disastrous. But Lourié should publish his memoirs. He was a kind of *valet de chambre* to Stravinsky, after all, and no one knows more about a man than his valet," though of course the sort of person who could be a camerlingo, or even a musical factotum, to I.S., would be unlikely to know very much about him. "Discovering that Stravinsky was a savage of genius (*'eine wilde Musik'* was Berg's description of *Petrushka*) Lourié set out to tame him, introducing him to Philosophy in the person of Maritain, and to Literature in other august persons; I remember seeing *Ulysses* in Stravinsky's studio in 1926, brought there, of course, by Lourié." (Not necessarily. I.S. and Joyce had many common Parisian acquaintances; George Antheil would have been as likely a donor of the book, or Henrietta Hirschman, a friend of I.S.'s for forty years and the sister of Joyce's secretary, Paul Léon.) "It was the old story of the man who explains latching on to the man who does. In this instance, fortunately, the genius was not tamed out of existence along with the savage. But there were portents, such as *Mavra*. What I do not understand is how Lourié could have had Stravinsky's musical esteem. But he *did* have it, was in fact the first person to be shown each new work, up to the time of *Perséphone*. Just how little progress was made at the Lourié *école* is another, almost unknown, matter, however, and it is one of the profound ironies of contemporary music that the savage of genius, the man who was all 'creative instinct' and 'natural talent,' came to be thought of as a mere arbiter of taste pontificating about the glories of Gounod."

It was Arthur Lourié, Suvchinsky might have added, who intrigued against V. just before her marriage to I.S., which is why the name is never mentioned in the I.S. household, and why I have no information to contribute myself.

"If Stravinsky had not gone to America in 1939," Suvchinsky continues, "he might have compromised himself politically. He was a frequent and welcome visitor to Blackshirt Italy during the Ethiopian and Spanish wars, after all, conducting at the Maggio Fiorentino as late as 1939, by which date that festival had become a loudly pro-Axis celebration. He even inscribed a copy of his *Croniques de ma Vie* for Mussolini. Was this out of pro-Fascist sentiments or because Mussolini's trains ran on time? Absolutely none of the first alternative, certainly, for he was deeply afraid of fascism, though more of the German than of the Italian kind. Still, these fears did not stop him from recording *Jeu de Cartes* with Furtwängler's orchestra in Berlin in 1938, by which time the orchestra had been purged of its Jews as well as of all good contemporary music including most of Stravinsky's; by which time, too, all of his colleagues with a scrap of political, if not moral, sense (and not least among them I.S.) were protesting Nazism.

"Apart from the immediate excuse of money, the explanation lies in his even deeper dread of Stalin, and it is the lecture on music in the USSR in the *Poètique musicale*, which convinces me that the fear of communism would eventually have driven him into the arms of the Occupier. He was a White Russian, after all, and his French friends, like T. S. Eliot's French friends, included Maurras and other former *Action française* writers, as well as Drieu la Rochelle and Lucien Daudet." (In fact, I.S. and Daudet were friends only at the time of *Petrushka;* it was Daudet who took the composer to visit the ex-Empress Eugénie in her Riviera villa.) "The political tendency of these associations is noted in Klaus Mann's *Journal,* by the way, and Mann's good friend Gide was equally well aware of them. The truth is that the friction between the authors of *Perséphone* was more political than artistic. In Stravinsky's eyes Gide was a COMMUNIST—it was at the time of Gide's first infatuation with the USSR—hence, *ni plus ni moins,* not only despicable but also dangerous. Now, from this alone, you can see that Stravinsky was not a political animal. Actually he did not have the remotest grasp of political facts, not the trace of a social concept. Which accounts, in part, for his turning to dogma, though of that, too, he understood precious little. 'I have no explanation of my own,' he used to say: 'Questions of that sort are for the Church to decide,' and he would quote Bossuet's 'The heretic is he who has an opinion.' And what did the Church decide to do about Hitler? To keep very quiet while he murdered Communists and Jews."

It is a passionate, if also a well-rehearsed, recital, not by any means having its maiden tryout. Clearly I am thought of as a plenipotentiary (rather than as a famulus, which is more often the case, or satellite, or jester), as well as a gray eminence who "operates" I.S. and is responsible for shanghaiing him into the "12-tone system" (as if anyone could even lead *that* horse to water, if it didn't want to go, let alone make it drink). The wording is for my benefit, too, though this hardly surprises me, for anyone who has spent as much as two minutes in the same room with I.S. has a theory about him, and a self-including story to put at the disposal of a potential biographer. But even from my non-impersonating and compendious, rather than complete, translation, it must be apparent that Suvchinsky's recital is the result of long-pent-up pressures. I.S.'s friendship was the central event of his life. Bereft of it, he would naturally swing to a critical viewpoint in the opposite direction, the direction, as it happened, of Boulez, the *enfant terrible* of the late Forties.

What of the content? Most of the daggers are rubber, it seems to me, though I cannot comment on the Suvchinsky version of the Lourié influence but only continue to suspect from my observations of Lourié at Tanglewood a decade ago, and judging from what I know of his music and writings, that the evaluation is exaggerated. As for the alleged perpendicular decline of I.S.'s music after the Russian period, that is the official French postwar view of it; and *Oedipus Rex* and the *Psalms* will be released from French quarantine only when some extremely daring antiquarian of the Seventies discovers that whether or not these masterpieces are neo-classic is beside the point.

The money question is less easily disposed of. Certainly I.S. can be oddly, aberrantly thrifty, and undoubtedly tradesmen *have* had to dun him for payment. But he can also be as extravagant as a grand duke, and is so improvident as to be regularly overdrawn at the bank. (His possessiveness is all-powerful, to be sure, as any photograph of his workroom shows, but the possessions he most wants are people, and he has rarely succeeded in his friendships, demanding too great a sacrifice and too strict a loyalty.) V. explains the money drive as an echo of the trauma of the war years when the coffers really were empty and he really was forced to grub around, but surely it is older and more anal than that. Whatever the explanation, and however formulated—"acts of charity" being classified under possessiveness nowadays—I.S.

has supported a whole welfare department of relatives for most of their lives and kept several destitute émigré friends in funds for at least as long as I have known him.

The imputed right-wing political sentiments are a more "vexed" question than Suvchinsky's account allows because of prior religious questions requiring disentanglement and differentiation of a kind that, understanding little of that side of I.S. myself, I am not able to undertake. I would agree that he does not understand political philosophy and the political medium, and that his socio-political parts did not grow up to match his genius parts; but then, it seems to me that the authoritarian mold of his mind is only spuriously related to politics. What it does relate to is the Church, and all that I can say positively about even that one aspect of his much greater religiosity is that he associates the institutional religion with his first wife and his guilt feelings concerning her, and that the Church influence seems to have been balanced by the "liberal" and "democratic" influence largely cultivated by the woman around whom his life since 1921 has revolved, for I.S. *is* influenced by the people he loves, and his capacity for change and growth is one of his most striking characteristics, along with, Suvchinsky notwithstanding, an inexhaustible intellectual curiosity.

Finally, the "no mind" diagnosis, the gravamen of the argument concerning I.S.'s supposed failure to understand Schoenberg's "general ideas," is in my opinion not even a factor; nor, for that matter, is the Schoenberg antimony wholly true, though of course I.S. was hardly among the original twelve-tone commandos. The real reasons were the circumstantial ones: I.S.'s musical isolation and—which is both cause and result of that isolation—his lack of communication with other composers. But the equipment itself was and is up to any job of understanding, the mind of the *Sacre* and the *Psalms* being, if anything, too subtle for such measurements.

Nor do I concede a penchant for paradox as an intellectual limitation in I.S.'s case; in fact it is hardly more than a mannerism, a device of social rather than mental behavior. But what Suvchinsky means by mind, in this instance, is a rhetorical discipline, and what I mean is something similar to Eliot's description of the mind of Henry James as so fine that no idea could violate it.

Still, this is the testimony of a man who was as close to I.S. at one time as I am now. By extension I am able to recognize everything and confirm much in Suvchinsky's picture. But it is another I.S. So, too, the I.S. *I* know would seem greatly transformed to Suvchinsky, who would also be able to see by looking ahead, as I am able to see by looking back, the "continuity of personality." But the differences lead me to wonder whether anyone has ever known more than one or another aspect of I.S. Even V., who can collate these views, is held apart from his deepest feelings by at least the length of each new composition.

1 9 5 8

May 22

Hollywood. Ernst Krenek for dinner, more suntanned than ever; I do not know how good a Catholic he is, but he certainly practices his heliolatry. We drink two bottles of Aigle-les-Murailles, after which he becomes an engaging memoirist of Webern, Berg, Karl Kraus, Loos, and especially Busoni. Describing Busoni's *soirées* in his Berlin residence shortly after the 1914–18 war, Krenek says that the composer sat between a fortune-telling mystic, and, for good luck, like Verdi's Prince of Mantua, a hunchback, and that this strange trinity was separated from the guests by a row of empty chairs. "Busoni did all of the talking, and was never less than brilliant; he had great qualities of imagination, and great visionary powers—far beyond his abilities in music. Coffee was served regularly, but once we were given *Sekt*, which had not been paid for; even as we were drinking it the merchant pounded on the door asking for his money."

Krenek himself is a man of great intellectual qualities, some of which are employed tonight as he explains to I.S. how he derived the time and density controls in his *Sestina* from the original twelve-note structure by multiplying and dividing the numbers of the semi-tones of the intervals. It does not really matter, either, that it has all been worked out well away from the music.

December 7

London. Dinner at Stephen Spender's with Graham Greene, who is so much taller than I.S. that an onlooker not already aware of the diminutive height of the one, might at a distance take the other to be an ex-center on a basketball team. Greene says he had been told that I.S. was in the audience at one of the New York previews of *The Potting Shed*, and regrets are exchanged that they had not met then. But conversation making is heavy going, lulls frequent. Greene's talk is topical, which is not unlooked for, but the I.S.'s have never heard of the Wolfenden debate, concerning which Greene suggests that T. S. Eliot and John Hayward should be induced to contribute a letter to *The Times* on the respectableness of two men keeping house together. He is more interesting on the difficulties of unblocking royalties in the bamboo-curtain countries, where *The Quiet American* is immensely popular: "It looks as if I will have to spend the rest of my days in China." But he intimidates the I.S.'s. They have read all of his books, starting with, because of their fascination with Mexico, *The Power and the Glory*, and they are attracted in advance to the author of them, if not by his obsessions with pity, fear, self-destruction, failure, the need to run away, the hollowness of physical love, the problem of Pelagian moral arguments. They do not know how to say *"Bonjour!"* to him in a way to make him talk, however, and, though not shy as a rule, they cannot bridge the shyness of the other along with their own. And Greene *is* shy: if he were aware of how much the I.S.'s admired his work, he would freeze altogether. As it is, he lends no support to the infrequent moments of, in any case, not exactly doubling-up general amusement, nor quite shows how he regards our own participation in them. The brows knit, instead, the jowls weigh down, and the saggy face sags a little more. When his implacable blue eyes focus on one of us, moreover, they are transparently seeing something else. It is a sad, wise, fanatical face, the mask of a man who has seen a great deal and knows the worst.

December 8

Dinner with the T. S. Eliots in their Kensington Gardens ground-floor flat. The name does not appear on the roster of tenants, but they are waiting for us in the hall when we arrive, and are holding hands. Their walls are bare except for bookshelves, and these are mainly in the dining room, "which is where arguments come up," Eliot says, "and the reason dictionaries and reference books should be kept there." As if to illustrate the contention, and in response to some specula-tions by I.S. concerning the word "paraclete," he fetches a well-worn Liddell and Scott from behind his own chair but offers the identical information himself before opening it. He also supplies apt and exact translations of the foreign expres-sions that occur regularly in I.S.'s talk, while disclaiming that he is a linguist: "I only pretended to be one in order to get a job in a bank." But he is a quiet man, slow in forming his remarks, which then trail off in diminuendo; the life in him is not in his voice, but in his clear, piercingly intelligent, gray eyes. He breathes heavily and harrumphs: "Hm," "Hmm," "Hmmm," deepening the significance, it seems, with each lengthening "m." His long, fidgety fingers fold and unfold, too, or touch tip to tip, which suddenly makes me aware that I.S.'s hands, otherwise remarkable for the large spread between the knuckles, are the least nervous I have ever seen.

Table talk is about taxes—I.S. says he feels very guilty on learning that tonight's dinner is not deductible—and writers. "Cocteau was very brilliant when I saw him last," Eliot remarks, "but I had the impression he was rehearsing for a more important occasion," to which I.S. adds that Cocteau is "a sincere liar." Eliot's anecdotes, otherwise, are all self-effacing. One of them is about a young woman who, "during the stop at Gander, on my last flight from New York, hovered nearer and nearer, until finally I invited her for coffee; I was then asked, with thesis-writers' relentlessness, for my recollections of Virginia Woolf." According to another story, Eliot was in a New York taxi one day with Djuna Barnes, when he "noticed that the driver had become engrossed in our conversation. After Miss Barnes left, the cabbie asked me whether 'that *woman* was a writer.'" Eliot says he was interested in I.S.'s comments, in one of our books, about Dylan Thomas, adding that "Thomas had the richest gift of humor of any contemporary poet. He might have written a great comedy, though whether he could have fashioned a libretto I am unable to say." Eliot then confesses that he cannot remember his own poetry, "because it was rewritten so many times I forget which version was final." We drink sherry before, claret during, whisky after, dinner. Eliot carves and serves the meat himself, and walks around the table like a wine steward to fill our glasses.

After dinner he brings a scrapbook bulging with photographs and clippings, and invites I.S. to compose something for it, saying that he writes in it himself every night.

A time for the evening under lamplight
(*The evening with the photograph album*).

For most of the evening I.S. refrains from medical talk, but once he mentions that his blood is too thick, which reminds Eliot that in 1911 a doctor in Munich told him that *his* blood was too thin.

I.S., in the car returning to Claridge's: "He is not the most exuberant man I have ever known, but I feel I have been with someone very pure."

1959

September 6

London. Dinner with the Eliots at Claridge's. T.S.E. looks younger and is livelier than last year, but he seems to think of himself as a hoary ancient with little time left. Social obligations, he says, are the bane of his existence. "I cannot accept lectures because the people who pay for them expect me to attend cocktail parties at which I am inevitably caught between someone asking what I think of existentialism and someone wanting to know what I *really* meant by such and such a line." A prominent critic is mentioned, and Eliot describes him as a brain-picker. "I know, because he tried to get me drunk and to pick mine. He is insanely jealous of all creative writers, and his own only good line must either have happened to him or been told to him by someone else. This occurs in one of his novels when a man stroking a woman's back exclaims how soft it is, and she rejoinders with 'What the Hell did you expect, scales?' "

On Pound's new *Cantos*, Eliot notes that "There are more Chinese characters than ever. Ezra is becoming the best Chinese poet in English." When I.S. relates his impressions of the Japanese theater, Eliot says he once watched a Noh dancer in a play by Yeats and was very moved by the performance: "One really could believe the dancer had become a bird." He asks I.S. about Japanese preferences in Western theater: "Ionesco, I suppose, and Tennessee Williams?" As for Büchner and Berg, he observes that "*Wozzeck* is too simple for a play but just simple enough for an opera."

He drinks a gin and tonic before, claret during, whisky after, dinner, which in his case is limited to a partridge, for while he enjoys sniffing the cheese platter, he does not, after deliberation and a final moment of indecision, actually choose one. He gazes at each of us in rotation, beaming affection in his wife's direction each time around. The Huxley name comes up, and he says that "I don't read Aldous; I am much too fond of him for that. He was very pessimistic when we saw him last. Too many people in the world already, and more all the time. So there *are* indeed, indeed"; and because one looks for special twists and ironies in everything he says, the echoed word seems to ring with extra meaning. Judging from his parting remarks about the weather—"Isn't it unusual? Why last year at this time . . ."—I think he would have enjoyed a chat on the subject. Describing his plans to visit his birthplace near St. Louis, he says that the house doesn't exist any more. "If ever a plaque is erected, it will have to go to one of the neighbors."

1 9 6 0

December 1

Paris. "Lunch" at the Boule d'Or with Suvchinsky and François-Michel, a brilliant writer who was Boulez's four-hand piano partner at one time, and who speaks Latin as fluently as French. At other tables: baby-faced North Americans, oily-faced South Americans, brewer's-bloom-faced (telangiectatic) Gauls. François Michel leaves me miles behind, both because the tempo of his talk is too fast, and because, with the exception of my contributions to his *Encyclopédie*, I know so little of what he is talking *about* (local literary *mesquineries*, Saussure's distinction between *langue* and *parole*, and Claudel, whom I.S. describes as a *"cochon incontestable"*). His gourmet talk, however, what I manage to digest of it, contains useful knowledge concerning such matters as *perdreaux* basting, the wisdom of asking for the less exercised left *patte* of the *poulet*, and of choosing the Gruyère close to the *croûte*—avoiding any cheese, of course, at the slightest whiff of ammonia. He complains that our wicker-cradled first bottle of wine has not been sufficiently aerated, though the glasses are like goldfish bowls, and this leads to a discussion of pre-phylloxera clarets, after which everyone begins to sniff, sip, debate the merits of body and bouquet, and report the reception to the palate, as if after a flagon of vodka that abused organ could differentiate between Lafite Rothschild and plonk. But after all, perhaps François Michel's can.

All told, we soak up, or down, two bottles of vodka, three of claret, two of Dom Perignon, and several slugs of Calvados —and, in consequence, are stupefied. The worst of this is that we have an appointment at five with Chagall, who has come expressly for it from Rouen. Fortunately V. realizes early on, finding herself in conversation with the South Americans at the adjoining table, that she is near the brink of inebriety herself; she takes no more, and is thus able to guy her debauched and reeling menfolk back to the hotel. (Testing one leg, then the other, the thought strikes me that I might turn to stone, on the analogy that certain chemical elements convert from one to another until stability is reached, at which point they become lead.) It is already four o'clock, however, by the time we arrive and steer I.S. to his bed, on which, after answering V.'s question, "Are you drunk?" (I.S.: "And how!") he goes out like a light. ("I saw stars, too," he recalls later, "and had a color-TV dream.") Trying to sober me up for the meeting, Suvchinsky and V. work over me on another bed as if I were a K.O.-ed boxer, Suvchinsky holding ice-filled compresses to my forehead in spite of my protestations on behalf of my sinuses and my insistence that the real trouble is in the medulla oblongata.

> *"They played him a sonata—let me see!*
> *'Medulla oblongata'—key of G."*

It is after five when, I.S. being beyond communication, I venture out alone with V. But though I get as far as Nicolas Nabokov's apartment, where the meeting is to take place, I am too queasy to enter and can only truckle and return ignominiously, as well as headswimmingly, back to the hotel.

An hour later, with the return of the valiant V., we learn that Rolf Liebermann, who had flown from Hamburg for the meeting, took the story as a great joke—"for which I will always love him," says V., adding with a feline scratch that "Chagall couldn't have behaved more pompously. And his wife looked at me as if I were depraved, or had come from a Roman orgy." "Wasn't *her* husband ever drunk?" I wanted to ask, and "What about all those upside-down roosters?"

1961

October 16

London. Dinner with the Eliots at the Savoy. The poet is more hunched than two years ago, leaning forward when he stands, as if from a yoke. The lines of his face are leaner and sharper, too, reminding us of one of those Hittite ceramic birds at the exhibition in Zurich last week, and his lips and large ears are damson.

He complains of the nuisance of having to refuse repeated invitations to the Tagore Centenary. "I took a volume of Tagore from the library, just to be certain I had not made a mistake, but I could make nothing of it. Difficult to tell that to the Indians, though, or indeed to admit that one does not put their man together with Dante and Shakespeare. I remember that Bill Yeats claimed to like Tagore, but he was making a case for the East at the time . . . I receive regular shipments of the works of new Indian poets, incidentally, together with letters inviting my comments. Once I replied, ripping the thing apart, and later found part of my by-no-means-complimentary letter appearing as a preface to the published poems! In payment for these criticisms I received a Kashmir shawl, which I returned, only to receive another and much better shawl with a note agreeing that the first one had not been worthy of me."

Tonight's dinner has been arranged to discuss a proposal that I.S. set to music "two lyrical stanzas," as Eliot calls them, from *Little Gidding*, though Eliot himself is "doubtful they can be set." Nothing further is said about this, however, and instead the poet and musician talk about favorite *romans policiers*, and plays of Voltaire neither of them has read. "I knocked down a complete Voltaire at auction when I first came to England," Eliot confesses, "but never came to pick it up. That has been on my conscience ever since." Both men are Simenon addicts, I.S. admitting he has read at least sixty of his books, and Eliot avowing that "I can read about Maigret when I can read nothing else." Another mutually admired sleuth is Perry Mason. "Gardner knows California law," says the author of *Prufrock*, "but Chandler was a better writer." Concerning the recent debate in the *TLS* on mistranslations in the *New English Bible*, Eliot owns to enjoying this sort of thing, "when I know, as I do now, that I have the right end of the stick." Suddenly Pound's name comes up, and Eliot confides that "Ezra was always a poor judge of people, and indeed of most things except poetry. He really did believe his monetary ideas would change the world—and weren't we all a bit tarred by that brush? But he had great gifts, and I owe more to him than to anyone. Which reminds me that I also owe him a letter; hm, hm, difficult to know what to say."

Eliot has a habit of exclaiming "Yes?" during each pause in the conversation, but once, after V. recounts some of our recent Yugoslavian adventures, and at the same time voices some criticisms of Switzerland, he interjects a whole sentence: "Yes, I see what you mean, but I like it because more than any other country it resembles what it used to be."

1965

June 5

Paris. We go to the SPECTACLE IGOR STRAWINSKY at the Opéra, which consists of *Le Sacre du printemps*, *Les Noces*, and *Renard*, all three staged by Béjart and conducted by Boulez. The *Noces* musicians are in the pit, the chorus in the center, wearing brown robes with cowls. The half-lowered backdrop, which seems to represent an *Arabian Nights* city—and is therefore too oriental by several thousand versts—is greatly indebted to Goncharova's curtain for the 1929 revival of the *Firebird*. No less remote are the village weddings of the title, as well as the whole character of the work; in fact the brides-maids, with their taffeta dresses and ermine muffs, might be ladies-in-waiting to a Tsarina. V., who was to have played the bride in the original performance and who rehearsed the part in Monaco, says that she stood stage center during the comb-ing and plaiting of the tresses, which were several yards long.

The second scene is no closer to the geographical target. The costumes of the "best men" are a cross between gauchos and Music Hall Cossacks, and their dance is half Siberian, half Argentine folk ballet. From the beginning of this scene to the end of the piece, the spectator's attention is divided by a choreographic device. Bride and groom, gotten up like fairy-tale royalty, are split in two; or, rather, doubled, like the Sorcerer's Apprentice, except that the doubles are nude, presumably to represent the betrothed pair's embodied visions (dirty thoughts?; in fact the text *is* coded, like "blues," with sexual meanings). But while this could be diverting in, for instance, a satire on a Victorian costume piece, it is wholly out of place in *Les Noces*. Dancing like shadows by the sides of their over-clothed projectors, the visions imply a depth which, no matter how shallow, is contradicted by a hard musical surface explicitly forbidding meandering psychological interiors. The gratuitous psychological dimension dilutes, or sells short, the severity of the musical emotion, which, at the end anyway, is tragic emotion of a rarefied kind. By contrast, the sentiment of tonight's staging is on the level of an exotic Musical. *Les Noces* is musically mechanized ritual. Failing to meet the demands of the score as such, the choreographer's next best course is to stage the piece straightforwardly as an album of village wedding scenes.

It follows that the thoughts, feelings, visions of people who are not individuals in the first place, but types, matter even less than they do. The visions are optically confusing, moreover, as the eye naturally prefers to travel with the nude *Doppelgängers* rather than with the over-clothed original. Finally, the naked thoughts obtrude too much, getting in the way of their thinkers, then taking over from the completely.

Judging by the costumes, the geography of the third tableau is even farther afield. The *gâteaux à la crème* hats might have been concocted by a Cambodian pastry cook, the bride's mother's minks by a Parisian furrier interested in the program credits. But the great scene of the two weeping mothers is ruined less by costumery than by an excessively slow tempo, when in fact no change is warranted at all.

The final scene is the worst. The backdrop is covered

with icons befitting a church of the Hagia Sophia class, the bride is veiled like a Muslim, and the groom is hatted like a Tibetan yak, perhaps to keep company with five no less oddly clad clowns—marriage brokers?—who pop on stage to "play" Pelegai. But the supreme vulgarity is appropriately saved for the very end. As I.S. conceived it, the wedded couple enter the nuptial chamber while the relatives and guests seat themselves on a bench against the wall outside the door. It is a creation of immobility unique in the theater, frozen in the music, frozen on the stage, and everlasting in its minute and a half of time. But instead of this realization of one of the simplest and most beautiful pages in modern music (drop the "modern," too), the visions are joined upstage to copulate in synchronicity with the piano chords. Commenting on this afterward, I.S. remarks that "the compromisers of art are the second-rate geniuses: stage directors, film directors, TV directors, orchestra directors."

The *Renard* staging is less offensive both because the scope for harm is so much smaller and because in this case a degree of experiment is justified. The backdrop, half lowered from the boom, exposes a collage of photographs, most prominently of Diaghilev, Astruc, Groucho Marx, Picasso's I.S. Orchestra and singers are perched on a pile of automobile tires, about twenty *pneus* high, at the back of the stage. (The screaming singers—all senses—are miraculously bad, incidentally, the voice of the tenor crying the cock's part being in worse tatters than the animal itself after the fox has mauled it, though only minutes ago the feat of finding a worse vocal quartet than that of *Les Noces* seemed unsurpassable.) In this version, the spectators are Stravinsky's *dramatis personae*, and they are given spectators' vantages to the rear and sides of the stage, forming a stage arena. The plot, a total enigma to me, is enacted by the animals' human representatives—more visions, I think—in Flapper Period bathing garb. This aquatic troupe is taxied on stage by a Hispano-Suiza during the introductory march and removed by it during the final one. The ballet world being what it is, the villain Renard—who has a marvelous slink and great guile—is a woman.

After the *"Spectacle,"* Boulez, who has conducted the entire program without visible exuviations—a literal example of "it wasn't any sweat"—tells us that part of his success formula is: "Be a Robespierre in rehearsals but a Danton in concerts." But *he* is Napoleonic.

1966

May 12

New York to Paris. Airplane conversations between strangers seem to follow a pattern. The first stage usually begins with a rummage for mutual acquaintances, shared opinions, shared impressions of places. The common knowledge even of a restaurant or hotel will help people to feel weighted together, proving to them that "the world is very small," when in fact it proves only that people of pro-rata incomes tend to be found in the same places, and hence on the same highways leading to those places. Stage two, distinguished from stage one by the settling-in-of-cocktails, moves on to exchanges of scraps of personal confidences. And sometimes to more than scraps. My remarkably unreticent neighbor, a New Man type —Foundation Representative, I think, or political economist, or Rand mathematician, the sort of person who would chat with you about Quine's set theory or Bohr's complementarity principle if you knew anything about them—manages to deliver himself of a very substantial installment of autobiography, between some twenty or so foot-trampling trips to the lavatory. (When it turns out he is on his way to an important lunch tomorrow in the Congo, I confess that I have had some "contact" with the Congo myself, but not that this was limited to flushing the toilet over it on a flight to Rhodesia.)

Stage two depends on the amount and effectiveness of the libations absorbed. Owing to the tensions of flight and the limbo psychology that abrogates not only responsibilities but even the sense of time, the Establishment Narcotic is an especially potent confessing drug in airplanes (to say nothing of its biochemical effects, on blood sugar for example, and the salt content in the hypothalamus). High-altitude alcohol seems to push forward suddenly remembered connections, stories, comments, all for a moment of supreme importance and all insisting on being voiced, but which turn away as peremptorily as a cat, and a moment later defy recalling. If we are but loosely in control of our thoughts ordinarily, how much less so are we under alcohol and over 40,000 feet?

Stage three, flirtation, depends on individuals, but a great deal of it transpires in airplanes. The reasons reinclude those for stages one and two, with the added factor that flying itself is sexually stimulating, both mentally—all flying dreams are sexual—and physically, if not in tingling sensations aroused by the wheels touching the ground, or in the pressure of braking, then at least in the desire to re-embrace life, each landing being a birth. The central sexual ingredient in air travel is none of these, however, but the stewardess, toward whom the male passenger harbors, and often openly attempts to navigate, the most ardent wishes.

The stewardess is not merely a new amalgam of receptionist, party hostess, geisha, waitress, mother, mistress, nurse (bringing napkins every few minutes as if symbolically changing our diapers), but an entirely new aspect, or hitherto unexploited aspect, of Woman. Just as landscape painting did not exist before Giotto, though landscapes evidently did, nor the cult of literary tears before *Manon Lescaut*, though the flow of actual ones must have been fairly constant, so the commercially invaluable combination of beauty and bravery was unknown before the age of air travel. A handsome girl, ever the most desirable traveling companion anyway, is now the most exemplary as well, her valor, or indifference, shaming the passenger and helping him to collar his cowardice.

Our stewardess's lecture on flotation seats and life-raft inflating, on the donning of life jackets and the manipulation of lanyards, sounds like so much fun-filled fashion modeling. But her perpetual cheeriness gives way for a moment nearing the French coast when the plane begins to bump coltishly and to yaw and shake. In fact the sternness of her command to buckle seat belts and gutter cigarettes is then in such contrast to her usual manner that I suddenly become aware of the Holy Bible on the magazine rack, along with *Playboy* and *Time*.

I.S. objects to the stewardess tone of voice, non-stop smile, salesmanship ("Your personal airline," she says, repeating the legend of this giant, totally impersonal airline), and interminable translations: "Captain Smith hopes you have enjoyed your flight. 'Bye now." "*Le capitaine* Smeet . . ." I might add that the busy path of the stewardesses to the cockpit with trays of vodka, wine, cognac, champagne, and even Pernod has not greatly increased *my* store of confidence in Hauptmann Schmidt.

I.S., who has been slaking his own thirst with several kinds of antifreeze, but is far from sozzled, talks to me about Chekhov, whom he is systematically rereading, and with whom he identifies to the extent of defending *Ivanov* against last night's Broadway cast: the wife who might have been reading from a teleprompter; the uncle who, judging by the way he picked each overly decrepit step, might have been on an obstacle course; and the Ivanov himself (Gielgud), whose main method of expressing bitterness and suffering was to curl his mustached lip, which, however, merely conveyed the impression that someone in his vicinity had made a rude smell. "Provincial Russians wanting to go to Moscow are no longer very spellbinding," says I.S., provoking no dissent from me. "Nevertheless, Chekhov manages to make us care whether they go or not, and he manages it, as he manages everything else, with the greatest tact."

Besides Chekhov, I.S.'s in-flight reading is confined to Michel Phillipot's monograph on himself, on every page of which he corrects, annotates, rephrases and rewrites whole chunks, deletes words and substitutes better ones of his own, polemicizes with the author and posterity. Not even Beethoven's marginal glosses,—"Oh you arch ass!" and "Double ass!" —were more vehement than these unsent valentines by I.S.

Approaching Paris, we drop from photophobic sunshine through the iridescence of an afterstorm and toward a cloud bank on which the shadow of the airplane flashes like a wheeling bird. Then, at a still lower layer of weather, we dive through the storm itself—which is like traveling backward in time. The encasing element creates an impression of the velocity of the plane and re-establishes its relativity, which is sobering, not least in the specific sense of the dispersion of alcoholic vapors. In consequence, the passengers' already pouchy faces seem to become pouchier and roomier for returning anxieties.

At Orly I watch an old woman standing as if hypnotized by the beam-controlled, electric-eye glass doors, but I notice that most older people, *i.e.*, with acquired rather than innate confidence in mechanics, fend with their hands as they approach the miracle.

Paris is the color of white skin from which black greasepaint has just been removed.

May 22

I.S. is complaining of a *crise de foie* today, as might be expected after so many bibulous meals, nor will he allow anyone to remain in ignorance of his faecal fears; his luncheon conversation includes an absorbing scatalogical disquisition, with digressions on purgatives and piles. But how much more at home he is in Paris than in Los Angeles! For one thing, he prefers the gender language, and for another, while he scoffs at French society, he is also entertained by it, especially by that climate of intrigue compared with which the smog-darkened atmosphere of Los Angeles seems pure and clean. In Paris, above all, conversation has not yet been superseded by television, though the cutting off of all that oral libido, the national satisfaction of the mouth, is in any case impossible to imagine. At the same time I wonder whether his Russian-ness is not at least as apparent here as his European-ness is in America, French social structures being so much more closed than American?

We drive to Chartres in the afternoon, but every approach to the cathedral is blocked by the booths of an agricultural fair. Returning through Maintenon, we eat Camembert sandwiches Chez Loulou, then go on to Paris 2, which is the French idea of American *luxe intégrale:* termitary architecture, swimming pools, shopping *géants*, and other tokens of *le bonheur*—as distinguished from *la culture*, which Americans cannot hope to understand, of course, let alone possess. In Paris 2, unlike Paris (*tout simple*), the bidets do not outnumber the bathrooms, the elevators do not hobble, and the telephone earpieces do not reverberate like seashells—"*Ne quittez pas, monsieur.*" This horrendous Utopia adjoins the toy village of Marie-Antoinette.

May 24

Athens. Lunch in the stuffy hotel dining room, where our two small cutlets are wheeled in on an egg-shaped silver platter the size of an iron lung. During the meal an elderly woman approaches our table flourishing a photograph of herself with I.S.'s brother Gury and reminding I.S. that they knew each other in St. Petersburg in 1900. Whatever, if any, his curiosity, I.S. is in a foul humor today and in no wise disposed to grapple with unforeseen reminders of the tenderest years of his past. He scolds the woman for disturbing him and sends her away, the upshot of which is that V., who is wholly unin-terested in her story, feels sorry for her and follows her to the lobby to hear it through to the bittersweet end. I.S.'s be-havior in such cases seems capricious and *is* in fact unpredic-table. Tomorrow he might have invited the intruder to a banquet.

We drive to Corinth in the afternoon, a five-hour jolt on a non-road in 1956, now a ninety-minute spin on a divided superhighway. Automobiles are a hundred times more numer-ous than a decade ago, and the jogging donkey carts of that remote date rarer in the same ratio. In fact all of Greece is so transformed, touristically speaking, that the view *of* the Hilton *from* the Acropolis is as frequently spoken of now as the other way around. It is even said that warning signs have had to be floated in the most popular vacationing waters against dropping anchor on the scuba divers.

Shrines survive along the road, nevertheless, and, near Athens, a few touchingly ugly churches with cypress-shaded cemeteries; all other buildings are covered with hoardings on their roadside exposures. Only the sweeping hillsides seem the same as ten years ago, which is to say stony and lacking in tilth. At Megara, the scent of pines, anticipated from memories of 1956, is swamped, if it exists, in the fetors of refining petroleum, then in clouds of spume blowing over small islands which look like crumbs fallen from the cake of the mainland.

At Nero's canal, the tourists lean over the sides of the bridge like seasick steamship passengers at the taffrails, and the proportion of tourists to natives at Corinth must be roughly equivalent to that of Persians to Greeks at Thermopylae. Where a decade ago I posed against a column of the then-deserted ruins—for an excitable photographer in an artist's smock, Lavallière cravat, and Taras Bulba mustaches, who ducked his head under a black tent to take the picture—tourists are posing and snapshooting each other by the hundreds. Returning to Athens we are held up at a railroad crossing by the toy-sized but clangorous and fuliginous—like black wool—Sparta Express(?).

May 26

Our concert, in the Amphitheater of Herodes Atticus, goes very smoothly, blessed by an ambrosial night and the circumstance that I am not, as so often, distracted by awareness of myself, as if from another plane or body, or from the helicopter of my superego, which can at times make a deafening "noise." A singer's mistake puts I.S. into a lather, unfortunately, and he brandishes his cane in answer to the manager's appeals to appear for additional applause-milking bows. After the concert I go to the Piraeus to hear bouzouki music.

June 2

Lisbon to Paris. Suvchinsky meets us at Orly, and we drive directly to the Boule d'Or. Suvchinsky's conversation quickly gravitates to Boulez. "He talks only about *les problèmes de la direction* nowadays," says Suvchinsky, "and though he has unquestionably mastered many of them, how can a man with both creative talent and brains want to be an orchestra conductor?" B. is in the throes of a *"crise de colère,* or *crise de* César-Napoléon," according to Suvchinsky, who gives it as the reason for the herpes zoster with which B. is now afflicted.[1] Suvchinsky has been calling B. in his bastion at Baden-Baden, attempting to stay him from sending an open letter blasting Malraux and, of all unblastable people, Milhaud. But Suvchinsky is less concerned with the vicissitudes of career maneuvering (he says) than with the dismissal of B.'s own music by the younger generation. " *'Bien décoratif,'* is what they say, and they compare the end of *Pli selon pli* to Ravel, and the *Improvisations* of Reynaldo Hahn."

This talk says more about a contemporary success story, a Julien Sorel updated, however, than about B., who naturally attracts the brambles formerly reserved for S., Q., and M. Toward the end of the dinner, and no doubt feeling guilty, following the pattern of gossip of this kind, Suvchinsky suddenly remembers how much we all love B., recalling the time he fetched I.S. with a car at the Gare de Lyon during the taxi strike of November 1956, and the time—August 1957 —when he played Stockhausen's fascicular piano piece for I.S. in the rue Beautreillis cubby hole.

[1] It is a viral disease, in fact, as we learned in December 1968 when I.S. caught it.

June 11

Walking in the rue St.-Honoré this morning, I am accosted by a display of Schoenberg recordings in a shop window. Then in the next instant I recognize them as *my* recordings, and in the instant after that I feel ill. Why does the sight of my name in print, or of a photograph of myself, or any kind of publicity concerning myself, or even of the sound of my voice on a playback or in an echo chamber during a long-distance telephone call, upset me so much? I put the question to I.S. later, but instead of explaining the neurosis he adds to its documentation, saying that I neglected to sign the first letter he received from me, because of which he had to track me down through Nicolas Nabokov.

I go with I.S., Xenakis, and Béjart to a screening of the CBS Stravinsky documentary for French critics, who condemn the film unanimously as an American-style cover story with interpolated gratifications for minority groups, music critics excepted. They seem to object to the popularizing diversionary gimmicks, above all: the reception by the Texas cowboys, the hansom ride in Central Park, the ballet of little girls—to whom, nevertheless, I.S.'s parting words, "Grow up well, little *demoiselles*," provide one of the film's most endearing moments. Nor do they approve the relentless hyperbole of the narration, the oh-so-famous Mister Balanchine, the great, great Mr. Benny Goodman, and now just look who this is, and in fact it is the Pope himself. Very pleased His Holiness was to be on American television, too, though the Vatican concert honored not only I.S. but also Malipiero and Milhaud, both unceremoniously shunted to a back row by the obliging Papal Public Relations Department at the request of the CBS cameramen. What the French critics see as most American of all, however, is the McLuhanite message of the TV screen itself, which says, in effect, that great artists are rewarded with riches, the company of the famous, TV biographies.

The critics reserve their praise entirely for the Giacometti episode, but as much for the reason that it is conducted in their language, I suspect, as for the relief it brings from the tone of an overly excited TV commercial surrounding it. Giacometti talks only of his failure, never notices the camera, never emerges from his absorption in his work. But none of today's viewers notices that in I.S.'s drawing of Giacometti the artist's eyes are closed, as if he were a dead man, which in fact was I.S.'s presentiment that May day of 1965, six months before the melancholy event.

"Is the film a true portrait of I.S.?" one of the disgruntled critics asks me afterward, meaning, I take it, that while I.S. has said and done everything he is seen to say and do, has the editing, cutting, transposition of contexts unduly distorted the resulting picture? I answer that the contexts of the critic-fustigating are immaterial, and that the drawing of a few more beads in the direction of Richard Strauss—"Strauss was a fine conductor"—requires no contextual preparation. I.S. had answered a student's question as to "what specifically" he disliked in the music of Strauss with, "I do not like the major works, and I do not like the minor works," adding, off-camera, "I dislike Strauss's over-homogenized confections."

The film inevitably offers many valuable reflections of I.S.'s mind. One such is a statement about preferring "the worst Communism" to anarchy. Another is his misquotation of Tertullian's "*Credo quia absurdum.*" ("I will give it to you in the original Latin[!] of St. Paul: '*Credo in absurdum.*'") The latter can be read as an indication of his dogmatic tendencies, and of his supposed respect for rubber-stamp forms (formulae, formats), time-hallowed ideas, apparent traditions; the received idea of I.S. as a composer for whom rules precede emotions, and frames come before pictures, is still widespread in Paris, but it is also, or was also, a self-promoted view, and a real hedge against rampant feelings.

The film misleads not in any out-of-context or too locally circumstantial remark, however, but in the implications of the Vatican episode, and in the inference that Poland was important in I.S.'s life and his return there something of a pilgrimage. The Throne of St. Peter, in a sudden, ill-advised gesture of recognition of the arts, decided to honor three composers of three faiths, choosing Milhaud to represent the Hebrew, I.S. the Orthodox Church, and Malipiero the Roman. But I.S. has not been *pratiquant* in *any* faith for more than a dozen years, and if religious affiliations could be classified by feelings rather than declarations and acts of worship, he might be put down as a lapsed Jansenist; in fact his beliefs are secret and defy labeling, but are now more Roman than Greek, all the same.

One frame in the Vatican sequence of the film deserves to be captioned. After the performance of the *Symphony of Psalms*, I.S. kneels to kiss the Fisherman's Ring but slips and momentarily loses balance. Seeing him totter, an old gentleman wearing a pince-nez steps forward from an aisle seat to help, blocking the center-view camera for an instant in the process. It is Giovacchino Forzano, librettist of *Gianni Schicchi*.

Considering the expenditure of so much footage elsewhere, it is a pity that the post-concert dinner at the Hilton by Puccini's nephew, Giulio Razzi, was not filmed. I.S., flanked by effusively and exclusively Italian-speaking ladies, both quite unknown to him, soon got very drunk, and as testimonial time drew round, his head was on his arm and his arm was on the table. V., seeing this state of affairs, came up behind him and whispered in his ear that he absolutely *had* to acknowledge the host's gratulations. This piece of intelligence took some time to sink in, but when it had, I.S. bravely raised

his head, slowly but clearly formed the syllables "*Gra-zi-e!*"
then sank back into his lees.

June 30

New York. The steam rising from open manholes and grates
of subway catacombs is like Doré's *Inferno*, and doormen's
whistles for taxicabs, like shrieks of Beelzebub, make the
picture lifelike, or afterlife-like. Unlike Dante's Florence and
Ravenna, however, which have been much the same way
for some time, New York is a never-completed city. "What
will it be like in five years?" I think aloud to my own driver,
as we wait in a traffic tangle. His answer is, "Mister, I'm wondering what it's going to be like in five minutes."

I spend the afternoon with Marianne Moore in a joint attempt to eliminate archaicisms in the Narrator's part in *The
Flood*. The poet is wispy, Twiggy-thin, and as bent as a
woman carrying a shoulder load in a Hiroshige print, but she
bustles about her apartment at high speed and works with
great energy and concentration. The book-lined walls are
embellished with pictures of birds and animals, and there are
a few photographs, one of them of a young, unfamiliarly
fleshy and smiling T. S. Eliot.

Miss Moore has marked scansions and circled words which,
as she contends, "can be read but should not be narrated."
Her own narration is not easy to understand; the alveolars do
not come through, the volume is small, and the delivery is
uninflected, if also refreshingly nonemphatic. She fails orally
to cross her *t*'s too ("cree-a-[t]-ure"), so that the unfocused
vowels surging around the unpronounced consonants are as

broad and undefined as the river—at springtime—whose name classifies her accent.

The blur in enunciation contrasts strongly to the matter enunciated, however, for her thought is marvelously distinct and her intellectual vigilance unflagging. Of the libretto generally, she commends the idea of assigning the lines from the Bible to a narrator and the guild-play lines to actors, saying that "The stylistic fusion of *Genesis*, Anonymous, and *Paradise Lost* is natural." She is also the first critic of the opus to catch the connection with *Timon* in the "salt flood" and to see the sea itself as the symbol of chaos. As for the replacements of words she rejects as too obscure for a textless audience, I concur in every instance, if only in gratitude for the pleasure and privilege of watching her work.

She fetches several dictionaries ("bulwarks")—one at a time, to my relief: those precarious, stilt-thin arms and legs—including German, for she has revised bits of the German translation as well. But only one of these tomes is used, a sere and yellowed rhyming dictionary, which she systematically ransacks, a long forefinger pointing like a fescue to keep her place as we discuss the candidacy of each word. Her method is to preserve the rhyme words wherever possible, and exchange the bodies of the lines, which is like bouts-rimés; only failing in that will she re-order the rhymes themselves. Quantities are not considered in these transpositions, and all purely musical ornaments and templates are ruthlessly expunged. Her aim is to eliminate ambiguity and obscurity, in achieving which stylistic questions may fall by the board, and even an anachronism or two be allowed in. Her rules, in short, are rules of thumb and ear: her thumb, her ear.

"I cannot use a word I feel contempt for," she stipulates, changing "Hares hopping gaily can go" to "And hopping briskly hares can go," and explaining that " 'briskly' has more dignity." She amends "Here cats can make it full carouse" to "Here cats make full carouse," and repairs

> *And here are bears, wolves set*
> *Apes, owls, marmoset*

to:

> *And here are bears, wolves, leveret,*
> *Ape, owl, and marmoset*

which may raise the question whether the singular might have been too sophisticated for the fifteenth-century guild plays, coupling being the *raison d'être* of the Ark. She also changes "Here are lions, leopards in" to "Here come lions . . ." and finally alters the "briskly" *versus* "gaily" stanza to:

> *Both cats and dogs also*
> *Otter, fox, fulmart, too,*
> *And, hopping briskly, hares can go.*

The most drastic revisions are reserved for Noah's last speech, where she re-renders "And multiply your seed shall ye" as "And so shall your lives be saved" (which lacks a syllable for the music), and "Sons, with your wives shall ye be stead" as "Sons, with your wives gain new estate." Objecting to "bairns," which the poet Basil Bunting is trying to keep in circulation, she adjusts "Your bairns shall then each other wed" to "The youth and maids shall then be wed." Finally she changes "And worship God in good degree" to "And thus your God be served," and "Shall forth be bred" to "Shall thus be bred."

Accompanying me to the street, Miss Moore provides a rare spectacle for the neighbors, I imagine, at least for the devotees of her extraordinary millinery. *La dame au tricorne* is bareheaded!

July 21

Santa Fe. I leave for El Paso in a chartered Cessna at 7 P.M., and from there at midnight for New York, joining a non-striking American Airlines plane on a flight from Mexico City. The worst of the Cessna is the noise, a skirmish of rasps and splutterings as we roll down the sizzling concrete-and-melting-tar runway and slowly lift into the sky, and thereafter a deafening drone. The flimsiness of the plane—the pilot has flung my bags aboard like a balloonsman loading ballast—and the thinness of its insulation are the more evident the greater the altitude. I feel pangs of acrophobia which, however, dissolve in an unnamed worse sensation when the plane is seized with paroxysms of shuddering. What is the meaning of those drops of oil shivering on the window, I ask, by pointing to them, but the pilot assures me that "It was like this three days ago." (A tertian ague, then?) He shouts this information above the roar of the motors; otherwise communication is by sign language, which includes a great deal of gesturing toward the instrument panel on his part, and a corresponding amount of ambiguous shrugging and head-shaking on mine, my mechanical aptitude being such that I hardly know the difference between a flooded carburetor and a flat tire.

Numbed by the noise, I begin to fly backward in time (like a positron, which is an electron traveling temporally backward) until, transported to a similar evening hour when, standing in a field loud with katydids and tightly holding my father's hand, I watch the take-off of the first airplane I had ever seen. The aviator spins the two-bladed propeller himself, running back from it several times before the motor, which makes stuttering, dynamite-like explosions, finally turns over.

I see myself as well, a short time later, much disturbed by the story of an ace stunt flyer and daredevil parachutist whose chute had failed to open and who had volleyed to his grave at the Kingston Airport a hundred yards from a horror-stricken crowd; this plummeting-man image, along with dreams of burning dirigibles, has remained in my mind's eye until now. In the same year, and in spite of this incident, I flew with my father in a Ford trimotor (my mother fainted when learning of our exploit afterward), rising over the city higher, it seems, than I have ever flown since, though I could see the Ashokan Reservoir and our house, which looked like a toy. I remember that we were unable to talk against the blast of the motors at that time, too, and that the noise bothered me more than the bumping or the paper bags marked For Sickness; I used to hide in the cellar or attic on the Fourth of July, and at the circus, waiting for the man to be catapulted from the cannon to a net, I suffered agonies of suspense— because of the explosion, I regret to say, rather than of the safety of the man. Then thirty-five years again hurtle by, and I am I, here and now, attributing the unlocking of memory to similarities of sensation between the two airplanes, and think-ing that the most evident difference now is that I am probably much greener in the gills.

Like a scenic-route bus driver, the pilot—who grips his steering wheel much less tightly than I grip mine, I now notice —points out the site of the first atomic explosion, and calls out the names of mountains, rivers, towns, sometimes shouting anecdotes connected with them, of which I usually fail to get the drift. Again as it was thirty-five years ago, we fly low enough to follow an automobile map and to construe details of the landscape as small as a haystack and a cow. Vast sheets of water gleam from the desert like metal reflectors. They are proofs of recent storms, as the choppiness, scudding clouds, and flashes as if from aerial bombardments, are promises of about-to-be ones. Suddenly the pilot begins to twiddle the dials and hammer the instrument panel with his fists as if it were a rigged pinball machine. Removing and shaking his earphones—his only "gear," for he is dressed like a rancher— he tells me that the radio is dead and that a landing at El Paso airport is unthinkable without it. Accordingly we head for a small strip along the river west of the city where, "if the weather is clear we should be able to touch down without difficulty." It *is* clear, clear*er* at any rate, a sliver of sunset still showing on one side of the plane while nets of stars ignite on the other, and the lights on the converging highways below turn on at a switch.

The Rio Grande coils blackly between the electrically gaudy American and the electrically faint Mexican cities. We come in, swaying like a swing, at hardly more than rooftop height, then bump down cushionlessly on a short, narrow, and ancient concrete strip, rebounding like a roller-coaster. "Fillerup?" asks a cowpoke with paprika freckles who slouches toward me as I emerge, weak-kneed, onto the wing and into a light warm rain. I count out two hundred and twenty dollars for the pilot and taxi to the main airport.

September 15

Louisville. The Leacock-Liebermann film of I.S., screened after our rehearsal this evening, is the most natural view of him, above all of his genial side, ever likely to be made, but like all one-man documentaries, it is essentially an obituary. It is also the least scripted, and least manipulated by technicians, advertisers, ax-grinders, of the filmed portraits of I.S.; in fact its only serious misrepresentation is that the original time sequence has not been preserved. It would be worth seeing for five remarks alone. The first is I.S.'s disarming explanation, in reply to a question about his anti-Wagnerism, that "Everybody who is creative does harm to something." The second is prompted by a question, raised during a tea party with Christopher Isherwood and Gerald Heard, about the creative process. "There is no creative process for me, only pleasure," he says, to which I remember that he added, off sound: "Imaginative processes have their laws, but if I could formulate them they might stop being useful to me." Then in response to a question as to whether he cares if his music is performed, the answer is: "Of course I am interested to hear if I was right or not." But the most valuable two remarks in the film come (transposed) at the end. "I am always happy when I am awakened," he says, "and it is the same with composing." Finally, the eighty-four-year-old composer says, "In the morning we think differently than in the evening. When I come to a difficulty I wait until tomorrow. I can wait as an insect can wait."

November 14

Honolulu. I.S. describes the tuning-up procedure before the orchestra plays, as "the great ritual of 'A' which, as soon as it has been observed, permits every chord thereafter to be out of tune." But Itzhak Perlman's playing of I.S.'s Violin Concerto at today's rehearsal pleases the composer as much as any performance of his music for a long time. Perlman having mentioned Isaac Stern in connection with his study of the Concerto, I.S. tells me later that he thinks of Stern physically as "still embryonic, a kind of unborn Beethoven."

A letter from L. rawly exposes what I have known for

some time, but out of vanity not been willing to admit, and I mind especially, and no less vainly, because other people had seen it so transparently. In fact, the whole episode has shown the amorist to be aging.

> *When amorists grow bald the amours shrink*
> *Into the compass and curriculum*
> *Of introspective exiles, lecturing*

Stevens's lines come to mind as, swimming across the warm lagoon, and warmer reef, to the surf (the loneliness of the long-distance swimmer), I find myself to be the only over-twenties, to say nothing of thirties and forties, in a group of still bald-chested surfboarding boys. This suddenly makes me aware that age differences had been suspended, and that the mask of age I must have been wearing against myself has now been lifted. But I must oust the feeling or cauterize it.

Will writing about it help? After all, one of the oldest forms of surgery is the Anatomy of Love, and an exploratory operation can at least discover whether the ego is tumerous. Thus:

1. All love is self-love; all talk of sacrifice for the other is rhetoric. ("Talk," yes. But the formulation is eighteenth-century, and the grounds on which such remarks could be made has been superseded by psychology.)

2. Love is like talent in that he who knows it truly, *i.e.*, has not mistaken an identity or used it as a form of conquest, can never lose it entirely. (Pointless, and the area of confusion is too large.)

3. We are more agreeable when in love than at less enchanted times, partly because the best of reality is intensified for us and the worst hidden. (Still *dix-huitième*, and worthless without statistics.)

4. The opposite of love is the fear of possessing or, which

is the same thing, being possessed. (Undevelopable in these terms.)

5. Love is uncharitable: we cannot beg it. (Cliché.)

6. The paradox of love is that we are more aware of its limitations during it than at any other time. (A Stendhal novel in this.)

7. Infidelity is natural to all "true" lovers, for "true" love is dependent and the deprivation of the other "unbearable," whence the recourse to substitutes, as exemplified in the supposed high incidence of posthumous cuckolding, and the need of all about-to-be-unfaithful wives or husbands to assure themselves and their adulterers that they really love the wives and husbands they are about to betray; the assurances are, of course, perfectly "sincere." (Too many hidden assumptions.)

8. Even a single experience of the depths of love's labours lost should have taught us that our feelings do and will change. We continue to pretend, nevertheless, that it is within our power to mortgage future feelings, as if we could promise a love that "death cannot abate" or pledge our love "forever," by which, even in love's exaggeration, we do not mean some extension beyond time, but an experience endlessly in it, and therefore above all, now. (Obvious.)

9. After the first fall, experience in love does not count in the sense that we do not learn any more from more of it. How otherwise explain Lothario's successiveness, and the length of Leporello's seed catalog? And how explain the experience of encountering a former till-death-do-us-part lover a cold interval later and wondering how we "ever could have"? (This is better.)

10. While our "rational" parts are fully aware of the circumstantiality of life, our far more powerful "irrational" ones prefer to cling to false absolutes, including the idea of an absolute love. (A parochial observation.)

11. Memory is no less circumstantial, and in the radically

different circumstances of Hawaii it is already dimmer and less poignant; even that last encapsulated moment together, our last exchange of love, is beginning to dissolve, as capsules will; and involuntary, purely glandular proclivities, the recognition of which made me feel disloyal only a week ago—active acknowledgment of the existence of anyone else representing a move away from L. and confirming the possibility of a post-L. world which in my "heart" I did not want—are now invested with a decidedly voluntary element, if not yet a full return to normal erotomania. (Personal.)

12. We talk about swallowing our vanity and our pride, but love is the bitterest and least digestible—it is more regularly and convincingly described as sickness than as health—of these in any case unnourishing metaphorical meals. (Literary.)

13. The unresponsive mistress may prove to have been a more fertile theme for poetry (Campion, Donne) than the fully cooperating, and aggressively abetting (in the line of Marvell's *To his Coy Mistress*), one. (*Ditto*, and remains to be seen.)

14. All lovers are ridiculous. (See 1–13 above.)

I empty out today's bag of platitudes—the circumstantial brain—on the beach, to escape not only the throb of Hawaiian music in the bar, but the people, too, for if the air is "like silk," as everyone says, and the sea "like satin," then the texture of the tourists is gunnysack. With this little exercise of penmanship, may I hope at last to be able to work? "Weeping Eros is the builder of cities," says Auden.

December 13

Hollywood. A visit from Yevgeny Yevtushenko, which the I.S.'s much enjoy, the family affection Russians are able to turn on at first acquaintance, even Russians holding such un-promisingly different views as the I.S.'s and Y.Y., amazing me once again. Yevgeny Alexandrovitch—the conversation is immediately on first-name terms—arrives with translator and publicity team in tow, but as soon as he has been pictured peeling his jacket under the tropical glare of his photographers' lamps, the entourage retires to another room. V. chats with him about Gorodetsky, Kuzmin, Vladimir Nabokov,[1] and other writers she had known in the Crimea during the Revolution, and of whom, she says later, Yev. Alex. reminded her. He listens carefully to her description of Osip Mandelstam in the Crimea in 1918. "Mandelstam was always ardent and always hungry, but as everyone was hungry at the time, I should have said even hungrier than other people. Having very few clothes, he parsimoniously hoarded the most presentable ones, which included an emergency shirt, as he called it, and a pair of almost-fully-soled shoes. Once he called on us wearing a raincoat and nothing else, then paced up and down by our cupboard the whole time like a peripatetic philosopher, not to keep warm but to find out—sniffing like a Platonic philosopher—whether our larder had any food. I also remember a train trip with him to Simferopol. The cars were so crowded with soldiers and refugees that babies sleeping on the floor were helmeted with pails to keep them from being accidentally crushed by people struggling to push through. I sat between Mandelstam and Sudeikine, who dressed me like a Moslem woman on account of the soldiers." Yevtushenko tops this tale with an account of Mandelstam's death, "drowned by bread, literally choking on it; his dying request was for *Russian* bread." (Y.Y.'s words, my italics.)

Of all the cultural ambassadors from the USSR to have visited the I.S.'s, Yevtushenko is the first to notice the contents of the house. In fact he looks at everything, lifting and inspecting objects as he might do in a flea market, and admiring

[1] Her English tutor in Paris was the novelist's brother, Serge Nabokov.

the paintings, especially one by V., thereby being presented with it on the spot, which is called Russian hospitality. Near the end of the visit he suffers one minor setback, when the talk suddenly turns to music and I.S. gives him a point-blank dismissal of Shostakovitch. But he recovers in time to mention several favorite compositions by I.S. himself.

Why am I recording this not very momentous encounter? I had not intended to, in any case, nor was I very attentive during it until I saw how animated the I.S.'s became speaking their *lingua materna* not, for a change, with other *émigrés,* but with a representative of the Russian political state. It seems to me that they were more natural with Yev. Alex. than they are with their closest American friends.

1 9 6 7

January 9

New York. A breath-fogging night. Dinner with Marcel Duchamp, who is tightlipped and *sec*, but in aspect only. And what an aspect! The profile might have been used for a Renaissance numismatic or medallion portrait, and the posture, the backward tilt of the head, is characteristic of equestrian heroes such as Pisanello's Leonello d'Este, which farfetched comparison I attribute partly to something equine about Duchamp himself, partly to his table talk about the armor of scorpions. He is neat, well barbered, tightly tailored. He sports a daunting pink shirt and blue necktie, too, though when complimented on the natty combination dismisses it as a Christmas present. A conversational opening is provided by mention of Giacometti, but when someone remarks that this mutually lamented friend must have been "a *triste* person," Duchamp objects to the word: "Not *triste*, tormented." Certainly neither description could ever have applied to the raptorial intelligence of Duchamp himself.

But what *are* the feelings of a man who when the talk gravitates to airplane crashes—I am flying tomorrow—contributes the thought that "Death in the air is a good way to go because you explode"? (*Vs.* death in bed from a heart attack because you implode?) They are not morbid feelings, certainly, the thought being purely logical to him, with no more emotional coloring than one of his chess moves. What may seem untrue to type in a crystallizing intellect such as his is the easy susceptibility to outside amusements. He tells a story of the Queen of England visiting an exhibition of his work at the Tate Gallery and questioning an embarrassed curator about an object that, as Her Majesty did not seem to see, was ithyphallic. But this drollery is quickly followed with the observation that "A freedom we are all much in need of at present is freedom from bad wit."

Tunneling a chimney through an after-dinner cigar with a large ice pick, he handles the awkward awl so adeptly that we watch him as if he were sculpting a new anti-masterpiece, which he is, but as he once destroyed the *Mona Lisa* with a mustache, so does the cigar destroy the Pisanello profile.

April 3

I drive from Boston to Kingston, and from there to my sister's home at New Paltz. "Samantha has recovered," she says, surprised herself to be pleased at the news. Samantha is a white rat rescued from a laboratory at Cornell by my niece, and since then living encaged, but far from all of the time, in New Paltz. Three mornings ago the rodent was discovered keeled over, breathing heavily, legs outstretched and deathly stiff. Until then Samantha had inspired only the strongest revulsion in my sister, but the sight of the stricken creature empowered her to reach into the cage, wrap the invalid in a blanket, and rush it to the veterinarian, even though worrying the while about bubonic plague. As it happened, the diagnosis was acute constipation, the treatment an injection of anti-biotics and a spoon-feeding of prune juice, after which the patient, tightly cuddled in a blanket, was discharged. This morning the legs began to flex, and tonight Samantha is her old self again, playing in the living room with the cat and dog, her best friends except when she receives more than her share of attention—which tends to bear out Lorenz's theory that real aggression takes place only within the species. My sister thinks that not having seen another rat for two years, Samantha may be assuming herself to be one of us, but, speaking for myself, I hope she takes me to be a sinking ship.

May 17

Toronto. A CBC concert in Massey Hall, I.S. conducting the *Pulcinella* Suite, after which I conduct *Oedipus Rex*. Leaving the hotel, I.S. happens to pass before a crowd come to stare at Princess Alexandra; what compounds the irony is that no one in it can be aware that the unscheduled parade of the little old man is a far rarer sight than the one they are waiting for, artistic geniuses being much harder to come by than merely well-born ladies.

At the Hall, one of the singers puts a question to I.S. about his "Wooden Indian staging concept of *Oedipus*," but I.S. denies that it is so different from his earlier theater works with voice. "The singers are in the pit and the dancers on the stage in *Renard, Les Noces, Pulcinella* as well, and the title part in *The Nightingale* should be performed in the same way. The music is more important than the action, as the words were more important than the action in Shakespeare."

For tonight's performance of *Oedipus* he asks us to repeat the *Gloria* before the Speaker, as in the original score, and he wants the first note of Oedipus's *"Invidia fortunam odit"* to begin with Tiresias's last note, though the original score warrants no overlapping at all. Tonight's performance convinces me that the repeat in Jocasta's aria and the repeat in the duet with Oedipus, both added in 1949, are miscalculations. But why were so many useful directions in the original score not retained in the 1949 edition? The indication to beat 2/2 at the 4/4 episode in the same duet, for instance, and to conduct the measure of Oedipus's 2 against the orchestra's 6 (1 before [58]) in 6, since it is slack and rhythmless in 3 or 2. Tonight's performance is vocally the most satisfying I have ever heard, from the chorus to Ernst Haefliger's Oedipus, *langsam* and *sehr ausdrucksvoll* as it is, Jean-Louis Barrault's Speaker, and Marilyn Horne's Jocasta, which not only is rich in tone, but is sustained at its stately metronomic tempo.

For the first time in his life I.S. conducts sitting down, but this probably gives him more trouble than he avoids by not standing. He *is* very unsteady on his feet, though, and in spite of the chair, he grips the podium railing with his left hand during much of the performance. V. is alarmed watching him, and remembering how vigorously he conducted in Chicago a mere five months ago. Worse still, as she can plainly see, the orchestra is not really following him but the *tempi* of my morning run-through of the piece. At the start of the *Tarantella* about half of the players interpret his first gesture as a one-beat, while the other half read it as a two-beat. This results in about ten measures of excruciating "augmentation," after which the playing thins out almost to the point of stopping completely.

The performance over, I.S. moves to a chair at the front of the stage, averts his eyes from triple-pronged TV exposure, listens to accolades in French and English of two dignitaries, is bemedaled. This ceremony very evidently affects him, as it would not have done a year ago; in fact he would have been contemptuous of it then. It is not merely the ceremony, either, but the special warmth of the audience whose applause and reluctance to let him go has distinctly said: "This is the last time we will ever see Igor Stravinsky." As I know him, no one is more aware of this than I.S.

During intermission he tells one of the medal conferers that he had an "occlusion" about two months ago, adding that his blood is "like purée." The remark startles us because until this instant no sign of a suspicion has been elicited from him that a stroke is what might have happened.

I am unable to sleep after the concert, seeing, as if on one side of a divided movie screen, the I.S. of the past skipping across the stage to the podium, his movements twice as fast as anyone else's, and in this, as in everything he did, his energy, physical and mental, leaving everyone around him far behind; and on the other side, I.S. tonight, old, frail, halting, and, I fear, conducting in public for the last time in his life. What makes his case the more disturbing is his terrifying self-awareness. A long decline and withering away would be a great cruelty to him.

May 24

New York. The findings of an electro-encephalogram and of other tests performed on I.S. yesterday are amazing, says his physician, Dr. Lewithin. There is no sign of senility, of the brain-softening normal in a man of his age, or any onset of brain sclerosis. But then, I.S. lives entirely in his brain. The receptivity tests have in fact shown his responses to be as rapid as they are in a man of thirty. I.S. is greatly interested in the encephalogram, which he compares to "an electronic score, with six-line staves and unreadable avant-garde notation," adding that the eighteen electrodes attached to his head made him look like "a bald woman trying to scare up a mane of hair."

At the same time, says the doctor, the composer's body is a ruin. Two blood-lettings and three Roentgen-ray treatments are scheduled for the week, and they are a matter of life and death, as I.S. knows—he is in fact already processing and overcoming the knowledge in his formidable psychological machinery. Armed with an understanding of the apprehensible biochemical facts, he will thus begin to "think positively," harnessing his powerful "esemplastic will" to all the favorable factors and ignoring the unfavorable. But the most difficult enemy to subdue is another part of the same mind, that powerful intelligence which has not aged with the body and remains so ruthlessly aware of it.

May 25

Attending to a medical problem of my own, I go this morning for X-rays of the kidneys, the first stage of which is a two-hour wait in a room permanently piped with very loud pop. Finally, served up semi-naked on a freezing platter to the photographing eye, I am interrogated about my susceptibilities to sodium injections; and now that it is too late to retreat am informed that "some people become violently ill." In the event, the injection, in the median cephalin vein, *is* followed by cramps, tumescence, hot flushes, vesical burning, and a tidal wave of nausea. (Psychologists would classify me as an "augmenter" rather than a "reducer," but I do not see how that helps.) At this point the radiologist warns "me"—actually carcass number so-and-so—that the slightest movement on my part during the next thirty minutes will destroy the test and oblige me to start over on another day, with three ounces of castor oil. I "endure," of course, but learn an hour later that I have prostatic calculi and must go on a *régime* of *Eau de Vittel.*

＊ ＊ ＊

To the Met in the evening, feeling slightly radioactive, to see the Royal Ballet's *Romeo and Juliet.* But the Met itself is the more arresting spectacle. The whole ensemble—lowest-bidder architecture, sculptured plaza, Chagalled foyer, retractable chandeliers—might have been intended for an Eastern European People's Republic, then sold to the capitalists by some sharp Ministry of Culture *apparatchik* who saw that it had gone wrong. Eastern Europe is where two principal ingredients of the ballet, Prokofiev's music and Nureyev's Slavic charm, do come from, of course. In fact, Nureyev's broad Slavic face is in striking contrast to the pinched Anglo-Saxon features of his fellow-dancers, just as the exhibition of his other main attractions (*Chacun à son gout*), the muscle-bound buttocks and steel-thewed thighs, is a contrast to the floor-length skirts which conceal the Juliet's charms and those of her attendant goslings.

The first act offers two opportunities for musical depth, Juliet's return to the deserted ballroom and the balcony scene. But Prokofiev makes nothing of either, merely substituting loudness for intensity of feeling, as if "passion" and "full orchestra" were synonymous. Moreover, the music accompanying Romeo's approach to the balcony is so over-agitated that for a moment it casts the hero as the villain. Being unable to perorate, too, Prokofiev provides only further repeats, in whose empty lengths even balletomanes must soon be lost. But I should have noted in the first place that the play is poor ballet material, as pantomime is a poor exchange for poetry. The choreographer seems to agree, at any rate in those instances when the dancers stand about gesturing like singers whose sound systems have gone dead.

June 18

Hotel del Coronado, Coronado Beach. "Are you Mr. Stokowski, the conductor?" the receptionist asks, and I.S. nods affirmatively. He is less amused later seeing his own name in a letter from Public Relations asking whether he would mind being photographed.

The hotel is old, but less so than local veneration, which seems to put it about on a par with Cheops, implies, and in fact it is exactly ten years younger than I.S. It might have come from another country, as well, but which one would be hard to settle. It sets out to be tropical, and overdoes it; and colonial-oriental, though, owing to prior knowledge that the original construction force was comprised largely of Chinese coolies, I may be over-ascribing the oriental side of it. The transoms, window ventilators, verandas, balconies, wicker furniture, valentine-lace panels, and tinder-box whole remind us of the Repulse Bay Hotel in Hong Kong, in any case, and only the ceiling fans like airplane propellers are missing. The pavilion tower, on the other hand, resembles a stave church in general shape and in its dark red shingles, but a Russian church in the cupola. The religion urged on the congregation inside is from Utah, however, each dressing table being furnished with a copy of *The Book of Mormon.*

Some congregation: "ex-passengers from the 'Queen Mary,'" says I.S., and the Coronado *is* spinsterish, prudish, dead-as-Lugano, and as sad as all old-fashioned resorts. We follow a creaky dark-oak and mahogany corridor to an elevator cage, then to a kind of Crystal Palace dining room in which a dozen or so occupied tables are huddled to one end against the gloom of two hundred or so unoccupied ones. Huge coronado-shaped chandeliers dangle from the high, woven-basket ceiling, but they shed precious little light. Because of the inhibiting emptiness of the room and the annoying sobriety of the other diners, we drink too much and become too effervescent ourselves.

Henry James wrote from the Coronado, in April 1905, of having been kept awake by the "languid list of the Pacific." But it is a loud rumble, especially from the waves curvetting against the rocks opposite my window. The beach is as wide as the Copacabana, and the sand is fine, soft, and apparently white, though footsoles tar after a few steps. At low or eddying tide the shore is a congeries of debris from "the ooze and bottom of the sea": lariats of kelp; piles of amber algae; chains of seaweed with spiculed, fin-shaped leaves; a plant from some fantastic underwater garden, with a long proboscis like that of a mosquito or the snout of an oiling can.

Jellyfish still quiver in the sand, some glycerine-like and purple-veined, some shaped like the human pancreas, some like *tête de veau;* amputated jellyfish tentacles look like soft icicles and are common. We uncover a dead gull, claws up as if to fight off an enemy, and a dead skate, its cuneal wings partly buried in the sand; as if in fear of the spirits of these birds, V. holds her camera over them like a Geiger counter. Live, all too live, are the beetle-size beach crabs which Japanese fishermen are gathering for bait, meanwhile leaving their tall fishing poles and pails of gasping perch untended in the dunes. I remember Auden once comparing himself to the beach crab (Talitrus), saying that, like it, he knew when it was meal time not by hunger but by knowing the time of day.

Scores of tent-like sails appear in the afternoon, tipping and careening in the wind. An airplane begins to skywrite, too, scraping a white path on the blue surface like a figure skater. But the wind strengthens, the aerial chalk blurs, and the drifting bits of alphabet are soon indistinguishable from natural clouds.

I.S.'s birthday party is launched with slugs of Stolychnaya vodka and docked with a cake, baked by Milène and brought into the room by her in a parade with V., who carries a tray with eighty-five lighted candles. We sing "Happy Birthday" and I.S. says that that makes it "*Son et lumière*." But he says little else, and it is hard to know his feelings.

After I.S. has cut the cake, we open some of the four hundred cables and telegrams that have been piling up all week from all over the world. But whereas, for example, the President of Germany has sent a two-page homage, no word has come from any public official in America, where "The poor procession without music goes." Nor, of course, has any message come from that despoliation of the desert in which I.S. has lived for twenty-seven years. In fact the only acknowledgement of the anniversary in his home community was a concert by the "Beverly Hills Symphony," conducted by himself four months ago at a greatly reduced fee not yet received. So let the record stand. While the greatest living composer's eighty-fifth birthday is being celebrated all over the world by entire festivals, and countless individual concerts and performances, no organization in the vale of smog-induced tears that *he* has so long honored by his residence so much as thought of dedicating a program to the event. Not the local—exceedingly local—Philharmonic, it goes without saying, but also not the Ojai Festivals, which were pleased to have him at a third of his normal fee at a time when they could use his name, but which had been distracted this year by the glare of momentarily more expensive but in the long run much cheaper attractions. In fact, the *art* critic of the *Los Angeles Times* alone recognized the necessity, for Los Angeles's sake, of a concert, but when permission was sought for the musicians to contribute their services for it, the Musicians' Union refused on grounds that it would "set a precedent." A precedent for whom? Is a deluge of Stravinskys imminent? In Los Angeles?

V. unwraps some of the gifts that have accumulated during the past weeks, identifying each of the senders for I.S. How utterly lost he would be without her! She translates bits of talk for him that he fails to catch, and supplies funny-sounding Russian synopses of American jokes. To be with her for a few minutes he will take the long walk to her studio and even brave the terebinthine fumes inside. And she is more kind and patient with him each ever-more-difficult day; she has begun to take him with her to the supermarket, for example, because he can hold on to the cart instead of his cane, and even push it, thus feeling useful to her.

The emotional strain of the birthday must have been very great, and at least some of the messages from old friends who broke down and said the things friends always want to say, but seldom do, must have moved him; Nadia Boulanger's letter, for example, was transparently about death. Now I.S. was never one to brood over the certainties of insurance companies, nor has he betrayed any sign of dotardly sentiment about his age today. Still, I will be happy to see him more combative again, which is why his answer to a well-wisher's question whether he would like to live to the same age (111) as his great-grandfather: "No, taxes are too high now" is reassuring; and why we are greatly relieved when, after the party, he says he is in a hurry to be rid of the birthday and resume composing.

July 15

Hollywood. Nureyev and Fonteyn come for aperitifs—directly from a rehearsal, which partly excuses his get-up: white tennis shorts, white sweater, white sandals. From the front he may be "faun-like," as is said, but seeing the back first, with the long, shaggy, Beardsley-period hair, one could take him for a tousled woman. He is quite unlike the thrasonical exhibitionist of newspaper copywriters, nevertheless, and in fact I have rarely seen anyone more gracious and gentle with I.S., to whom his first words are: "This is a very great honor for me; I only hope I am not taking your time."

He talks about Bronislava Nijinska's revival of *Les Noces*, saying he has learned a great deal from it himself. The I.S.'s then talk about their red-carpet reception in the USSR, and this makes him uneasy. When V. quotes Nancy Mitford on the "clean feeling in the Soviet Union that money doesn't matter," he cannot help breaking in. "Of course it doesn't. There is nothing to buy: no automobiles, no houses, not even food." But he speaks gratefully of Mme Furtseva, the Culture Minister, who discovered him during the Bolshoi Ballet's season in Paris. "One afternoon at a reception for the dancers she pointed to me and told one of her minions: 'Next time this one will dance the solo.' That did it." Explaining his defection shortly after, he says that "the Soviet dancers were quartered in a very poor hotel near the Place de la Bastille, where we never saw anything of Paris. Then one day I learned how to use the Métro and took it to the Champs-Élysées. Walking from there to the Seine, I resolved never to leave; Paris seemed to me the most wonderful place on earth. But tell me, why are Russian *émigrés*, in Paris, and California, and everywhere else so nostalgic for a Russia most of them have never seen?" V. suggests that part of the reason is in Russian literature, and it is true that many of the refugees she knows exist in a world of Russian books and have never learned other languages. Nureyev's rejoinder is that "A refugee should live according to the way of life in the country of his adoption." Just as *he* lives?

Next to I.S., who is as thin and shrunken as Mahatma Gandhi, Nureyev is impertinently healthy-looking. Entering the room, he identifies a postcard-size Klimt, and he continues to study the art objects on tables and walls, glancing back and forth from them to I.S., as if trying to crack the "object language" of the house—people being implied by their possessions, after all—and which is simply I.S.'s obsession with the minuscule. Dame Margot, very lissome and lovely, describes her arrest in San Francisco a few days ago on suspicion of possessing marijuana, saying that she was searched skin-deep by a jailoress who claimed Dame Margot was her "idol."

I.S. had wanted to avoid the visit, at first, but he was especially lively during it, partly because of a hint from V. that his state of health is reported nowadays, a consideration that had never seemed to occur to him before.

❊ ❊ ❊

In the evening we listen to Fischer-Dieskau recordings of parts of *Winterreise, Dichterliebe,* and the Opus 39 *Liederkreis,* as well as a batch of Brahms *Lieder,* and the *Spanisches Liederbuch.* I.S.'s fingers play along with the piano in the

Schumann songs, of which he asks to hear *Am leuchtenden Sommermorgen* three times. He also cues vocal entrances, flips pages back in search of a detail or comparison, and two or three times turns ahead impatiently to the next song. His response to anything that strikes him as exceptionally fine is a staccato grunt, but a related type of noise turns into a groan when something displeases him, or is *too* beautiful. ("Beautiful, but not for me," is a characteristic remark, a standard one, for example, in reference to Chopin.) *The Prophet Bird* in the *Waldszenen* delights him, for example, and earns several staccato approvals, but *The Wayside Inn* is too much Schumann doing his thing: "The AAA sign of approval over the door." And Brahms wearies him on the whole—"too many *Regenlied*, and compared to Schumann it is formalism; what I admire most in Brahms is his knowledge, which isn't quite the right thing"—but he likes *Herbstgefühl*, and admits *Du sprichst* and the third of the *Ernste Gesange*. Of the Wolf songs he falls heavily for *"Herr was trägt der Boden hier."* [1]

July 26

Santa Fe. Tonight, in prickly heat and dry lightning, and after four weeks of rehearsing, I conduct the American première of the original version of *Cardillac*. Tonight, anyway, my feelings are that in spite of a few patches of really wretched music, umpteen patches of indifferent music, and the composer's lack of aptitude for the theater, the opera

---

[1] In May 1968, in San Francisco, he arranged the piano part of this song, along with that of *Wunden trägst du mein Geliebter*, for three clarinets, two horns, and solo string quintet. One of his reasons, so he said at the time, was that "Wolf used octaves only for more sound . . . He had a marvelous ear and a marvelous sense of invention, but very little technique."

somehow still succeeds. (Could a performer esteem a work any less than that and still perform it?) It is at least stage-worthy; and silly and imperfect as the libretto may be, it is nevertheless a real one, unlike that of *Mathis*. It inspires Hindemith, moreover, which is no mean feat; in fact he sur-passes himself at times, his routine self running after, even if rarely catching up to, his inspired self.

The general weaknesses are summarized by the dull-as-potatoes overture. First of all, the units of form and the rhythm are square and block-like, which is well suited to the pedestrian pace, at least. The music is so bottom-heavy, too, that the bass line seems to have been written first, and the orchestration emphasizes this weight in the stern, the tuba playing almost as continuously, it seems, as the flute. But nearly every line is doubled many times over, and octavized and double-octavized (the piccolo fifing away at 16 *va.*).

The plot is stronger than the characterizations. Except for Cardillac and the chorus, in fact, the roles are all manikins unbreathed on by any form of life. The opera might be presented to greater advantage if the first act were treated as a prologue or masque. Its plot and characters are self-contained and, figuratively speaking, the action could all take place before the curtain, like the Prologue in *Ariadne*. The other acts could then stand as two equally balanced scenes, which would help to concentrate the evening as well as spot-light Cardillac's own musico-dramatic position in not singing until the second act.

The scope and proportions of the opening scene are too large for the balance of the act. This largeness is filled, more-over, by a relentless and inexhaustible flow not of invention but of notes, which hit or miss and are expended like flak. In the second, overbalanced, part of the act, the Countess and Cavalier are introduced in a formal recitative, but this is stylistically misleading since it is the only one in the opera. The minuet following it shows, however, that Hindemith has at least been listening to operas, in this case *La Bohème*:

Piccolo (8va)

Contributions are levied on Gershwin in this scene, too, and the villainous muted brass in the Cavalier's portion of the recitative derives, no matter how weakly, from *Wozzeck*— compared to which *Cardillac* is about as profound as the supposedly sound-reflecting pool behind the orchestra pit: *e.g.*, two inches deep. *Wozzeck* is the source of supply for the percussion endings to Acts I and II, as well, and for the tavern music in Act III, where the borrowings from Lully sound remarkably Teutonic.

The vocal line of the Cavalier's aria is moderately interesting, but the piece is marred by such crudities as the thrice-repeated trumpet toots:

3 times

and at times is almost sunk by its own orchestral weight. The Copland generation seems to have found the Countess's aria irresistible, for which reason, in part, the "openness" and "simplicity" of the original no longer rate very high among its more intoxicating qualities.

The *Pantomime* that concludes the act is the most unaccountable event in the opera. A concert piece, pleasant enough by itself, it contains no message whatever concerning the dramatic action, and even gives the impression of having come from another opus, a dance-suite "*im alten Stil*," say, and of being included by mistake after some overworked packer at the Hindemith factory mixed up the parts.

The orchestral introduction to the scene of Cardillac *chez lui* describes the goldsmith's tinkerings with comic over-explicitness, and the aria itself, an unalloyed disaster, adds egregiously corny saxophone and glockenspiel parts to the description and dissolves all hope of keeping a straight mien. (Mine only, apparently: the gravity of the audience is quite untried.) Nor are the seductions of the vocal part strong enough to give the piece the popularity ("Cardillac's Song") the composer was so obviously after. The metallurgical discussion with the Gold Merchant that follows is inaudible because of the orchestra, but their duet is a good piece, and the setting for the best instrumental idea in the score, the trio for violin, viola, and piano at [H].

The aria of Cardillac's daughter is not much of a Siren song, and the tables, chairs, and walls she sings about add little color to the musical or dramatic arguments. But the aria is an instrumental piece in the first place, a trio-concerto, and its instrumental frame is awkwardly large. Hindemith seems not to have trusted voices or his ability to write for them. Whether or not the duet of Mlle Cardillac and the Officer *is* unintentionally comic, as I think, the happy warrior's musical style:

is a cardboard cutout of the Hussar in *Mavra; Mavra,* incidentally, is a glaring influence on *Cardillac,* beginning with the *orchestre d'harmonie* with light upper strings, except that *Mavra* is spare and as light as thistledown in comparison. The next scene, Cardillac *père et fille,* matriculates in a fugal exercise that is the *vade mecum* of contrapuntal boringness. Plod as he will, strive as only he can strive, Hindemith simply cannot yield a drop of passion—which is to say, music.

The royal visit to Cardillac's workshop is music at least, and the device of restricting the singing to Cardillac while the others are in dumb show is theatrically effective. But the subsequent piece reverts to the *Mavra* style with very bad results, and the solo scene of the crazy Cellini, now a mad-genius inventor of the comic strips, is even worse. His theme song from the beginning of the act returns bedizened with a convulsively comic string obbligato, and this is followed by a jazz coda that is literally indescribable since it is impossible to know the dramatic intentions of the music.

Act III takes place on higher ground, but the musical timings are fumbled. Whereas an acre of preparatory musical landscape was traversed before the entrance, wholly undramatic, of Mlle Cardillac, here the music allotted to transfer the chorus from the *coulisses* to the stage scarcely suffices to get the tenors on. And the Gold Merchant's cry to the Watchmen, for whatever reasons of misapplied economy, occurs *simultaneously* with the dialogue between Cardillac and the Officer, hence is *not* heard. The instrumentation of the Gold Merchant's aria is intolerably cumbersome, I should add, and the Quartet, a relatively promising piece initially, and one in which the composer is obviously trying to scale a peak (blowing very hard into his hands to stave off frostbite, actually), concludes in the most galumphing cadences imaginable. But the scene of the Daughter and the Officer contains good music, nor is the adjective to be attributed entirely to scarcity value; whether merely coincidentally or not, it is the only music in the opera to draw on rhythmic fluidity, metrical irregularity, and dynamic nuances.

The offstage music contains some good soldierly rallying pieces, but tonight's offstage conductor seems to have had an attack of offstage fright. Finally, the last scene redeems much: not the choral rejoinders on *Frère Jacques* (in the minor mode, as in Mahler) or the music following the deranged

Cellini's mob-murder, but the requiem lullaby, which is as moving, even luxuriating, as anything Hindemith wrote. It raises the opera almost to shoulder level at the very end, which is where the lift counts most.

July 27

I leave a party for the Cardillac cast at 1 A.M. and, not being able to sleep, impatiently scribble the foregoing opinions: I expect to forget the opera very quickly, but if I should en-counter it again I will want to compare old and new impressions. Then during breakfast comes the horrifying news of an unscheduled Wagnerian finale: a fire, apparently starting at about 3 A.M., has burned the stage and auditorium to the ground, incinerating the *Cardillac* sets, costumes, and orchestra parts as well, along with violas, cellos, basses, harps, and in fact everything combustible in the theater area, which is now a sickening prospect of ashes and charred remains. Our second performance being canceled, I drive to Albuquerque and fly to Los Angeles.

Seeing the I.S.'s again after even a short separation moves me nowadays almost more than I can bear. They are the two most marvelous people in the world, the last survivors of a richer and better humanity, a whole continent in themselves. But they are so old and creaky and fragile now, and so terribly alone. They know the hour of my flight, and when to expect me; if I am late they will go to the window again and again and play their rounds of solitaire more anxiously. When I do arrive, the sight of them in the doorway, to which they come at the sound of my taxi, is upsetting. They seem, especially after that ride through the junk yard and the dreck of Los

Angeles, so desperately out of place as well as out of time, for I tend to think about them, when I am away, as they were in the past. To see them after an interval, therefore, is a sudden acute reminder of age, a reminder full of the pain of impending loss. I simply cannot accept their passing as natural, as I have had no insurmountable trouble doing in other cases, but then, to me, I.S. is himself a part of the order of nature. Dinner with them tonight is sad, all the sadder because they are so happy to see me.

August 21

New York. An alarming call from V. during my recording session tonight saying it has been discovered that I.S. has a bleeding ulcer, that he has been taken to the Cedars of Lebanon, and that he has lost more than half of his blood. I arrange to fly back immediately.

September 13

Hollywood. The fourteen days in the hospital and nine subsequent days in bed at home have been extremely weakening. I.S. has lost eighteen pounds—one wonders from where, since he was so tiny anyway—not much of which can be regained on his present frugal diet. His rib cage reminds us of photographs of Buchenwald, and he complains that every nerve ending in his skin-and-bones body is raw and painful. The hematocrit still stands at only 35, too, whereas the platelet count has risen to 1,200,000. The one component of the blood is anemic, in other words, and the other too rich, and to complicate matters further, the indicated medication for each is "counter-indicated" for the other. His uremic acid level is high, as well, and each finger of the left hand throbs like toothache from what has now been diagnosed as gout. Worst of all, and unspeakably depressing to observe, is the defeat, I pray only temporary, of that powerful will. He does not even read today, and when I switch on the television for him to watch his favorite African animal program, he refuses to turn toward the screen, saying "I only like to look at it in Vera's room." He tells V. that he saw his birth certificate in a dream last night, and it was "very yellow."

V. has draped a towel, with a print of a cat on it, over the couch in his room, as if to represent her *in absentia*, though she seldom is absent anymore, and this *does* seem to raise his spirits when she is out of the room. How fitting, if it is so destined, that his last creations should be a statement of religious belief, and that a Requiem, and then a personal piece for the human being who has meant most in his life.

September 25

A marked upturn today symptomized by an old-time tantrum over some of the contents of the mail: a fulsome fan letter; a self-paying *Who's Who* form; a request to fill in a sexual questionnaire (I.S. is regularly circularized for this); a tape of a "ballad composed on a harmonica by an airline pilot during flight," herewith submitted for I.S.'s opinion, which is: "I will be afraid to fly again." Reaching for a Kleenex and finding it to be the last in the container, he flings the empty box to the floor. V. gently admonishes him, as one would a small child, telling him that the box will probably have to remain where it is until a pile accumulates, "Then perhaps the thrower will realize that we have no one to pick up such things."

The night table at the side of the bed holds an array of pens, music pads, pliers, secateurs, as well as the Fabergé gold clock which Tsar Alexander II gave to and inscribed for I.S.'s father, and the small gold cross and silver roundel of the Virgin which I.S. has worn around his neck since his baptism. Books, dictionaries, boxes of Man Size Kleenex are stacked on the floor around the bed. To remind him of the necessity of drinking water, sheets of paper reading "water" and "H_2O" in V.'s hand are taped to the walls and furniture, clipped to the wastebasket with Tchaikovsky's picture on it, and strewn and propped everywhere else. V.'s Russian translations of medicine schedules are attached both to the head of the bedstead and to a dressing table otherwise crowded with trays, thermos bottles, glasses and cartons of milk with Mickey Mouse straws in them, packages of crackers, paper cups for quarter-hourly doses of Gelusil, plastic and glass vials of medicine. I.S. keeps his own pharmaceutical inventory and his own records of the medicines he consumes, entering this information in a red diary, which extraordinary chronicle sometimes takes note even of a sneeze or a cough. On better days, prescriptions are spelled out in full, and reactions elaborated in detail, but on worse ones the identifications are brief: "Took one *foncée* capsule at 2:30, two white ones at 3:45."

He sits up for most of the afternoon today, telling me with some of his old zest that Hideki, our cook, has taught him the Japanese ideogram for noise, which turns out to be the ideogram for woman repeated three times. He also talks about Gorky's *The Mother*, which he is rereading. "I read it when it was first published, and am trying it again now probably because I want to go back into myself. But it is not good. Gorky is certainly not the 'big' writer I had hoped he might be, the writer that Tolstoy still is even at his worst. Gorky's indifference to 'style' is legitimate, of course, but he invents nothing new to replace what he dislikes, and it is more important to show what you like than what you dislike." The comparison with Tolstoy brings to mind Gorky's famous remark about his great predecessor, which, I suddenly realize, exactly describes my own feelings about I.S.: "I am not an orphan on the earth as long as this man lives on it."

George Balanchine comes for dinner, snorting and sniffing as if from hay fever, twitching as if he might be getting the *tic douloureux*. In check pants, silver-buckle shoes, double-breasted blue jacket with gold buttons, sideburns to the ear lobes, he looks a spiv, but on arrival puts in a half-hour of very conservative piano practice. He describes the *Salome* ballet, now planned for Suzanne Farrell, using mudra-like movements, and asks me to suggest music for it by Berg; but *Reigen*, the only possibility I can think of, is too large orchestrally, and like the Variations and Adagio from *Lulu*, which he has also been considering, is too brooding in character and too explicit dramatically. I suspect Balachine's conception no doubt hinges on the circumstance that the seven-veil striptease, like that of Astarte-Ishtar, would nowadays conclude in a complete disrobing, and that the dance would be able to show Salome, like the Queen in *Alice* ("Off with his head!"), really wanting a different part of the victim than the one she gets. Herod, too, could be revealed as the archetypal Humbert Humbert marrying the mother for the daughter (or the Baron de Charlus buttering up Mme de Surgis because of her sons), which may be the prototype of a problem in Mr. B.'s own history.

Mr. B. asks for I.S.'s new piece, and in reply to the composer's damper that very little of it is finished, says he would settle for two minutes of music because "they are bound to be an atomic pill." I.S. shows him the score of *The Owl and the Pussy-Cat,* saying the song "should be impersonated, a little hooted, a little mee-owed, a little grunted for the pig." Mr. B. then asks a number of questions about *Russlan,* which he plans to direct in Hamburg. He still looks to I.S. for ideas, as well he might, considering that some of his most successful ballets—*e.g.,* the Bizet *Symphony in C*—came from suggestions by I.S.

When Mr. B. first enters I.S.'s bedroom, I.S., very self-conscious about his loss of weight, says: "As you see, like all Americans I am reducing."

October 8

At about 4 P.M., I.S. complains of a chill, and his teeth, as he says, begin to "*klapper.*" By 5 P.M. he has a 101° temperature, which, in his weakened state, is very alarming; he can hardly navigate across the room now, and his shoulders and torso are as fleshless as a coat hanger: pneumonia or even influenza could kill him. His lungs seem to be clear, however, and the fulminant pains he complains of are obviously abdominal. But when I ask him to describe them, he sits bolt upright and says "FEAR." Soon after this he begins to micturate every few minutes, which could indicate an infection from bladder crystals formed by the high uric acid.

Re-entering the room at 7 P.M., I find him praying "*Gospodi, Gospodi,*" over and over, with his head turned to the wall. At length a doctor arrives and prescribes Gantrisin. At the beginning of the doctor's examination I.S.'s pulse is fast, but as soon as he is convinced that a bladder infection is the true complaint, the pulse rate drops to normal and the temperature to a bit below; he has had a death scare, and was as frightened of flu and pneumonia as we were. All night long, says V., who spends it on a couch at the foot of his bed, he twists, turns, fumbles with the sheets trying to make a nest, but is unable to forget the specter.

A man is no readier to leave his life because it has been rich, long, and perfectly fulfilled, but rather the contrary, and the more so in I.S.'s case because of his knowledge (and ours) that there is more of it in him. Nor do "naturalness" and "justice" enter into consideration, except from afar, where the termination of a life of sixty-five years of continual creation certainly seems more just than the savage extinction of wholly unfulfilled young lives in a senseless war. But what may seem the most natural of events at a distance can be the most unnatural at close range. At any age and in any circumstances, death is immeasurable loss; or, if I even *try* to measure the loss of I.S., it comes out to something very like life itself. And special pleading though it be, the consequences of his existence will bring joy to future millions, whereas many if not most other existences only succeed in compounding the misery. But, strangely, I find neither compensation nor consolation in that thought.

> . . . *blown husk that is finished*
> *But the light sings eternal* . . .

says Mr. Pound, but the eternal light does not matter to me now, only the life which I pray will go on in that . . . well, I.S. is still far from a husk.

I realize now that in recent years I have so often hidden my true feelings for him precisely because of the dread of this moment. Yesterday evening those feelings came irrepressibly flooding out as the result of an extraordinarily clear hour with him, during which he talked to me and discussed his ideas with me in the way it used to be between us years ago. I understood then that he has no thoughts of *not* going on. And he can go on of course, in that undamaged and undaunted mind of his, but only there, which is the tragedy.

Ever since I have known them, I.S. and V. have kissed each other at first sight of every new moon, a promise of renewal. The moon is new tonight, but they do not see it, and there does not seem to be *any* future.

October 28

I.S. is very keen and alert at dinner with Suvchinsky, as he has been since the arrival of his old friend yesterday. We listen to *Les Noces* together, and, after I.S. goes to bed, to the *Requiem Canticles*. The latter, Suvchinsky suggests, "are ritualistic in an ancient, atavistic way, without being either Pagan or Christian, but also without intentionally avoiding both, as *King Lear* seems to do. The Postlude," he continues, "is one of those endings, like that of *Les Noces*, which do not end, or end in infinity, and in which Stravinsky adds a dimension to Western music, beyond the classic composers. Think, for comparison, of the ending of a Beethoven or Brahms symphony, which simply thumps more loudly on each repeat."

Suvchinsky contends that a neurosis is at the root of I.S.'s passion for order, and we discuss a relevant new study on "Religious Order and Mental Disorder in a South Wales Rural Community" (in *Social Anthropology of Complex Societies*). He argues, further, and it is a major reversal for him, that I.S.'s Russian background constituted a greater handicap to his development as a composer than the misunderstanding and

opposition that were the lot of Schoenberg. "If you had seen
what he came from in Russia, in both the family and musical
senses, you would believe in genius." (I already do.) "Stravinsky's creative psychology was fully formed by the time
of the *Firebird*, nevertheless, and it never veered in any essential thereafter. He was a 'walled-in' artist from the beginning
. . . Of course, he never formulated a doctrine of neo-
classicism, but simply made music out of whatever came to
hand, which was all he *could* do, given the limitations of the
music from which he sprang . . . But it is high time to explode
the Diaghilev myth. So far from his having discovered Stravinsky, Stravinsky happened to him, and Diaghilev never
really understood how big Stravinsky's genius was." And with
this, Suvchinsky repeats I.S.'s story about Diaghilev's reaction
to the ending of *Petrushka:* " 'But you finish with a question?' " "Well," I.S. used to add, "at least he understood that
much."

November 2

I.S.'s "gouty" left hand has suddenly turned black. A new
team of doctors, after consultation early this morning, attributes the discoloration to circulatory blockage from a
sludge of platelets, a rate of some 2,000,000 at last count,
versus a normal of 200,000. The finger pains of the past eight
weeks were caused not by gout, in other words, but by circulatory failure, and the anti-gout medicines were not merely
powerless to relieve the hand but were dangerous for the
ulcer. The discovery is infuriating as well as frustrating. Why
was a gout specialist not called two months ago, and a competent vascular-cardiologist? Or if not two months, then as
soon as the colchicine and the wonder-drug medications for

gout failed to alleviate the pain? Furthermore, is sudden gout even a remotely reasonable prognosis for a man of I.S.'s build, temperament, and lifelong hard habits? And finally, how could the four expert doctors, whom I would not trust now with a hangnail, accept the gout theory and overlook the possibility of circulatory blockage in a man who has suffered from polycythemia for twelve years and whose platelet count is two millions? That is a miracle of modern science.

It is decided to try to dilate the coagulated capillaries by blocking the nerve with Novocain injections, and as this entails a risk in a man of I.S.'s age, the operation can only be performed in the hospital. Choking with tears and fears, I pack his bag and take him there in early afternoon, practically carrying him from his room to the car, for he is heavily drugged and scarcely able to walk.

The injection is not administered until seven o'clock, after a second consilium with a second vascular-cardiologist, but when we return to the hospital at eleven, the fingers are even more horribly black. The surgeons now speak of it as gangrene and mention the gruesome possibility of amputation, further warning us of a high danger of pneumonia, I.S. having been in bed for so long. I take V. home, then go home myself, but I cannot pass I.S.'s studio and bedroom, or look at his dark window from my room, or, of course, sleep; and when going to bed I remember and use all of my childhood prayers.

November 3

The finger color has improved slightly after the third Novocain injection, but the hand is still gangrenous. Sick as he is, however, and despite the haze of pain-killing sedations, I.S.

shines like a beacon, replying precisely, ironically, originally, I.S.-ishly, to the forensic inquisition of his doctors, and replying to them in English and German, moreover, and to myself and V. in French and Russian, without once mixing or confusing the languages or fumbling for a word. To one of the new neurosurgeons who asks if he dreams under the drugs, his answer, to our great relief, is that he does (I.S. is a hyperactive dreamer) and that the dreams are "mostly good." When the doctors leave the room for a consultation, he asks V. if she has been painting today, dropping his voice to a whisper, apparently without sense of his own volume, except that he overhears *our* whispering, even through the pall of the drugs.

His extreme fastidiousness is giving him no end of trouble. He insists on staying in the *gabinetto* unaided, and even on brushing his teeth unseen, and he charges me to explain to the nurse that he does not mean to be rude but is unable to converse with her. To me he says: "I can offer you nothing here but *ennuis*." As we leave him, the nurse, noticing my anxiety and probably seeing me trying to stifle my feelings, follows me into the corridor with the advice that "It is a mistake to get so involved," as if "involving" oneself were a matter of choice, and as if a non-involved life, if it were possible, would be worth living.

November 5

The index finger is slightly less black this morning, and the palm of the hand is a little rosier; the nerve will not be blocked today. As the amelioration is ascribed in some degree to a trickle of alcohol in the intravenous fluid, it is further decided that I.S. should be allowed to taste the stuff, if it *can* be tasted through the milk he would have to swallow before and after. Accordingly he is to receive three half-jiggers of Scotch, at wide intervals, and each one blended to obliteration with milk. The prescription provokes a great flap among the floor nurses, who say that it is the first time in the history of the hospital that "drink" has been administered in the social fashion.

But I.S. is untrusting, nor will he take my word for the contents of the bottle. We have to uncork it and hold it to his nose, after which we can almost see his olfactory bulb turning on. What follows is a Finnegans wake. He sits up as if from smelling salts after a dead faint, eyes widening with each inward waft. To prove that we are not misleading him with a stratagem of flavoring or perfume, I play Petronius and sample some of the liquid in front of his eyes, after which the head nurse fills a paper cup to the halfway mark, inserts a straw, and holds it to his mouth. I.S., drugged to the bones as he is with codeine, Darvon, Demerol, nevertheless protests the miserable dram—"Half?"—then, resigning himself to it, throws out the straw, and with inimitable I.S.-ian panache touches his paper cup to mine, and in distinction to the torturous sipping of milk and medicines during the past three months downs the whisky at one gulp. A smile spreads over his face, it seems for the first time in an age, and we tell him that a new era has begun, imitating Goethe on the beginning of the French Revolution: "From today forward, a new chapter in the history of mankind . . ." But in fact the whisky, strongly opposed by the gastro-enterologist, is a desperate expedient, almost the last trick up those white surgical sleeves.

The left index finger is blue-black above the last joint today, but the others are almost normal, and the nacreous, color-of-death streaks in the palm of the hand have disappeared. He insists that all of the fingers still hurt, adding characteristically that "Each pain has its own manner." No less characteristic is his response to a doctor who asks if he can endure the pains from three to five minutes longer without more codeine. Out of a profound stupor—his eyes roll like ball bearings when he tries to open them—but out of a fathomless vitality also, comes the accepted challenge: *"Five minutes."*

Returning to the hospital in the afternoon, I spoon-feed I.S., and hold his bad hand: he says the warmth diminishes the pain. Always a naturally affectionate, as well as a deeply lonely man, feeling now pours out of him. And not a little of it pours into me, for we are very close now, as we were in our first years together; he asks me to sit by him all the time, and will allow me to leave only if I promise to return immediately. This directness of feeling, which each of us would be the first to flee in other circumstances, makes it difficult to check my not notoriously suffusion-prone eyes, an absurd propensity that I try to excuse by arguing that death is different in I.S.'s case because he can still create: witness the sketches on his piano, and his talk even now about his musical ideas. And in truth it is this power of creation in him that has always fascinated me, a fascination that all creative people must exercise over all uncreative people. But this is not the principal reason why I cannot bear to have the light extinguished of this most intensely alive human being I have ever known, to whom my own life has been closer than to anyone else since childhood, and who for twenty years has been the most important person in it. The uppermost of my feelings are simply those of love for my best friend, and admiration for the fight and the will and the courage and the guts of the old man.

To what extent death is in his thoughts I have no idea; that will appear later, if he lives. But it is clear that much of his mental suffering in late years is caused by the absence of a proper sense of himself as aged. In his own mind he is not eighty-five.

* * *

A resurrection has occurred between our second and third visits tonight, and of all providential ironies the whisky may have turned the tide. His face has more color, his hand grasp is firmer, his voice is stronger, his conversation is quicker, and his criticisms of the nurses are as caustic as they would have been a year ago. He wants to know the date, and, on hearing it, seems as surprised as Rip Van Winkle was on being told how long *he* had slept; only yesterday I.S. was uncertain he was even in the hospital, at one point asking the name of the hotel and the city. The finger is clearer tonight, and as the doctors concur in ascribing at least some of the improvement to the whisky, we tipple once more. He eats with appetite, too, but pushes a cup of Postum away calling it a *"horreur indescriptible."*

November 6

To stimulate circulation, I.S.'s mattress vibrates from an electric current, and his left arm is thickly swaddled in cotton. A fluid of glucose, vitamins, alcohol, vasodilators flows through a tube intravenously attached to his right arm, which is also bandaged in several places and as needle-marked as the "golden" arm of a "mainliner." His watch is on his right wrist now, too, having been transferred from the bad arm after the struggle, but he has still not allowed his rings to be removed from the painful left fingers, except during an X-ray, and then virtually by force.

We spend the entire day in the hot, badly lighted, medicine-flavored stale room, and return again in the evening, after attending a concert in the Museum to hear *Le Sacre du printemps* in the four-hand version. The Museum program also includes a group of Schubert songs, sung not only with no *Schwärmerei* but also with no voice; Webern's piano minuet, which seems self-mannered and is just long enough for the thought to cross the mind that no composer has ever been so quickly and so cruelly picked so clean; Stockhausen's *Adieu*, which contains some novel instrumental suggestions of weeping; and I.S.'s *Pastorale*, which, with quarter rather than eighth notes as the unit of beat, is nearly twice too fast for the *gopak* character of the piece. The performance of the *Sacre* is rousing, even if the timbre is monotonous, the main lines frequently lost or overbalanced, and the *tempi*, pianos not being able to sustain, generally too fast. But the effect on me, and of the concert as a whole, is extremely depressing. It has made I.S. himself seem remote and expendable and made me wonder if his music can ever have an independent existence for me as it has for the audience. The evening is a foretaste of a time in which his absence will be felt and re-gretted by no one but me; which means quite simply that I have never been able to separate the man and his music.

At the hospital afterward we find him drugged but lucid; Suvchinsky describes him as a *"flambeau."* The room being as stifling as a greenhouse, we do not stay, and because I.S. begs us to, with imploring looks as well as words, the separa-tion is very painful.

November 11

The patients' list today includes Jennifer Jones, brought in last night like Botticelli's Venus, still dripping from the sea.

The nurses are goggle-eyed in consequence, not with scientific amazement at her apparent amphibiousness, nor phenomenon of anadyomene, but for the banal reason that Miss Jones is a "movie star."

I.S. has a new nurse today, a tough old trout with scabrous tongue and the personality of a warden. She treats him as if he were a very ancient, puling baby, and deeply offends his decorum with remarks such as "Do you use Poly-Grip on your dentures?" and "I've wiped more bottoms in my time . . ." The patient is a lever of compensation in her own life, as I have come to think most patients are for most nurses; she clearly resents V.'s place next to the bed and the rapt gaze of I.S. toward V., as if she were a peri from another world. "Can you see this?" V. asks, holding up a book of photographs for him to peruse, and he says, "I think so, but I would rather look at you." And now I am beginning to fear that V. will collapse, unless I can find a way of spreading her burden.

November 13

A *Dies Irae*, the worst since August. A new abscission must have occurred in the index finger, which is blacker than ever. Equally upsetting is I.S.'s semi-delirium. His sense of time and sense of distance are virtually inoperant, and his memory has become a total jumble. He repeatedly asks where he is, and confounds names and places, partly because of verbal resemblances; thus "Dr. Marcus" starts him off on Markevitch. He talks to the nurses in Russian, too, mistaking them for V. Worst of all, he says he cannot see, and he is clearly unable at times to identify objects in the room, and even ourselves. Once he tells me that "I have left my passport behind and cannot return."

Fearing he has had a major stroke I ask for a consultation, convene the two neurosurgeons, and return to the hospital in the evening to witness their examination. The result is an amazing display of an always amazing and still very much intact mind. It is true that I.S. has always been fond of medical interrogations, but tonight he rises to the occasion with some impish *mots d'esprit* as well. Dr. Rothenberg: "Will you answer a few silly questions, Mr. Stravinsky?" I.S.: "No." But the questions come. "Do you see double, Mr. Stravinsky?" "Yes." "How long has this been going on?" "All my life, when I am *soûl*." "What month and year is it?" Here the best I.S. can say is "autumn." "Did you see people or animals in the room at any time today, and realize later that they weren't there?" "Yes. Two boys were sitting in that chair all after-noon." "Did you see a black cat?" "No." But he claims to see vivid mixtures of color in the curtain even now, at the same time telling us that he knows the curtain was a drab brown yesterday. Dr. Rothenberg proceeds to examine his eyes with lights and to test his ability to read a paragraph from a book, but the reading proves to be very laborious because he sees the letters a half-inch to the left of the print at the same time as the print itself. What distresses him still more, he confesses, is his inability to relate events. "Something is wrong both in my sense of time and in the reasoning faculty," he says, and goes on to describe the symptoms of this mental state with an awareness and a power of reason that a philosopher a fourth of his age and in perfect health might envy. In fact one of the doctors, in the interests of an analogy I fail to follow, puts a question to him about time in music but bungles his concepts, whereupon I.S. sets him straight by distinguishing "time as a matter of speed, and rhythm as a matter of design."

The doctors seek to assure him that his new complaints are due entirely to the effects of his new drugs. "I am *consolé*," he finally concedes, adding that "I looked hard in myself for

the cause of the failure and was anguished because I was unable to reason about it exactly enough.[1] I want to be more
exact in my thoughts." But *is* he "*consolé*"? He pleads for "a
more powerful pill, so that I do not have to think about it
any more tonight." But stronger sedatives are forbidden because of the danger of pneumonia if he fails to move enough.

The examination has allayed V.'s worst fears for a bit. Certainly his imagination is unimpaired, and his repartee says the
same for his spirit. But it is no less obvious that he has had a
new thrombosis. And what of that black finger and of the
effects of more pain and more drugs when he has already
been saturated with both for so long? As Exeter says of the
King:

> *Now he weighs time*
> *Even to the utmost grain.*

November 14

Finally, eight weeks late, I.S. is injected arterially with radioactive phosphorus, by a doctor wearing a rubber suit and what
looks like a welder's helmet. Three nurses wheel the patient
to a lead-lined room in the basement, making me think of the
three queens accompanying Arthur to Avalon. Afterward, a
thrice-daily series of abdominal and subcutaneous heparin injections is begun.

The mental wanderings are worse than yesterday. Before

---

[1] Intellectual self-accusation was a great trial during his convalescence, the
slightest memory failure provoking him to fits of anger. In Zurich almost
a year later, he had a nightmare, after failing to recall some incident during
a discussion at table. Hearing him get up, I went to his room and found him
sitting on the edge of his bed with his truss in his hand to use against the
guards who, in his dream, were coming to take him to the madhouse.

the trip to the X-ray room, he asks us to look after his wallet, which of course he has not had on his person in months; the mistake probably betrays a habit of concern about his pocket valuables when disrobed for X-rays in the past. On the return to the room, however, he asks if we have "enough *Frantsuzski Geld* to tip the porters." Then, when dinner comes, he insists on eating from his own tray, thinking he is in his room at home, and when V. says it isn't there, he points to where she can find it. As we leave for dinner ourselves, he asks to come to the restaurant with us. I tell him he will be able to very soon, and after considering this for a moment, he replies, heartbreakingly, "I realize I am not able to eat with you, but I could watch." He also begs to be taken for a "promenade" in the car, and no doubt troubled by his mistake in thinking he was home, asks how it is there now. Very bad, I say, for we miss him all the time. "You remember how you used to describe us as a '*trio con brio*'? Well, please hurry and get well so we can be one again."

He has a bad period of hallucinations, a side effect of the heparin, the doctors say. He apprehends people who are not present but fails to see us and his nurses when we are only inches away, and once he asks why there are two watches on his right wrist from which even the one has now been removed. V. says that his Russian comments are "nonsensical" and "delirious," which greatly upsets her, of course, nor is she impressed by my argument that this unreality is better for him now than truth. Then suddenly, in the midst of the rambling, he drops a remark showing such a perfect sense of reality that we know his mind is holding on tight. Over-hearing us mention a certain music critic, whose name has not come up in years, he wants to know whether the said critic is dead or alive. "Dead," says V., but I.S. is doubtful. "No, he is probably alive and in Argentina."

The mind seems to be divided into two parts, of which only

that part dealing with the outer world and the present is confused. And surely this is natural, considering the disruption of the time sense by drugs and medicine schedules, and the dislocation in consequence of staring at hospital walls, which are not so unlike the walls of his bedroom at home.

The other, the creative part of the mind is undisturbed. In the evening, during one of his lucid spells, I tell him that the BBC wants him to compose six to ten seconds of music to be used with a multicolored eye by Picasso as the signature of a new color-television channel. The creative mind instantly seizes the idea and moves ahead with it like a prow. "The time problem interests me, the six seconds ruling out chords and rhythms in any conventional sense, but of course many notes can be used at a time. An eye means transparency, too, and that the sound should be produced by very high instruments, possibly by flutes, compared to which oboes are greasy and clarinets oily."

I leaf through a book of Watteau drawings with him, and though he sees little, he complains that the reproductions do not show scale. What annoys him still more is a phrase in the commentary about the greater sophistication in the appreciation of Watteau at present. "Whatever comes later is automatically more sophisticated," he says "which later-comers should remember as they look forward, as well as back."

November 18

The depredations are showing; I.S. is so thin now that his nose seems to have grown, and his long-untrimmed mustache overhangs his lip, suggesting a walrus or fox terrier. But the finger remains blue-black, and it is painful, less so in the mornings when he is still comatose from the sedatives of the night before. As for the intensity of the pain, the doctors assure us that he performs for our sympathy, which is normal patient behavior, and that he has often dispatched a nurse for codeine or Darvon, only to fall asleep before she has had time to give it to him. Some pain he has, nevertheless, and he moans from it throughout the afternoon. Once the nurse gives him a pill, warns him it is a big one, goes to fetch water to help it down, but when she returns, I.S. says "Already done."

The result of yesterday's midnight consultation, which introduced a new vascular surgeon into the medical-opinion pool, is a compounding of new ingredients in the I.V., the commencement of arm and hand exercises, and the application of mild heating therapy to the entire integument of the forearm and hand. Thanks to computerized filing systems, too, a former victim of the same ailment has been traced, and his case history, treatment, progress, studied and compared. The man was I.S.'s junior by twenty years, and his hand became gangrenous after a coronary. We also learn from his deposition that recovery was extremely slow and that in the matter of pain he would "prefer ten coronaries to that ache in the fingers."

The change in the I.V. fluid since the midnight medical pow-wow is having a soporific effect. The new strategy is to keep the patient "under" until the radioactive phosphorus begins to work, which is like waiting in a heavily besieged fort for the relief column of cavalry. But why am *I* suffering so much, asks a new nurse, young and analysis-jargonized ("accident-prone," "fantasize," "intropunitive")? Father figure? Identification? I do not give my answer, which is simply that I love him, for the primitive word would be translated into a neurotic symptom.

But what *are* the answers to her questions? To use Rank's terminology, wasn't there a narcissistic basis for the object-choice of I.S. in the first place, meaning twenty years ago, and, to use Freud's terminology, isn't there some identification of my ego with the disappearing object? Perhaps, and certainly I can fool my ego as well as the next person. But the main hinge of Freud's explanation, the transformation of the object-loss into the mourner's ego-loss, certainly does not apply.

November 19

The new I.V. formula, with the new anticoagulant, Pris-coline, has not changed the finger color, but it makes I.S. so drowsy that we get only a few words out of him the whole day. When we first enter the room, he says, "They are giving me phenobarbital now, probably to keep me polite," later adding, as if he were reading our own minds: "My impression is that the doctors haven't the faintest notion what to do." At one point he describes the finger pain as "crackling," and at another as "needling," but I suspect that a really resourceful nurse could keep him off painkillers entirely. He displays the finger ceremoniously to the new, analysis-wise but otherwise resourceless one, saying "*We* can't touch it." Still, the blind-ness is far more frightening than the finger. He identifies us by our voices, hardly turning his head to left or right, while what he *does* see—the anti-corona of someone walking past the bed—is not there.

November 20

"Where are you?" he asks, hearing me enter the room this morning, and as I reach the bed he puts his good hand to my face as if he were totally blind. He is so heavily drugged, too, that speech occurs only at great intervals. Once he wakes up saying, "How long will it last?" and again, "How much longer?" Then for the first time in all these months: "I don't want to live this way." I try to make him believe that he will soon be home and composing, but he nods his head weakly toward his hand, saying: "I need my hand; I am maimed in my hand." I am more worried about his eyes, nevertheless, and most worried of all about the amount of fight left in him; already, as Lear says, "The oldest hath borne most."

November 23

It is Thanksgiving Day in the most wonderful possible way: the long-prayed-for miracle has happened. Not once in seventy-two hours has I.S. complained of pain or taken a pain-killer, and the finger color has returned almost to normal. His sight is not normal, and he is still unable to distinguish faces in what seems to be, as he describes it, a dioramic blur; but his eyes turn much more rapidly toward, and focus more quickly on, us than a few days ago. He sits in a chair for a while, which makes him look much thinner than in the bed. Milène reads to him, too, and he is quick to pounce on her mistakes in Russian pronunciation. Incredible man! Only three days ago he was in a semi-coma, his left hand a half-silted estuary of gangrene, his body worn out by months of pain; but as Suvchinsky said, he himself was a torch. And he has come out of it, actually recrossed the Styx. "How much is it costing?" he asks me suddenly, and in all these weeks no words have sounded so good. I.S. is back in decimal-system reality. Thank God.

He is pepped up from glucose and jumpy, brittle, anxious, ready to fly off the handle at any and everything. "I have had enough medical philosophy," he tells one of his physicians, and to a nurse who advises him to "Relax," his retort is: "What? And leave the driving to *you?*" He is suffering drug withdrawal, of course, and a mountain of aftereffects, but I like the friction.

V. is ill and in bed today, with flu, she says, though it is more likely battle fatigue. The crisis of last weekend was too much for her, and she has kept her fear inside too long.

November 28

I go at noon to bring I.S. home, but his departure is delayed by requests for autographs from every nurse on the floor, which he gives, even embellishing some with musical notations. Outdoors, out from that stultifying hospital at last, he is as pale as junket; dressed in a suit, he looks terribly thin, shrunken, and frail.

As I lead him from the car into the house he says that it must seem to me as if I am "towing a wreck," but weak as he is, he props himself on the couch and will not go to bed. He is contemptuous of his medicines and balks at his doses of milk, saying "Milk is the Jesus Christ of the affair," to which profanity V. responds with: "Now at least we see how much better you are." But he will not have any of that. "Not better, bitter," he corrects. But when V. plays some games of Patience to divert him and asks him to keep the tally for her in his head, his scores, she says—and meaning no pun—are perfect.

He asks about the newspapers (which say that Zadkine,

another coeval, has died) and the post. The latter contains a package from André Malraux, a copy of *Anti-Mémoires* with the author's dedication: *"Pour* Igor Stravinsky, *avec mon admiration fidèle."* But I.S. jumps on this. "When was he ever *'fidèle'?* He once said that music is a minor art." And so I.S. is still I.S.

Later in the day the doctors call to congratulate themselves, but he flummoxes them, too, as he has done at every stage, telling them that "The finger and the eyes are from the same cause." In fact the chief neurosurgeon corroborates this to me privately, saying that there have been not one but three thromboses, and that some peripheral vision in the left eye is permanently lost. I.S. himself is less distressed by his poor sight, at the moment, however, than by a gas pain, and when the doctors attempt to remind him that he has not suffered alone, he snaps at them with, "Maybe, but you don't have this gas pain." (Apostrophizing them later, he adds that "It was very well-paid suffering for them.") But he is beginning to talk like a doctor himself. "Is the pain merely spasmodic," he asks at one point, "or could it be organic?" One of the medics tells him, in parting, that "Healing takes longer at eighty-five, Mr. Stravinsky," but I.S. turns on this with "Damn eighty-five."

He watches *Daktari* in V.'s room tonight, but tosses and turns in his bed afterward, tormented, he says, about the state of his mind. At eleven o'clock I go to V. to see if she is all right, and find her room dark and herself quietly crying, the tears streaming down her face. Not once during the whole horrible ordeal did she ever lose control, and only now is it clear that she was losing belief and only continued to pray that he would ever be home again. After an hour of trying to talk her into some "peace of mind," I am summoned by the night nurse to help with I.S., who is not sleeping in spite of his pills. I try to fake some more good cheer with him, but

he says he is "in a bad way psychologically." When finally I
leave him, he answers my last inane "Please stop worrying"
with "I am not worrying any more, only waiting," which
wrenching remark kills the possibility of any sleep of my
own. "Old people are attached to life," says Sophocles, condemning it as a fault.

December 1

Hallelujah! The platelets have fallen to 900,000, and the white
count—"my blood policemen," as I.S. tells it, though he is
also using such non-metaphorical terms as oenosyllophyl—is
down to 17,000, this from 37,000 only a few days ago. His
diet is less strict now, too, and thenceforth the taste of milk
is to be cut with larger swigs of Scotch. The news raises I.S.
out of the apathy and black melancholy into which he had
fallen the day after the homecoming, when he had apparently
expected to be able to skip rope. After dinner we listen to
Opus 131 and the *Dichterliebe*, the first music heard in the
house since he entered the hospital. And with the music he
comes to life, grunting agreement with Beethoven at various
moments in the quartet and beating time with his left hand,
which is protected by an outsized mitten, like the claw of a
fiddler crab. He has not been able to read words, but his eyes
travel with the score, being guided, of course, by a rather
exceptional ear.

December 6

It is a marvelous day, warm and brilliantly sunny, while the San Bernardino Mountains glitter with new snow like Kilimanjaro. But leave-taking is the hardest I have ever been through. It will be for only a few days, I tell I.S., blaming his music as the reason for the trip in the first place; to which he says, *"Je crâche sur ma musique."*

December 15

New York. To the Met's new *Carmen*, as the opera is still billed, though both musically and visually it lacks all trace of the traditional character of the piece. A bull ring of Colosseum proportions is the set for the whole opera. In the first act it is used as an esplanade for couples strolling at fashion-model pace and dressed in lavish Goya and Manet costumes. In apposition to this preposterously rich apparel, the children are gotten up like Cruikshank chimney sweeps or the waifs in newspaper photographs advertising starving Indians or Greeks.

The principal shortcomings of the musical reading are that the *tempi* are too fast, the orchestra is too loud, the performance is too innocent of nuances, shadings, inflections of any kind. The singers and the orchestra are seldom synchronized, moreover, though Maestro Mehta strives heroically to bring them together, with thrusting chest and jaw, and prize-fighterly cues to cymbals and brass. Nor is Grace Bumblebee's beautiful voice enough equipment for the role; she does not charm, seduce, or move like the sultry heroine.

But no matter. The Met audience, corporation presidents and blue-rinse spouses, applauds each ill-conceived and worse-executed stage trick as if the music did not exist.

December 16

Hollywood. Meeting me at the door, V. says that I.S. has been waiting for me since early morning but became tired and fell asleep. He is awake when I enter his room, nevertheless, and he actually sheds some tears when he sees me. He is utterly changed, better than I ever hoped to see him again. V. says a delayed shock has occurred, dropping a veil over the worst of the illness and eradicating all memory of the hospital. In fact he suddenly refused to believe he had been ill at all, on the grounds that he had had no temperature, and while remembering that we were all much concerned about his hand, did not recollect that it had ever pained him. He flexes the hand as we converse, tightening and loosening its grip on a toy-sized football.

The greatest difference is in communication. Talk flows from him now, whereas two weeks ago he would follow the conversations around him abjectly at best and contribute little himself. Telling me about a Christmas letter from the conductor James Sample, he recalls several incidents touching the lessons in composition which he gave to Sample's father-in-law more than twenty-five years ago, and describes how he wrote much of his pupil's symphony for him. After dinner we listen to the quartet movement which I.S. calls the *Sehr grosse Fuge*, and to the Debussy *Études* which, not for the first time, he identifies as his favorite piano opus in the music of this century. He says he dreamed about Debussy a few nights ago and remembered the powerful scent of his Eau de Cologne when they last embraced.

Both I.S. and V. seem happier and are looking better than at any time since August, for which I thank God and I.S.'s invincible spirit.

December 25

It now seems likely that the viral infection to which I.S. is supposed to have succumbed on the nineteenth, and against which he was murderously dosed with antibiotics, was a new thrombosis, but it is difficult to be certain precisely because of the debilitating effects of the anti-viral drugs. He is extremely low, in any case, seems to have aphasia at worst, and at best, forms words with great difficulty. He cannot walk at all without the nurse, but resolves to come to the dinner table because it is V.'s birthday and Christmas; apropos of the latter he says, disapprovingly, that "Christianity is a system, but Christ is not a system." His only other words during the whole, horribly depressing meal are a *cri de coeur:* "Something new has happened to me. What is it? I was walking so well last week." Leaving the table he says *"Ne bougez pas!"* then climbs slowly up the stairs with the help of the nurse, and again all the way back down, bringing me a Christmas present: "A gold clasp," he says. "It belonged to my father and to his father"; and he apologizes because it isn't wrapped.

It seems so brutal that, having endured so much, and reaching the threshold of recovery—walking again unaided and even mentally digesting his ordeal—this brave and miraculous man should again be struck back. What can we do now except to pray that the thread by which his life seems again to be suspended will prove, as it did before, to be as strong as someone else's rope? When I greet V. with "Merry Christmas and Happy Birthday" this morning her response is: "I went to his room a few minutes ago to see if he was still breathing and thanked God that he was."

1 9 6 8

January 1

I.S. is none the worse today for his 12:01 sip of champagne, but he releases a thunderclap by remarking that certain legal actions of which he has just learned "were necessary in case I had died in the hospital." The word never crossed his lips during the struggle, of course. Then at lunch when the nurse prods him to exercise his bad finger, he says: "I will be able to use the finger only when I can get it out of my mind."

One of I.S.'s Christmas presents is a chirruping canary.[1] When I remark rather acidly on the impressive volume of its "song," I.S. challenges the word: "There are musical elements in it—pitch, color, intensities, rhythmic patterns—but the result isn't 'song.' Nevertheless, the bird gives notice before signing off."

We listen to *Messiah* in the evening, and although I.S. tends to resist Handelian grandeur—"Handel was the pop-tune, and the commercial composer," he says, "Bach the inward one"— he cannot resist this excellent performance (by Colin Davis,

[1] Bequeathed to the S.'s' friend, and neighbor, the writer William Inge, the following September.

whose *tempi* and articulation are generally good, but who does nothing about *notes inégales*). We listen to bits of *Hercules*, too—Dejanira's mad scene, Iole's recitative "Forgive me, gen'rous victor"—but give up because the performance is excruciating.

January 16

Stephen Spender telephones from London, asking I.S. to answer the Litvinov appeal. I.S. consents, tells me what he wishes to say, and together we draft a statement, a version of which he and V. then translate into Russian to record next week for the BBC:

> I remember the suffering of my teacher Rimsky-Korsakov from both the threat and the actual exercise of Tsarist censorship. Now, sixty years later, while the world stands in admiration of so many achievements of the Revolution, Russian writers and readers still live under the censor's Reign of Terror.
>
> But the spirit of the Revolution is with the condemned writers, who must be counted among their country's most valuable patriots, if only for the reason that they love her language; except that writers cannot live, and neither a poetry nor a people can grow, under censorship.
>
> The Soviet Union can prove its greatness far more profoundly by pardoning the condemned writers than by the conquest of all outer space.

Privately I.S. denies that Tsarist and Soviet censorship are even comparable. "There was hope under the old regime, now there is none . . . But what an idiotic idea is this 'patriotism.' The world being what it is, how can a writer or anyone else be patriotic?"

January 25

We play Schubert's E-minor four-hand Fugue and some of the F-minor Fantasy together this afternoon, after which I.S. confesses that he does not want to go on with his own piano opus because he has "a bigger piece in mind." No further information about this newer composition is forthcoming beyond the assurance that it is not to be a string quartet. As for the abandoned piano opus, he says that "I had no sooner forbidden myself to use octaves in one piece when I saw the richness I could get from them, and I used them in the next piece all the time."

V. is disturbed because I.S. cannot remember where they were married. But why should he remember New Bedford, Mass., from a visit which lasted only a few hours and took place twenty-eight years ago? Furthermore, after nineteen years of what amounted to matrimony, anyway, the ceremony could hardly be expected to constitute the most indelible of events. Still, the lapse *is* curious in that the day before the thromboses, in November, he began to talk about his life in Massachusetts in 1939–40, a subject rarely mentioned, and to talk about it with exceptional distinctness. Is this merely the long arm of coincidence, or were the cells encoded with those particular memories in that particular file of the information bank undergoing exposure as a result of strain just before the eclipse?

Listening to *Pelléas* after dinner, I.S. says that he likes it much more than the last time he heard it. When was that? I ask. "With Debussy."

February 10

San Francisco. The view from our hotel rooms features an electric letterboard flashing time and temperatures in the name of Equitable Life Assurance; a second electric sign that intersperses news of local and world disasters with appeals to drink, smoke, wipe, and deodorize with products that are better, bigger, newer, cheaper, sexier; tomorrow's skyscrapers —slanted jibs of cranes, girders, showers of sparks from welders—dwarfing today's skyscrapers and promising more and larger executive suites; a column, possibly a reject for a Central American version of the Place Vendôme, capped by a globe bearing a coyly draped and dancing but disproportionately diminutive dancing nymph carrying a thyrsis and trident.

A hurdy-gurdy performing to the benches of Union Square below reminds I.S. that this Low-Fi but loud music machine—it is audible even above the demolition squads— "was so popular in St. Petersburg that it was not an uncommon sound or sight to find more than one competitor grinding at the same time, as in *Petrushka*. Sometimes they were accompanied by dancers, too, and as a child I watched more than one hurdy-gurdy ballerina from my window, and with my brother Gury threw coins tied in a rag to the *artiste*." Another, much louder, concert is pealed up to us in late afternoon by off-key carillons somewhere in the all-too-near environs. This angelus consists entirely of the principal theme of Tchaikovsky in B-flat minor, and because of it even the pigeons flee their eyases on the ledge below us, whether it be anthropomorphism to say so or not.

"Loud" is again the word for tonight's Chinese New Year parade, some of the firecrackers suggesting not merely an old-

fashioned Fourth of July but the blunderbusses and cannon-
ades of the Revolution itself. The wail and din of Chinese
music combine ominously with the subterranean rumble of
the cable-car chains, too; but the procession itself is ominous,
with its real (caged) gorilla—this is "the year of the monkey"
—and sinuous, scaly, and block-long cardboard dragon (to
propitiate Confucius knows what malevolent powers). Some
of the marchers carry paper hares and paper tigers, and some
of the onlookers hold clumps of balloons resembling models of
molecular structures. But San Francisco itself has a Chinese
aspect tonight in the shapes of hills under the nesting fog, in
the stylized Chinese clouds, and in the Chinese moon over the
Bay.

We visit the Haight-Ashbury and the Barbary Coast North
Shore tourist districts. The former might be a movie set for
an earlier America. The nomadic, semi-pastoral people carry
duffel bags and guitars, and they wear long hair and Smith
Brothers beards, frontiersmen's leggings, Civil War capes,
dungarees, Indian ruanas and headbands (there is berdache,
or Indian transvestism, too). A sign in a store window here
reads: MIRRORS FOR SALE, NEW AND USED. The North Shore
is utterly different, catering to that privilege of businessmen,
the tax-deducted night out. It is a flesh market, sold on the
hoof. There are advertisements for "Bottomless Shoe Shines"
and "Topless Weddings," for "Thoroughly Naked Millie,"
"Miss Freudian Slip," "Naked Orphan Fanny," "The Nude
Bat Girl" (what is the *added* attraction of an aliped?). One
establishment lures its customers with a sparsely clad, busty,
and curvaceous girl standing in a glass telephone booth ele-
vated to about twenty-five feet on the street front. In fact,
we are lured here for a moment ourselves, though more, or
so we say, to observe the scopophiliac audience than the en-
tertainment, which is very dull and which, with all the potential lactation, would be a more useful place for babies.

February 11

A Navy training jet has grazed the Bay Bridge in thick early-morning fog and drowned. Hardly any traces of debris are found, and though frogmen discover an oil slick—a clue to them, as spilled blood would be to the police in a murder case—the plane is not recovered by nightfall.

We drive to Muir Woods, over the red bridge from which known *salto mortale* number 340-odd has been tabulated this week; the number of unknown opters of this way out (down) is estimated from between three to ten times as many. San Francisco, from the bridge, is a white, Arabian, city, and Muir Woods is a small pocket of Natural resistance.

At the evening rehearsal of his "Requicles" in Oakland, I.S. says that the *Libera me* sounds like a mob scene, and he asks the chorus to speak in triplets, and to speak, not mumble; but then the words come out as if from a cheering section at a football game.

Germain Prévost, the violist and a friend of I.S.'s for fifty years, tells me that he finds the composer spectral and weak-voiced, but less peaked than might have been expected after such an illness. It is true that I.S. has never regained his full voice (there were spells of total aphonia in the hospital), but we are accustomed to the new timbre now and do not notice the difference. Undoubtedly he strikes other people as very thin, too, though to us, comparing the present with a few weeks ago, the face seems almost bloated, as in the portrait by Auberjonois, who made him look fish-like, slanting the eyes and distorting the head like the sculptures of Lepenski Vir. "Eat more," the portly Prévost advises, and I.S. says that he swallows two raw eggs "like oysters" each morning. Prévost's autograph album, submitted for fresh inscriptions, contains a manuscript poem by Schoenberg, and the chronicle of a concert tour in the Twenties featuring I.S.'s *Concertino*. What most impressed Prévost about the *Concertino* was I.S.'s demand and receipt of five hundred francs for each performance.

After the rehearsal, talking about love in the Pill paradise to K., a member of the Sexual Freedom League, I put forward the *a priori* (*a* Priapic?) opinion that groups such as hers are expressions of reaction to Salic laws, hence more important to women than to men because they give women the freedom to choose. "Obviously," says K., an informed student of mating behavior and advocate of sexual freedom à la Fourier, "the point for men is that the prospect of new females increases the possible number of copulations—*brevis voluptas* —as is the case with other male mammals, bulls, for example, being able to mount new cows [and Pasiphaës?] shortly after dismounting old ones, and while still unable to remount the old ones." Whatever the truth of these contentions—and apriorism is overcome not by more philosophy but by experiment—K. believes that all participants in group sex suffer from third-sex repressions. She also says that group sex is engaged in in total silence, and that names are never used. Pot is seldom taken at Bay Area League meetings (orgies?), she says, but she justifies her own occasional use of it by citing the laudanum-taking of De Quincey, Coleridge, Elizabeth Barrett. K.'s talk has made me feel very antique.

February 13

At the concert, when I.S. stands to acknowledge the ovation and, Russian style, applaud his applauders, the audience rises, too, and blocks the composer, who is probably the smallest man in the hall, from the view of all except his immediate neighbors. Emotional dangers beset him from several sides tonight, the concert marking at the same time his first appearance in public since May, first exposure to live music-making, first audition of the *Requiem Canticles* since Princeton. No wonder he is trembling slightly in the car afterward. Back in the hotel, however, he shows signs of having had a boost from the experience, and a badly needed restoration of confidence. V. says she is now convinced that he can and will compose again.[1]

His comments on the concert show that, as always, it is impossible to know what is going on in the engine room when the view is limited to the top deck. "The Symphony in Three Movements is naïve in construction," he says, which emboldens V. to ask if he entertains a similar opinion concerning the *Scherzo à la Russe*. The answer is no. "The *Scherzo* is exactly what it should be." He is well aware that only a small part of the ovation can have been generated by the *Canticles*. "People come first to see if *you* are still there, and second to see if you are still there in the music, hoping, of course, that you aren't." With this he begins to autograph a pile of scores, pirated editions of his early ballets mostly. Buccaneering not being injury enough, one of the stolen publications of *Le Sacre* adds the insult of subtitling it a "Ballet Suite." I await an outburst, but, untrue to form, the composer calmly and neatly blacks out the offending description, saying, "Why not call it gavotte?" Singing a score of *Petrushka*, he

---

[1] On April 17 he began to compose an extra instrumental prelude to the *Requiem Canticles,* for a performance of the work in memory of Dr. Martin Luther King. He started with the first two notes of the violin solo in the *Canticles,* the same interval that appears in so much of Stravinsky's mourning music, and the same notes that he identifies in an interview (see p. 72) as the first he was to play on the piano after his illness. The prelude was abandoned when he saw that it could not be completed in time for the May 2 performance date.

tells me that one of his aunts, "married to a man with whiskers like a Schnauzer," refused to see the ballet because she was "not going to the theater to look at a lot of peasants."

February 21

New York. To *Die Walküre* at the Met, two acts of it, that is, for it affects me like chloroform. Visual interest is sustained in the first act, for a time, by the arboreal confusion in Hunding's tree house. The two limbs sprouting like phalloi from either side of this mammoth log—the only one, incidentally, in the whole forest primeval—appear to have been grafted from a cactus (*Girl of the Golden West?*). Now I agree that a Plantagenet profusion of branches was probably not to be expected, but the poverty of connection implied by only two, and those from a cactus!, is really too poor and too bastard. Besides, there *must* be another part of the forest. The tree is hewn through at the base, moreover, not merely like the redwood that straddles a highway somewhere in northern California, but as openly as the Eiffel Tower. Siegmund's sword, uneasily sheathed in the shin bark, is hardly as big as a thorn, in proportion, but it is a most sensitive thorn, blushing at every mention of its name, flickering and gleaming at every hint of the "sword motive." No one is surprised, therefore, that when finally extracted, after much strenuous but unconvincing tugging, it comes out as highly charged electrically as a bolt from Thor.

The "action" in the Fricka scene, what I see of it in my sleepless moments, takes place on what might be the rim of a recumbent flying saucer, or other UFO; but whatever it is dwarfs the gods who, by my prejudices, should look like

Giulio Romano giants in a clouded skyscape. The duel takes place in a kind of mobile Monument Valley, where two great monoliths come together most effectively.

March 3

Hollywood. "I have been thinking about the Picasso eye," says I.S., out of the azure, and as the subject has not been mentioned since the hospital, the remark falls across the conversation like a news caption on a television screen during a detergent "opera." "A thousand notes could be spent in those few seconds, but what matters is that the form—the music must begin and end, after all—reminds the listener of an eye. I have considered many ways of composing it and many kinds of measurement. But my brain is not clear enough yet, and my body has to be re-educated. I was thinking as I left my bed this morning that I walk like a turtle."

At *The Graduate* tonight, as always at the cinema, it is impossible to restrain I.S. from commenting aloud, and from loudly and frequently applying to V. for Russian translations. At one point he provokes a chorus of shooshes and a scramble for new seats. In fairness to our fleeing neighbors, too, it must be admitted that his observations are annoyingly detached (if also marvelously acute, especially on errors of length) or probably would be to anyone engrossed in the film.

I leave the theater ahead of the I.S.'s to bail out the car from the parking lot and meet them at the curb. I return to find them drawing blank stares from people filtering inside on a long queue, people as faceless and undifferentiated, even by the effects of Crest on their grins, as eggs on a conveyor belt; which makes the two old people seem more radically differentiated than ever, and turns the flow of my own abundant philoprogenitiveness away from the egg faces and toward them; and which further makes the old man's desire even to *go* to the movies (and it is his second time for *The Graduate*) seem like a manifestation of the same tremendous life force that compelled him, at the age of most of these eggs, to stay home and compose *Le Sacre du printemps*.

March 21

Phoenix. We are suffering from euphoria, for a change, due, we think, to differences of climatology (if the word can be borrowed back from political jargon) and the sudden excess, after Los Angeles, of chemical-free and even orange-blossom-scented air. Another explanation for the feeling of looseness is inadvertently proposed by the pretty, snub-nosed photographer who meets the I.S.'s at the airport. She says that certain supersensitive small parts of her cameras come unfastened during flights. What then, *I* say, of the effects of flight on such a comparatively sensitive appurtenance as the human nervous system?

We stay in the Casa Blanca Inn, in the desert near, and with a view in zoom-lens distinctiveness of, two humps of rock inevitably called Camelback Mountain. The Inn's mosque-shaped central building, as well as each outlying motel unit, is protected by spiny saguaro, prickly pear, bristling ocotillo, tall cucumber-shaped and small porcupine-shaped cactus—a statement that probably reflects my low tolerance of the golfers who appear to be our only Inn mates. Beyond the swimming pools, the fairway and the putting greens, the desert is tinged with lupines and golden poppies. In Arizona, the color of spring is gold.

Just how mortal the desert can be is made clear by a traffic warning: DON'T END UP A LITTLE WHITE CROSS—unless, of course, the sign was erected by a society of agnostics or by B'nai B'rith. We refrain from questioning our driver on this point, in any case, because to do so would be to interrupt an exceedingly slow-moving disquisition on the, as it turns out, not inconsiderable differences between buttes and mesas; and we are already late for the dress rehearsal of the *Rake*.

This takes place in an auditorium designed by Frank Lloyd Wright for, it is said, an emergent African republic that in the event failed to emerge. It was completed by Wright's pupils three years ago and is something of a freak, perhaps because no impious modifications of the master's plans were introduced in consideration of the change of destination. The building would certainly look better in Cairo or adjoining the Casa Blanca Inn. Then, on second glance, whatever it is seems to be more sea- than earth-going; a stranded ark, for instance: the side entrances are in the form of gangplanks and the wall lights are shaped like portholes. For a building so recently finished, in any case, it is astonishingly tacky and out of date (Wright the irrepressible stuccodore), and the atmosphere it provides is more appropriate to a Ziegfield folly than a "mod" opera.

Before beginning the rehearsal, I introduce I.S. to the assembled cast, chorus, orchestra, bystanders; except that the only person actually to stand, out of respect to the composer, and older man, is our friend Robert Tobin; which means that some of those present have undoubtedly taken Mr. Tobin (who is distinguished-looking) to *be* the composer.

We go to a diner, following the rehearsal, but the food— plastic shrimps, chopped-rubber-tire hamburgers, a "short-cake" made of old pancakes—is a "front" for juke boxes with video screens showing "conservative strip tease." Finding no restaurant open after the performance, we go to bed hungry. At 3 A.M., V. is awakened by a noise she thinks was made by a rat, but it is I.S., half starved, nibbling a *gaufrette*.

❋ ❋ ❋

The musical reading of the opera is excellent and would have been even better with some fifty more rehearsals and several other changes of circumstance. The Rake's English, for one of them, is unintelligible, owing in part to tracheal congestion, judging by the struggles with mucosities and the emanations of Vicks reaching to about the thirtieth row. Perhaps from the same cause his pitch is only intermittently *not* a quarter-tone flat, but the fitfully in-tune notes, obtained at the cost of an excruciating *fortissimo*, are worse. The harpsichord is distinguished by a no less painful pitch discrepancy, but in the other direction, and the instrument is amplified to something near the level of the Mormon Tabernacle organ at triple *f*. In the first scene a singer anticipates an entrance by several beats, and the others follow him, sheep-like, instead of taking their cues from the orchestra, with the result that the dénouement occurs rather sooner on stage than in the pit. In spite of this, I.S. tells me at intermission that he feels as if he were "in a *fauteuil*" when I am conducting the opera. But at times tonight I feel as if *I* am on the edge of a very wobbly chair.

I.S. likes the male Baba vocally ("voyce of unpaved Eunuch," as Clotten says in *Cymbeline*), and the sound *is* good, except for the alarmingly clamant bark on the A in *alt*. "After all," says I.S., "the opera takes place in the age of Farinelli, when operatic sex swapping was conventional." True, but in the period of tonight's staging, universal transvestism constitutes a stronger justification for the switch. Whether or not unnerved by considerations involving his, or her, muliebrity—or bilateralism—tonight's Baba is forgetful. "Speak to me," she croons, and the Rake, dependably flat, wonders "Why?" but gets only a freezingly long pause, then a backing up, by Baba, for yet another try at "Speak to me," as if she had suddenly found herself to be extremely fond of that particular line. At this point, and because her next lines are *a cappella*, I clear my throat and prepare to give way to the swell of lyricism myself.

But the breakfast scene is too campy with a male Baba, and anyway—a more fundamental objection—the opera needs a second woman, even a bearded one. Then, too, hermaphroditism seems to be less happily represented by the division down the middle, as the case is here, than by the over-endowing of the female, as in the replica of the Hellenistic reclining nude in the Villa Borghese. In last year's Boston performances, the resurrected Baba—after the hibernation under the wig—was projected on the curtain through closed-circuit television. This suggested psychic manifestations and ectoplasmic transsubstantiation, and was superior as an idea to the new one, in which the garrulous androgyne reappears on a standard-size television set exactly like the evening news. Incidentally, the running commentary of photographic slides during the breakfast scene now includes a view of Baba doing a sit-in at the *Last Supper*.

The psychedelic lighting has been greatly improved since Boston, however, and so, on the whole, has the stage management, despite minor logistic failures in chasing people on and off the sets in time, no doubt blamable on green thumbs in the local stage crew. Half of the scenery is rather surprisingly carted off *during* the cabaletta, for instance, word probably having got back that intermission had already begun, which indeed it would have if Anne had been two inches farther upstage and hence carried along. Nor are mishaps of the sort confined to people. In the best tradition of Environmental

Theater ("all the world's a stage"), objects are continually dropping in, falling down, bursting, all apparently of their own accord. Even the Rolls-Royce hearse enters too fast, recoiling from its stage blocks like the El Capitan jerking to a stop as it almost overshoots a station. But at least the Rolls does not catch fire, as it did in Boston, where apparently a Fundamentalist was trying to smoke out Shadow, forgetting that the brumous pit is his natural element, and obliging the stagehands to jimmy the windows in an all-too-real rescue operation.

❋ ❋ ❋

As each performance occasions further thoughts about the opera itself, this one leaves me with the conviction that the lack of dimension in the characters is a graver weakness than any fault of dramatic structure. In any case, the rustiness, or even the absence, of a few dramatic hinges is not necessarily calamitous in a form as dependent on suspensions of disbelief as opera, to say nothing of the unrealities and fairy-tale premises of this particular opera. The Rake's three wishes have not become less silly over the years, to be sure. Nor has the nursery-rhyme plot—"a year and a day hence"—grown more compatible with Hogarth and Everyman, however well it suits the Faustian element in the mixture. What does stick out more than it used to is the Rake's unbusinesslike agreement to the leap-year pact. In fact, it now seems inconceivable, and is certainly not putting too naturalistic an interpretation on the opera, that the Rake can accept Shadow with no notion of who he is, and with no further questions about that long-forgotten uncle, the mysterious benefactor, who does not re-enter the Rake's thoughts until the graveyard scene: not inconceivable in a fairy tale, but certainly in a dramatic spectacle inviting a degree of audience concern over the fate of the characters. Shadow's "We will settle our account" follows too quickly Truelove's "the sooner that you settle your estate," incidentally, and when the Rake's hash *is* finally "settled," Shadow's gift of an escape clause—"only what you yourself acknowledge to be just"—is forgotten. Still, these are technical mistakes, not violations of the genre, and the opera survives them.

Thanks to the music, it also survives the one-dimensionalism of the characters, but the strain is greater. While no one in the opera is a believable person, Shadow, Baba, and Sellem, who least need and least pretend to be, are more so than the hero and heroine; by the time of their final exits, in fact, this exotic trio has won a substantial measure of our sympathy and aroused our desire to know more about them. All three are intelligent and engaging, and Sellem, who could have been tiresome in the hands of another composer, is so much the opposite that we regret his failure to appear in the Epilogue— in so far as it is worth regretting anything about the Epilogue besides its existence. (In this staging he reappears as the turnkey in Bedlam.) Still, all three are strictly one-dimensional, for Shadow's confidences to the audience hardly invest him with an extra layer of depth, though they do form a stylistic link with the Epilogue, hence are a clue to staging it, if it must be staged. In spite of his parsonical black, and that other well-known clerical disguise, a bad case of Pulpit's Disease, the "king of tears" cuts a more dashing figure than the Rake, and the role is by a long shot the stageworthiest in the opera.

Audience involvement reaches its highest intensity at the Rake's demise, nevertheless, because at this juncture the drama is real and the poetry and music are both perfect in themselves and perfectly fused. But until the graveyard scene, sympathy for the Rake is minimal, our interest in him being confined to his music. His first aria exposes him as a cad, after all ("Why should I labor for what in the end/She will give me for nothing, if she be my friend"), and from the dramatic point of view, a marplot, for the aria spoils true "love interest." Nor is he very clever; in fact in the bread-machine episode, the parable of the Multiplication of Loaves, his intelligence appears to be so perilously low that when Shadow compares notes with the audience—"My master is a fool as you can see"—the latter, accustomed to suffer operatic fools gladly for their music, is convinced that this one will end up in Bedlam from natural causes.

Anne is no less vacuous. But she is strangely blinkered, too, and she and the Rake go through the middle part of the opera passing each other like ships in the night. Clearly the Rake is happier with Shadow, as the Don is with Leporello; at any rate, the callousness of his description of his former betrothed as "only a milkmaid" seems to me unthinkable under any other interpretation of his sexual temperament. Partly for the same reason one cannot feel bitterly sorry for her, and for this and other reasons as well—for example when she can say nothing more about the Rake's betrayal than "It is I who was unworthy"—we wish her Godspeed back to the dairy.

❅ ❅ ❅

Whether or not the words are, or can be, superior to the meanings, verbal infelicities are by no means rare.[1] Some of the difficulty appears to be with the period of the language,

---

[1] On the other hand, most of the once awkward-seeming musical accentuations of them are no longer ruffling. I should add that at the time of the *Rake*, Stravinsky was steeped in Elizabethan music, which offered him precedents aplenty in the matter of accented weak syllables: Morley's "and sweet wild ros*es*," for example, and Wilbye's "with smiling glan*ces*." His tendency to favor the French scansion of franglais words, as in the allocation of only one note to "uncle" was more of a problem when he first started to compose. It is at the opposite extreme from Handel's German habit of pronouncing *everything*, making a dissyllable, for example, even of "whole."

the pastiche of which is at times stilted ("Nick . . . you have some scheme afoot"), and at other times too broad, as in the inclusion of quotations from *Henry IV, Part 2* ("I am exceeding weary") and Dryden's version of Book VI of the *Aeneid* ("Restore the age of gold"). Period aside, some lines are ambiguous to the ear. Thus, "Let all who will, make their joy here [hear?] of your glad tidings." Another example is "Bowers of paper only seals repair," which conjures a vision of sea lions, until we begin to wonder what a bower of paper might be (a Wall Street office building stocked with lavatory tissue for a "ticker-tape" parade?). Ambiguous, too, in the reference of the plural pronoun, is Truelove's "While they're in mind I'll tell you of his needs," which sounds as if it had been written in German first; and Shadow's "Lawyers crouched like gardeners to pay" is remarkably cryptic, considering the dramatic business in hand. In this scene, incidentally, Shadow reacts to the word "God" in Truelove's "May God bless you" by interrupting the conversation, but at the beginning of the next scene he refers to himself as the Rake's "godfather," which is not a likely irony for him at this point. Nor, two scenes later, is Shadow's image, "the giddy multitude driven by the unpredictable Must of their pleasures," altogether waterproof. I do not doubt that the sensation of giddiness may have been felt at some time by the gray majority as a whole (though I do not entirely believe it, either), but certainly the predictability of its pleasures is absolute and foregone.

Whether the double meanings are intentional I cannot say. Certainly the Ophelian repressions betrayed in Anne's dreams of wedded bliss—"The joyous fount I see that brings increase," and "the touch of his" (his what?)—seem to be, and so does Shadow's question to the Rake, "Does your machine look anything like this?" Long before the Rake can confirm that of course it does, the audience knows the answer, in this performance at least, and in this prepuce-less age (unaware that foreskins were Pharaonic trophies, as scalps were to the Sioux), for the machine is a modern phallic fantasy, not in design only but also in operation; it lights up with each discharge of bread loaf like a one-armed bandit registering a jackpot, thus identifying sex and money as well. Naturally it wins the loudest and most spontaneous applause of any of the performers.

But the words, words, words, themselves are a verbal fault compared to which these are peccadillos. The audience is regularly told more (as well as less) than it needs to know. (So is the score reader. "The crowd murmuring," says a marginal direction before the line "We've never been through such a hectic day," but try murmuring "hectic" for a start.) Thus the Rake's soliloquy at the beginning of Act II is full of good lines, but for a poetry reading at the "Y": few of them count dramatically, and the shape of the scene is imposed entirely by the music. The next scene, too, Shadow's tripartite aria, depends exclusively on the music, the verbal argument being almost purely rhetorical and the dramatic action nonexistent. On the other hand, when the words *are* dramatic and active, which is the case in the Bedlam scene, the effect is powerful enough to carry the weight of all the failures.

* * *

As for the staging, not all of the "mod" correspondences are successful, but many fit surprisingly well, and even those that do not are to some extent redeemed by the evidence of a lively imagination. This much must be said because the reviewer's ploy is to make heavy weather of the unorthodoxy and to pose as a defender of the sacred original, which he has heretofore loathed. This must be said, as well, simply because *any* proof of imagination in opera is rare and in need of support; American patronage tends to help the workshop and the study group rather than the real thing. Miss Caldwell's imagination is evident all the way from her programming—in following the Boston *Lulu* with *I Puritani*, for example, and this year in saluting the Mexican Olympics with *Montezuma's Revenge*— to her last desperate improvisations on opening night. She has authority, too, and superb musicianship, as proved by the *Tosca* she conducted a few days ago on no notice, when the scheduled maestro turned up so much the worse for drink— the offstage life of Miss Caldwell's company is more theatrical than the on—that he had to be ejected from the theater, a building so poorly insulated, however, that his vociferations from a new location outside were distinctly audible in the quieter moments in Act I.

The first act goes down remarkably well "mod." At least *something* happens in that starchy first scene, and if the Hell's Angels motorbike and the Harold Lloyd-era Rolls are gimmicks, then gimmicks are useful in teasing some life into a formality ("O clement love") bordering on parody. Pop Truelove, a lunchpail-carrying, aitch-dropping railroad worker, is an improvement, too, being a somewhat less absurdly portentous father-in-law figure than "Dear Father Truelove." This change in social position raises a difficulty at the end of the opera, however, because he appears there in Sunday clothes—after not having been seen since Act I, scene I, some two and a half hours earlier, and then wearing overalls. Programs rustle all over the theater when he himself fails to give any immediate clue, for his daughter's misbetrothal has turned him tight-lipped, and he contributes only four words to the Epilogue.

The beginning of the second scene is even more convincing "mod," partly because the discothèque dances (boogaloo, swim, funky Broadway) fit the corny march music as well as spoof it. But one episode fails. When Shadow, acting as MC, has adjusted a reverb mike to the Rake for his *ad lib* song, and "Love, too quickly betrayed" gets underway (sung more than a hint flat throughout), the "mod" apparatus suddenly seems tawdry and irrelevant. But, then, the stage looks forlorn whenever the music engages any depth of feeling. Shadow is not baleful enough in these surroundings, I might add, and it is precisely at the end of this scene that he should first gloat a bit and bare his fangs.

The third tableau is cumbersome. We do not need the Big Dipper or an ocean of pallid lighting to know that it is night. Good diction would be lodestar enough, and in fact would obviate the scene shift in the first place, for it is six minutes in coming and then lasts only nine. The one rule here, to which all other considerations must be sacrificed, is not to interrupt the transition from strings to wind trio. Anne's two plummy arias can be delivered in front of the curtain and, come to think of it, that is the best place for them in any case.

The first scene of Act II, the Rake wringing his withers in his London pad, is very busy with lights and other distractions, not all of them intentional. They detract from the mood of the music, too, without making a wordy and undramatic scene less so. Nor is the street scene short on visual targets, though the stage picture was more effective in Boston where filmed rain made it still more complex. The crowd could be more nondescript than it is, more like a troupe from *8½*, though the Rake's neighborhood is not necessarily one likely to be invaded by protest marchers. Finally, it still seems to me that Ingmar Bergman's two-act division, concluding the first part with this scene, is the best way to shape the opera.

The auction is Miss Caldwell's most complete success. Sellem—Hawaiian shirt, hippy beads, gardenia over the ear—is a combination pop Guru, con man, TV automobile salesman. He sits crosslegged on a Simeon-like stylite hoisted from stage level, and as he reels off the objects under the gavel, photographs of them are flashed on the curtain in the manner of a fast-moving slide lecture. The bidders infiltrate the audience, in Café La Mama style, moving closer to the orchestra as each lot is knocked down, until they stand by the pit itself for the balance of promises and a better view of the resuscitated Baba on TV.

The graveyard, on the grounds of an abandoned, weed-fronded church, is for automobiles, and the lighting is supplied entirely by the headlamps of Shadow's Rolls-Royce hearse. The idea is a brilliant one, but the execution is marred by the trap-door crudity of Shadow's descent and by his back-to-audience position which denies even a glimpse of Satanic transformation; in a staging as tricked out with effects as this one, surely a sulphurous whiff, or earth rattling could have been devised at this point, where something really is needed. The switch from cemeteries for people to cemeteries for automobiles renders Shadow's rope useless, incidentally, unless he had intended to perform an Indian rope trick: the set has no tree, or yardarm, or hangman's drop.

The Bedlam scene is weak and scrimpy, I regret to report, and the "mod" style itself founders in it, the only time in the opera. Nothing after the curtain is as good as the montage of projections before it, of green embryonic faces like those in Tchelichev's *Hide and Seek,* then of Hogarth's madmen.[1] Nor is the stage picture convincing. It is dominated by the Harley-Davidson, now thickly bandaged, hence Surrealist as an art object, coy as a dramatic object, and awkward as a utility, the gauzed pillion being a clumsy throne for "Venus."

Throughout the scene the madmen shield themselves from the audience and each other—even group therapy has broken down—lying behind the ends of hospital beds. These bed-

[1] Not the least recommendation of the visual performance of the opera is that the black-and-white sets imitate eighteenth-century engravings, burin lines and all.

stead grilles are handy, if too transparent, symbols for sickness and isolation, tombstones, and prison bars, but they are ineffective for the simple reason that the patients never appear. Visual scale is missing, too, so that what the picture suggests is a baby hospital full of bassinets. And anyway, isolation to this extent is the wrong idea. The lunatics are a chorus, and Miss Caldwell's Odyssean first conception, which was that all of them together should weave a shroud or other fabric—crazy quilt?—would at least have refined the choral performance. But the scene would still lack movement. The choruses are dance pieces, after all, even "Madmen's words are all untrue." Whether Balanchine ballet—the Minuet is a fast, quirky dance as Stravinsky conceived it—or Peter Brook hoppings about and holy-rollings on the floor, like chickens turning on a spit, some kind of movement is indispensable. That goes for the Mourning Chorus as well. (How beautiful are the suspensions in the bassoons and English horn at the end of this piece!) "Tread softly round his bier," the madmen chant, but no one in this mysterious asylum even shows himself.

The Epilogue is a disaster. But a photograph of I.S. playing cards, flashed across the curtain at the end—I.S., the artist, finessing his work, and I.S., indomitable—trumps it and is a real *coup de théâtre.*

March 31

Hollywood. Twenty years ago today I first met the "Stravs," that same day on which Auden delivered the book of the *Rake*. To mark the event I.S. gives me the sketches of *"The Owl and the Pussicat [sic]*," calling them a "vicennalian" present. But the greatest gift is that we are celebrating together as, a short time ago, with I.S. straddling two worlds in Death's Row at the hospital, I hardly dared hope we would.

At dinner, Christopher Isherwood, still boyish, his eyebrows now like tussocks, asks how such an anniversary is to be designated, and we decide to call it a marriage of Craft and Art. As the I.S.'s have a corner and more in Isherwood's autobiography, Isherwood asks them for *their* impressions of *me* at that first meeting. But the I.S.'s are able to recall only that I was "very nervous, hardly said a word, and had apparently never touched alcohol before!" Well, I am still nervous at times, but I do talk a bit now and then, and I do not invariably refuse a glass or two of certain kinds of anodyne. Finally Isherwood wants to know "whether it was love at first sight," and I am happy to say that all three of us at the same time answer YES.

APPENDIX A

Diary   Addenda   (1968)

September 29. Zurich. Our hotel, the Dolder Grand, belongs to the Engelbert Humperdinck period (the *original* Engelbert Humperdinck), judging by the gingerbread towers, but the period of the weather is the Wet Age. Mists and fog alternate with drizzle and pelting rains, and vapors deliquesce from the pollarded chestnut trees and golf-green lawns below the hotel like steam from doused fires. At noon today, as if in response to the morning-long barrage of church bells, a sudden wind sweeps the snow peaks and sends sailboats skeetering over the lake. It sends me outdoors, too, and into the woods—more Humperdinck —where the shuffling leaves take me back thirty years.

The hotel seems to have been prophylactically insulated against any form of mirth, and whether as insurance against leaks, or for the sins they may have beheld, the rooms are diurnally punished with turibund rug-scourgings and vacuumings. Nor are the tidy-ings-up, at various unpredictably inconvenient times during the day—the bedspreads resmoothed, the pillows newly primped, the Kleenex freshly pressed—really intended for any other purpose than to make *us* feel otiose and immoral. But the Dolder would be a perfect retreat in which to knit a novel, as V. says, and it *is* a good place to put on weight, which is what I.S. needs. In fact the restaurant is a holdout on a grand scale against quick-fix, pre-cooked, and semi-reconstituted airplane meals. Kangaroo-tail soup, roast thrush, smoked swallows' nests (an acquired taste), and saddle of chamois *poivrade* (served with *pommes* Goethe, *pointes d'asperges* Eisenhower, or other cultural side dishes) are regularly available, along with the perennial *Birchermuesli*. Considered simply as a room, too, the restaurant compares favorably with the rest of the hotel, the lounge being a gallery for *September Morn*-type pictures, and the bar a mausoleum with pianist.

Our fellow boarders include a Libyan prince who looks like Sam Jaffe as Gunga Din, and a sister of the late King Farouk, who looks like nobody knows what, for the reason that she has not left her room in eight years or exposed more of herself than a phantasmal arm extended from behind a door to receive a letter or telegram and give a tip. According to our Austrian *Stubenmädchen*, the Princess bolts herself in the lavatory during meal deliveries and room cleaning. The *Stubenmädchen* reports great quantities of books, too, and racks of never-worn Parisian dresses, and she romantically attributes the Princess's purdah, or super-Garbo seclusion, to blighted love.

Shah Pahlevi is another of the hotel regulars, partly, it is said, because of vast personal fortunes in local banks, access to which is probably assured by a permanently revved-up 727 on the palace runway back home. (Our room waiter's description of the Shah's entourage reminds me of a Saudi prince and fellow hotel guest of ours in Geneva in 1951, whose caravan included a portable harem complete with eunuchs who camped in the hallway outside the royal concubines' doors—where monogamous guests leave their shoes. I remember seeing four of the royal Fatimas one day in the back seat of a six-door Cadillac parked in front of the Hotel des Bergues. They were wearing black robes, black triangular veils, and gold bracelets, and one of them was pouring water from a gold jug—which, I suppose, is the Royal Arabian equivalent of a thermos bottle.)

October 7. We overhear an American in the bar telling a companion about one of Zurich's temples of the gnomes. "You enter by a special door," he says, "where a guard impounds your passport and obliges you to write the number of your account on a paper. When your handwriting has been verified, and your face identified against a photograph, another guard escorts you to a conference room—incarcerates you there, in fact, to the extent that he continues to stand watch outside the door; the bank wishes to protect the privacy of its celebrated depositors, as well as spare them embarrassing encounters with each other, the Shah bumping into General Franco, for instance, or Truman Capote colliding with Gore Vidal. The room, you imagine, must be rented out in the evenings to abortionists or psychoanalysts, when not occupied by the usury squads of the Swiss Monetary Police. Then, discovering it to be soundproof—a clank of chains next door, or even a murder, would not be heard—you realize that, off hours, it must serve some still more sinister purpose, such as a confessional cell for high-ranking criminals.

"The furniture is sparse: a leather couch, a leather-backed chair, a table containing picture-magazines of Swiss scenery and skiing resorts, mimeographed sheets of stock market quotations, and a telephone—severed, no doubt, or tuned to a record saying 'normal service will never be resumed.' At some point you are aware of a peculiar aroma—money, obviously, except that apart from those market averages, nothing in the bank even hints at anything so crass. One of the very last features you are likely to notice is the bars outside the window, if you *do* notice them, for they are the most discreet bars imaginable. They alone remind you of the bullion somewhere below, and of all those nests, glittering with golden eggs, of the rich and super rich.

"When he arrives, your banker—eyes sterling cold, clothes as crisp as newly minted money—immediately puts you on sufferance by requiring you to recite your account number, as if it were a password in a speakeasy or the combination to a safe. He is courteous but uninterceptible, male-voiced but sexless, and the mini-skirted secretary who joins him after the inspection of credentials is so cold she would probably copulate adiabatically. She brings a folder containing the numbered but nameless records of your investments, which you are allowed to study but not to remove. In fact no documents of any kind are exchanged; instead you receive an accounting in the mail, unsigned but with a printed card: 'Compliments of the Schweizerische Bank Verein.' Then, as soon as your business has been transacted, you are bundled out of a back door, after an all-clear from the guard lest in that instant Harold Wilson be entering or leaving as well."

October 10. On the way to Lucerne today, I.S. expresses the need of a "Watyer Closyet"—Russia evidently had so few of these facilities that it did not bother to make up its own name— but he rejects an Esso station after discovering that a "previous user has had very poor aim." A similar complaint could be made about the swan-fouled lakeside walk in Lucerne, except that this looks deliberate, an act of mass excremental retaliation for the polluting of the boat basin, from which apparently even the youngest cygnets have soiled their down.

The caretaker of Wagner's villa at Triebschen is unbelieving after reading I.S.'s signature in the visitor's book, but she recovers her composure (and composer) in time, and guides us through. The collection of musical instruments on the second floor contains many beautiful objects by Renaissance and Baroque craftsmen, along with such Wagnerian instruments as the tenor *Tuben*, not only of the *Ring* but also of *Le Sacre du printemps*.

October 11. Zurich. I.S. receives the manuscript full score of *Le Sacre du printemps* from his son in Geneva today, but the sight of penciled changes made during the first rehearsals reminds him of the première, which thought so irritates him that he adds a P.S. on the last page, berating the first audience for "the derision with which it greeted this music in the Théâtre des Champs-Élysées, Paris, Spring 1913." The score is bound in red morocco and linen, and many pages are reinforced with transparent tape. The *Russische Musikverlag* stamp is on several pages, too, the manuscript having been lent out to conductors and used in performances. Among those penciled pre-première amendments are the following additions: the trombone parts two measures before [22]; the bass drum part one measure before [22], and, *ibidem*, the *fermata* on the F (*not* sustained by the tubas in this score); the piccolo trumpet part at the beginning of the *Jeu de rapt;* the horn and trumpet parts in the first two measures of [62].

The title "Khorovod Game" has been deleted here, and replaced by *Jeu de rapt*, but at what date I.S. no longer remembers. *Spring Rounds* is called simply "Khorovod," too, while the music at [64] still bears the separate heading "*Eedoot-Veedoot*," and the *Dance of the Earth* is still "*Vyplyasyvaniye Zemlee*," with no translation supplied. Finally, the manuscript title of the *Action rituelle* is "Consecration of the Place," while the title of the *Evocation* is unhelpfully more specific than the published version: *viz:* "The Evocation of the *Human* Ancestors."

The only major revision shown in the autograph is at [28], where the quarter-note theme was first composed for horns, and where, in rewriting it for trumpets, Stravinsky cancels the entire page (18 measures) and rescores it on an inserted one—which, however, is bound the wrong way around. I might mention that the eighth notes in the *Kiss of the Earth* are in the solo cello part here, rather than in the solo bass; that the bassoon lead-in to the *Action rituelle* is marked *forte;* that the bass drummer in the *Evocation* is directed to use a wooden stick and to touch the head of the drum with his hand to try to produce a pitch close to B-flat; that the score specifies four timpanists, the timpani notes in the main part of the *Danse sacrale* being doubled.

A note on the title page of Part Two advises the publisher that "Pages 69–87, containing the *Danse sacrale*, will be sent shortly," and that the music between [86] and [88] is out of sequence. The score is signed and dated "8 III/23 II 1913" (*sic*) at the end of the *Danse sacrale*, and signed, dated, and located, "Clarens, 16/29 III 1913," at the end of the third measure of [85].

October 19. To Einsiedeln, crossing the lake on the causeway at Rapperswil, where V. photographs the cloister and Schloss. The valleys are still green but the vineyards are yellowing and the ivy is already mulberry red. South of the lake the road is clogged with wains and army trucks.

The exterior of the Benedictine monastery at Einsiedeln— "*Coenobiu Eremitaru*," on old maps—reminds me of the Escorial, except for the church front with volutes like treble clefs, which is typical South German Baroque. The interior is disappointing, partly because we have anticipated the gleaming white and gold of Wies and the other Bavarian masterpieces, but a choir of shavelings, kneeling before the Madonna and Child in the nave chapel, is singing a Vesper service with the greatest refinement of intonation I think I have ever heard. Outside again, in the arcades which form a semicircular approach to the church, we buy photographs from a man who manages to inject so much kindness into the transaction that he sticks in my mind, together with the idolatrous choristers, for the rest of the day.

October 23. Paris. Our rooms at the Ritz are not merely holding actions against the "de-erotization of the environment" (Marcuse), but veritable love nests, as strategically mirrored as brothels, though in style like Gavarni's foyer at the Opéra. The beds—pink-silk spreads, goddess figureheads on the footboards— are double. (So, in a squeeze, are the *chaises longues*.) Moreover, the allotment of space for the boudoirs would be unthinkable in any city except Paris, and unthinkable *there* since about 1900. Erotically conducive, as well, are the log-grate fireplaces, the coved doors, the carnival-mask (*cache-sexe*) lampshades, the key-and-keyhole light switches, the cushion footrests for the *maquillage* and dressing tables, the chain in the bathtub to summon the *femme de chambre*, the bedside push button for *service privé*, and—not least—the view from the window of one of the largest phallic monuments in Europe, in the Place Vendôme. Less erotic, certainly, even allowing for kinks, are the umbrella stand, the chandelier, the five-minute choke of the wall clock, the tarnished gilt moldings, the striped upholstery, and the escritoire; but the only serious *an*aphrodisiac is the price.

According to the doorman, the hotel had only nineteen guests during last May's revolution-that-got-away, but the staff of four hundred was always on the job. Sugar had to be rationed from the second day, he says, but while he elaborates on this hardship, I wonder about the continuing provocation, to Cohn-Bendit and company, in the steady flow of Mercedes, Rolls, and Alfa Romeos stopping at the entranceway.

October 26. Tonight's concert in the Théâtre de la Musique is the culminating event of a *"journée* Xenakis." The other principal event is billed as a discussion-debate, which does not entail any lobbing back and forth, evidently, but only some very heavy "questions" that are really self-answering statements much longer than the "replies." Pop-cult hero Lévi-Strauss himself attends the debate, and young people, dandy rather than hippie, overflow both affairs. They lather into a Beatles-type hysteria several times at the concert but were perhaps already in it beforehand, as any casual connection between the character of their responses and the contents of the program is slight. I sit not far from Messiaen, in a loge apparently designed for people with no knees.

Few contemporary composers can survive the exposure of a one-man concert, let alone a one-man day, and Xenakis is not among them. But this difficulty is nowhere dealt with or acknowledged in the purple program folders, whose Xeroxed sheafs of press clippings, biographia, film-strip photos of the master at work, and a booklet of Pataphysical bull entitled *"La pensée de Xenakis"* spill across the stage most effectively later in the evening, however, when jettisoned there by the protesting minority.

One of the publicity releases assures the reader that Xenakis's "time" is "in some cybernetic future." But tonight's reception shows all too patently that his time is right now, and that the future, cybernetic or otherwise, is precisely what he will soon have to worry about—as soon, in fact, as the next performance. Again, despite all the advance warnings about the abstruseness of the composer's cogitations and the inaccessibility of his mathematical methods, the music itself is often devastatingly predictable (in fashionable cant: "The mind makes probabilistic assessments") and astonishingly naïve, the latter being the case with several timpani rolls of the type that one had thought to have gone out with the *Symphonie fantastique.*

The centerpiece of the program is an avalanche of electronic noise called *Bohor*, which if pronounced as one syllable is also a description of the effect. As an experiment in sonic torture it is even louder than *Hair*, being inflicted by "quadruple stereophony"—bruited by eight loudspeakers shaped like dryers in a beauty salon and aimed at the audience like death-ray machines. A jet motor seems to switch on *in* one's penetralia, and one expects to explode. One stops one's ears, of course, but that only tires one's arms. When the theater itself begins to tremble like a tuning fork, many non-swingers head for the exits—as I would myself, except that I go on thinking from second to second that it cannot last a second longer. It seems obvious after a while, inasmuch as the noise is so little varied, that the machine must be stuck, or the tape derailed. But whatever the explanation, *Bohor* should be played, or detonated, if at all, in a football stadium for an audience in air-raid shelters several miles away.

One point of interest would be to compare impressions of duration (ten minutes? an hour?), but even that is frustrated. When the aural holocaust has finally subsided, the outburst of booing, jeering, catcalling—accompanied by a hail of program folders like the refuse thrown into a bull ring after a bad corrida —nearly equals *Bohor* in volume. The counterassault (*"Bis!"* from the Beatlemaniac majority) hardly gets underway when the string orchestra returns to the stage, and the demonstration turns to whistles imitating the slow glissades, which are mostly what the strings play. Then as the conductor signals the start of the next piece, a shout, *"Du* Mozart!"—a "plant," I suspect—goes up and is answered by a rich assortment of uncomplimentary epithets including *"Con!"* Nevertheless, and surprisingly, the opus passes without further outside incident. And without much inside incident either. In fact, the layout of contrasting blocks of sound-effects is much the same in every piece; "contrasting," moreover, misleadingly implies movement. If this is "sound architecture," as described, then it should go back to the drawing board.

But the real trouble with the concert after *Bohor* is that the live players, the "trad" instruments, and the concert routine itself seem glaringly obsolete. The conductor's straight beat-patterns, for example, have no evident bearing on the rhythms. Nor are the instruments functionally well adapted to their work; the design of a violin, after all, and its tuning in fifths, correspond to an evolution in music itself. In sum, Xenakis's *"pensée"* seems more fittingly served by filters, sonotrons, oscillators, potentiometers, sine-wave generators, ring modulators, and the other hardware.

The composer comes on stage for his ovations wearing the blue-denim uniform of a factory worker and footgear showing him to be ready for tennis. Well aware, however, that the turn-over in the reputation stock market is more rapid on the Paris Bourse than anywhere in the world, he emerges afterward inveighing against the Parisian process of becoming *à la mode*. BE-COMING?

I emerge thinking about Verdi's "Progress could be in the reverse direction." I think about it, with diminishing interest, until 2 A.M., in fact, at which hour girls for hire—"shop workers who want to buy more clothes," says R.—are trying to give a basic idea of their wares in nearly every doorway of the rue de la Paix all the way back to the Ritz.

November 18. Pompano Beach, Florida. The state of culture as it is advertised on the mental five and ten of U.S. #1A: a "U-$Save Shopping Center"; a "Drive-in Funeral Home"; a "Jungle Garden Safari" ("See 100 Lions In The Wild"); a "Wigwam Village" selling "plastic driftwood"; a First Church of Christ Scientist selling a sermon: WHERE WILL YOU SPEND ETERNITY?; invitations to swim, bowl, yacht, roller-skate, have your fortune told, play shuffleboard, miniature golf, jai alai.

I go to the beach, despite the wilting heat, the louring sky, the paralyzing blue-bladder hydrozoans (Portuguese men of war), and too many people—a breed peculiar to the peninsula, though not bred here, whose talk, judging from my (involuntary) eaves-dropping, is confined to Dow-Jones averages, the weather, and "back-home."

APPENDIX B

Virgil Thomson by Virgil Thomson*

This self-portrait by the ranking critic-composer is indispensable to anyone concerned with the contemporary musical scene and how it got that way. To others it can be recommended for its skillful characterizations of the intellectual moods and its distinctions between the fashion symptoms and the main lines of development, of Paris and New York between the wars. As a chronicle of that period it must be one of the most readable in existence. Unlike many authors of indispensable books, Mr. Thomson is perspicuous, enviably fluent, and nearly always engaging.

An autobiographer differs from his book-simulacrum both because of the exigencies of artistic selection and the discrepancies between his own and other people's versions of himself; hence his "I am" is a convention for "I portray myself as," a convention the reader generally accepts. The reader might question it at times, however, in connection with the intellectual character analysis served up in this book. The author portrays himself as (and, I am convinced, is in fact) an independent, one who has made his own way in both life and art. At the same time he is intellectually *mondain* and extrovert, vain of his place among "the knowing ones." He records no serious self-doubts or inner trials, whether or not he was beset by them, standing at the

*New York: Alfred A. Knopf; 1966.

opposite pole of contrast in this from, say, Maurice Sachs, who traveled in some of the same, or overlapping, circles. Mr. Thomson is never really intimate, and though the reader neither expects nor requires him to be, he feels, nevertheless, that the author has much more about him than he is willing to give in a book.

What Mr. Thomson does give is a well-balanced view of a career in relation to its time. This widens the appeal and vendibility of the book, of course, but the absence of the inner picture is not entirely explained by that. Neither is it entirely a matter of choice. Certain features of the face we are shown are too obvious to be taken at face value. I mean, for example, the display of self-confidence and the air of knowing all along that one need only bide one's time and keep the pedestal polished; and the descriptions, supported by dollops of outside opinion (Christian Bérard: "Virgil speaks the truth"), of virtues, skills, successes; and, last but far from least, the determination to avoid false modesty: "I remained for two decades quite possibly the finest choral conductor of them all . . ."; "I wrote the best exam on orchestration ever seen . . ."; "The title essay for my next book is probably the best statement now in print of the whole experience of hearing music . . ." As I said, some of these features are exhibited too obviously, as if the author badly needed to believe them.

Mr. Thomson is also, at times, disarmingly frank ("I thought perhaps my presence in a post so prominent [music critic of the *Herald Tribune*] might stimulate the performance of my works"), but for calculated effects. Effects also govern the citings of adverse judgments of his work, unless I have misunderstood the feelings they aroused in him. In fact, he is warmly touchy about the neglect of his music, as all composers are. But apart from that, the body temperature of the book is cool. No argument is blurred by passion, no episode soured by angry or indignant notes. The more surprising, therefore, are the author's periodic bouts of "frustration grippe." He is never down for long, though, this lucky-starred one who, as he says of himself after his safe exodus from wartime France, "lands on his feet."

Do I make him sound overbearing? If so, blame the clumsiness of my language; *his* language not only saves him from the imputation but is felicity itself, even when most mannered and gay: "I practiced up a fine prelude and fugue"; "Harlem was full of lovely people. So was the WPA. The times were for sweetness and joy in work"—which reminds me of the Japanese commandant in *The River Kwai*.

In many biographies the reader is tempted to skip the family background. To do that here, eliminating the hero's early days in Arcadian Missouri, would be to rob Mr. Thomson's discovery of Paris of its contrasting force (and, incidentally, to remove the setting of the book's best quip, Thomson *mère* on first hearing John Cage's prepared piano: "It's pretty but I never would have thought of doing it"). Paris discovered, the story centers there, then moves back and forth to New York, and the author, comparing the two cities, is at his epigrammatic best. Some of his pictures are enlarged for detail with excerpts from his own newsletters of the time, and all of them are enlivened with thumbnail portraits. That of Gertrude Stein is the most vivid, and a new view of her is exposed, and an old score settled, by printing her correspondence concerning the financial arrangements of their collaboration. At no time during these negotiations did Miss Stein risk the Stein style, one notes, and though the prose parses as it seldom does otherwise, the woman behind it shows herself as hard as nails.

A number of aesthetic formulations are encountered along the way. Mr. Thomson invokes a "spontaneity which can be original if it comes from self-containment." He believes, too, that "if a text is set correctly for the sound of it, the meaning will take care of itself." As a film composer—for Mr. Thomson is a man of parts—he subscribes to the theory that "landscape should be rendered through the music of its people." What he divulges of his own composing procedures is less satisfactory and not always plausible ("I let the piece write itself"), and now, while Mr. Thomson's new opera is awaited, readers will be disappointed to find no hint concerning the substitutes for the hymn-tune harmony which was the charm of his first two efforts in that form. But while the statement that he selects chords "for their tensile strength" is unobjectionable so far as it goes (which is nowhere), he explains nothing at all by claiming that his "skill was to be employed not for protecting composers who had invested in the dissonant manner . . ." *Whose* dissonant manner? (there are many), and were its investors in need of Mr. Thomson's protection? And what are we to make of the following? "Before I could lay out the score I had to decide what instruments to use." Well, yes, goodness me, you certainly *would* have to do that.

The roundup chapters ramble a bit, tidying odds and ends, but the last offers valuable comment on the current scene, as well as an intelligent barometric forecast. Mr. Thomson argues the need both for a comparative musicology and a musical sociology, a "clarification of music's varied roles in our civilization." And he enters an eloquent plea for the "recognition of art and artists as national wealth." Who, we might suggest, could more ably serve a bureau of the arts in furthering these aims than Virgil Thomson? And not only serve it but adorn, for though he compares himself in his freshman days at the *"Trib"* to a "stormy petrel," he was then and still is a bird of some very fine plumage.

APPENDIX C

Lulu: Notes on the Drama [1]

Is the book worthy of Berg? Or is *Lulu* as much of a disappointment after *Wozzeck*, dramatically speaking, as *Titus Andronicus*
would be after *King Lear*?

The composer himself had misgivings about the Wedekind
plays. They were too long for what he felt to be his natural
musical dimensions, and the task of reducing the two plays to
one, hence of building a new dramatic shape and a new structure
of the dénouement, was a formidable one. And Wedekind's
slow-moving period pieces would have to be renovated into a
swift-moving Berg libretto. That Berg succeeded in the reconstruction of the book seems to me indisputable, but the work cost
him an unconscionable amount of time as well as those misgivings.

Why did he choose the plays in the first place, and are the
characters and their motives interesting enough to warrant complex musical treatment? My own answers to the second are
equivocal and will be reserved for my notes on the characters,
but to the first the only answer that accounts for Berg's final

---

1 Written at the time of the first American performance of the opera,
which I conducted, in Santa Fe, July 1963. Shortly afterward, Mr. George
Perle informed me of his efforts on behalf of the publication of Act III, and
in ensuing correspondence I discovered his study of the opera to have
penetrated so far beyond mine that the essay for which these notes were
being gathered need not be written. I print the notes in spite of that
disclaimer, nevertheless, because the angle from which they attempt to
view the opera is unfamiliar.

overriding of all objections is that Lulu herself is a subject for music, in much the same sense as Don Juan. She was, furthermore, the contemporary version of that *Ewig weibliche* ideal which had had such a fruitful effect on Berg's own musical lineage, especially on Mahler, who was temperamentally closer to Berg than any other composer, including Schoenberg. Secondarily, Lulu was a contemporary subject, in her social and moral situation (the sensational content of the plays—sex and violence—has helped to keep them contemporary), which Berg required as well. Finally, he must have been actuated by at least two other considerations, one simply being that the plays gave him an opportunity to try his hand in new genres, the other that he found in them the touchstones of identification required by his creative psychology.

The nub of any criticism of *Lulu* is in the question of Berg's own sympathies, for the degree of our involvement will inevitably reflect the degree of commitment of the composer's feelings. Until Act III is restored, however, the question cannot be pursued all the way, or even far enough, and it is obviously very imprudent to conjecture, as I do now, that even *with* that act, a number of puzzles and objections will remain unresolved.[2] So long as Lulu's own musical character is not fully known, then to some degree the character of the opera as a whole must continue to be a matter of speculation, and the staging of even the first two acts at certain points continues to be tentative. But where ambiguities might still flaw Berg's masterpiece after we have it complete, as I suspect, I predict that in the completed work both Lulu and Geschwitz attain a dimension of tragedy denied them in the truncation which now stands.

[2] The contents of Act III are less mysterious than the reasons for its suppression. The dramatic events were long since known from Wedekind, after all, and even if they were not, Act III is hardly likely morally to unhinge anyone who has not yet been so effected by Acts I and II; which is to assume that the censorship now in force is on moral grounds. Berg's libretto exists, in any case, and the music matching it has been described, measure for measure, by Mr. Perle.

A hint of the enlargement of Lulu's character that might be awaited in Act III seems to have been divulged by the transformation in her following the prison experience. Certainly this new and more poignant Lulu extends at least the promise of a deeper engagement of our sympathies. Yet the new mood hardly endures to the end of the scene, while the libretto of the next two scenes (Act III) reads like more Graustark or *guignol*. In fact the mood at the end of the same scene [3] (end of Act II) is a prime example of what I hold to be the obscurity of Berg's own feelings. First of all, the propriety in Lulu's question "Isn't this the couch on which your father bled to death?" is out of character, I think, even as a taunt, or display of sheer bitchiness. But the serious objection to the line is its risibility. It brings the audience to the brink of laughter, and would push it over, except for the orchestral *crescendo* that covers its tracks. Now whatever Wedekind, who regularly mixed tragedy and farce, thought to effect by the line, Berg cannot at this point have intended a joke (as, for example, Wagner must have with Siegfried's exclamation on first seeing Brünnhilde: *"Das ist kein Mann"*). Nor is it easy to believe that he expected the question to produce a shudder; it could not have sounded *that* much less corny in 1934, and is probably less corny now in fact, thanks to sick humor.[4]

Then what *does* Berg mean here, and for that matter, throughout the *Hymne?* Is simple satire intended, as the text might lead one to assume? The answers are that Berg is not Wedekind, and that the composer's satire is generally straightforward. The quotation of the *Merry Widow* rhythm ♩ ♪ ♩♪ ♩ in Lulu's cavatina is an instance (the not *very* Grim Reaper, from the relict's point of view, having harvested two husbands in Act I); others are the snare drum crash in Schoen's *"Lebensabend"* aria, and the thump of the bass drum in Alwa's aria just before the let's-drop-the-subject music (ms. 285, which, incidentally, resembles ms. 661–2 in *Von Heute auf Morgen*). But to return to Lulu's too heavily ironic question about the couch, if Black Comedy was

---

[3] The "amoralism" of which is strikingly similar, incidentally, to the duet *"Pur ti moro, pur ti godo"* as the end of Monteverdi's *The Coronation of Poppea.*
[4] Breton's *Anthologie de l'humour noir* dates from 1940.

intended, the genre has not been established, and the ambiguity is fatal.

The question of the composer's commitment of his emotional gravity is complicated by his psycho-pathological need (as it *seems* to me) to build "real-life" identifications into his work. Thus he identifies himself with Alwa, not merely by profession and the reference to *Wozzeck*, but by the music with which Alwa is characterized. To me, at any rate, and without attempting to substantiate the point with the analysis it requires, the features of the musical self-portrait in the Chamber Concerto are similar to those in the musical picture of Alwa. (*cf.*, the "Berg" segment of the Motto from the Concerto and ms. 243 in Act II.) Alwa's remark to Lulu, "I feel your form as a musical form" ("symphonic form" in Wedekind) may be counted as a further identification (Berg feeling the form of *Lulu*), and psychoanalysts would dig up still another in the parallel that Alwa's character loosens in the absence of his father, Schoen, even as the character of the Schoenberg technique loosens in the absence (the departure for America) of Berg's musical father, Schoenberg.

Berg also identifies himself with Schigolch through the bond of asthma. And to some extent he may have identified Geschwitz with his own sister, Smaragda Berg. To take these two connections a step further and combine them in a larger speculation, Geschwitz may represent repressions in Berg himself relating, in turn to his asthma.[5] Last but not least, Berg identified with his heroine. "Loulou, *c'est moi*," he might have said, as Flaubert (a now certified case of repressed homosexuality) *did* say, except that the name he used was that of *his* most famous heroine. And finally Berg carried this ultimate identification to the somewhat extreme point of actually dying on the same night, Christmas Eve,[6] as his leading lady.

[5] Berg's *Letters To His Wife* (Faber, 1969) reveal that he was concerned with homosexuality and displayed masochistic tendencies. The *Letters* also show that the element of "sensuality" is what had originally attracted him in the Lulu plays, some twenty years before conceiving his opera. The *Letters* reveal, moreover, that Berg knew Freud, and had read Lombroso and *Psychopathia Sexualis*.

[6] The same night, incidentally, on which Van Gogh hacked off part of his ear to give to a brothel inmate.

✲ ✲ ✲

Wedekind's intentions are not mysterious. Furthermore, he draws the same picture, in the same social-satire terms, employing the same nefarious characters and the same circus ring in a later play, *The Marquis of Keith.* There the cynicism (the moralist's mode *par excellence*) is epitomized in the line "Sin is what mythologists call bad business," a line that Brecht might have stuffed, along with a cigar, into the sound box of one of his American gangsters.[7] But Wedekind's Lulu is earthbound and one-dimensional. Her claims on our sympathies are bounded exactly at the point where the music creates other dimensions for her, in her flights of erotic fantasy, and in dramatic ironies possible only in music. Ambiguities notwithstanding, Berg's conception of the drama and its people is immeasurably more profound than Wedekind's.

A critique of the opera should begin with a comparison of the libretto and the plays and explaining the musical and dramatic reasoning behind each of Berg's alterations. What, for the most obvious example, is the difference between the period of the plays and the period of the libretto? Wedekind wrote *Earth Spirit* [8] soon after Jack the Ripper's five prostitute murders (1888), and *Pandora's Box* occupied him throughout the Nineties; the period of the scenario is the gaslit decade. But Berg updates the book, in places, to a time when telephones were in ordinary use and Freudianisms were household words. Moreover, his use of these modernizing trappings is so effective as to cause regret that he did not wholly and openly transpose the opera to Isherwood's Berlin, thus turning Lulu into a vamp. A late-Twenties, early-Thirties date would suit the style of Schoen's death, too, as the Doktor was thought to be at the Stock Exchange and, like many

[7] Critics have regretted the missed opportunity of collaboration between Berg and Brecht, but Brecht's socialist realism was too tidily objective for the composer. The "decadent," "morbid," "effete" Wedekind was closer to Berg's taste and time. I note in passing that Brecht's obituary for Wedekind evokes the balladeer singing songs of social content to his own lute accompaniment.

[8] *Erdgeist* is Goethe's word, of course, and Wedekind obviously intends to borrow the meaning, from *Faust*, of the life principle, which also includes death and destruction.

a ruined investor of those years, he carried a revolver. In any case, the telephone obbligato, Schoen's call to his city editor with the news of the Painter's suicide, and the use of that quaint turn of Viennese argot, "persecution complex," is a brilliant device, musically and dramatically. Both the instrument of communication and the language are anachronistic in the flamboyantly *fin de siècle* setting, of course, but in other respects, such as the circus format and the cabaret dirty ditty (the *Dirnenliebe* lute song in Act III), Wedekind is more up to date than Berg's updating. Nor have all of the targets of Wedekind's social crusade fallen from sight as yet; Geschwitzes are still a top topic in and out of the theater.

The Prologue is the musical and dramatic key to the opera, and the animal symbolisms—serpent, tiger, bear, crocodile—it attaches to the characters should be kept in mind throughout, along with the Animal Trainer's excoriation of the *dramatis personae* as "monsters" and "soulless creatures." But the Prologue does not impress itself at that depth, and in my opinion fails to constitute the frame of reference Berg intended; once the story proper has begun, we no more think in terms of these animal symbols than we think of Petrushka as a sawdust puppet. As is the case with other prologues, too, Shakespeare's included, we tend to forget the predictions and to miss the clues. In fact many people think of the beginning of the opera as the scene with the Painter (as many listeners remember the beginning of Mozart's G-minor Symphony from the violins instead of the lower strings). Nor are the musical identities of the cast, as presented in animal skins, very firmly imprinted on the memory. In sum, the Prologue lacks weight for its length, the initial excitement of the Animal Trainer's advertisements peters out, and the piece is a very long way from the truly referential musico-dramatic beginning of, for example, Wagner's Norn scene.

The Prologue associates Lulu, the serpent,[9] with chromatic

---

[9] In the Santa Fe production, the cage with widespread bars from which she hisses at the Animal Trainer would seem to be more suited to a tigress.

music in the strings, a cliché for sinuousity. The same music recurs in association with Schigolch, in the second scene of the first act—also in the strings, partly as an *aide-mémoire*, for the return follows an extended woodwind nonet. Recognition of the derivation is vital, the Lulu-Schigolch relationship, whatever it is, being one of the opera's most potent mysteries. The chromatic motive is cardinal to the symbol system of the whole opera, moreover, for Lulu the serpent is also Eve the seducer, a character whose mysterious origins and suggestions of other-worldliness constitute still another musically fertile mystery. Lulu's otherworldly yearnings, and her "earth weariness," which Schigolch shares, are in fact the opera's most powerful enlargements of the heroine, and they inspire some of Berg's greatest music. The serpentine string motive appears next in association with Schoen (I, 531), I should add, and then becomes the theme of the stage-band music, and of the Sextet. But by this time who remembers that old bore the Animal Trainer?

Lulu marks a return to so-called closed and self-contained forms and, no less important, to forms that are primarily vocal and operatic (as those of *Wozzeck* were primarily symphonic): cavatinas, canzonettas, duettinos, etc. In this regard, the influence of *Von Heute auf Morgen* is basic, and not only in the nature of the forms but also in the vocal style, above all of Lulu herself; it is in its vocal side, if in no other, that *Lulu* surpasses *Wozzeck*. Nevertheless, the strophic aria which Berg favors (*cf.* Schoen's *furioso*) still offers a type of development—successive verses being comparable to further stages of variation—similar to that of instrumental forms.

Lulu restores as well such other operatic conventions as the love duet, the concerted ensemble, the *buffo* scene (the sniggering trio-canon lullaby), and even the stage-whispered double aside (I, 578), all of which the composer of *Wozzeck*, at the time of *Wozzeck*, would most likely have banished as artificialities. Wagnerian conventions are utilized, too, as well as these Italianate conventions of the pre-Wagnerian unreform. Thus the opera is *leit*-motivic. And thus whole blocks of music—that of Schigolch and his familiars, for example—are translated from one scene to another, just as parts of scenes are re-employed in successive operas of the *Ring;* and recapitulations of this kind may be expected to occur on a more extensive scale in Act III. But *Lulu* reflects still another, very unexpected musico-dramatic source. The conversations without music—the Painter's letter reading and talk about money—as well as some of those "over" music (the melodramas), are reminiscent of operetta, and so, at least in one instance, Lulu's brief scene of domesticity with the Painter, is the music.

Berg's obsession with musical palindromes is given its greatest opportunities in *Lulu.* In fact, the dramatic structure of the opera as a whole is based on the principle, the deceased major characters of the dénouement (the Painter, Dr. Schoen), as well as four minor characters deceased and extant (the Medizinalrat, the Prince, the Wardrobe Attendant, the Theater Manager), being reincarnated in the *catastrophe* in complementary roles. This dual-role (in one case treble-role) repeatability, with its endless possibilities, uniquely within the power of music, of dramatic irony and dramatic cross-reference, must have constituted one of the book's strongest attractions for the composer. As dramatic technique, incidentally, the device has been revived by the contemporary theater of illusion, above all by Genet to whom a role *is* a costume.

If Act III reworks earlier materials, as I have predicated, then it may be expected to cast reflections on the earlier, pre-metempsychosical existences of each multiple-role character. One of the properties in the decor of the first scene is *"Ein höher Spiegel,"* and a high musical mirror is exactly what Berg would be likely to provide. Musical mirrors are standard furniture in the first two acts. The largest of them, the *Monoritmica*, the Sextet, the *Kammerdiener* episode, the film-music *Ostinato*, are complete musical and dramatic units in themselves, and the smallest—hand mirrors and pocket glasses (the clarinet at II, 606, for example)— are found with great frequency.

Palindromes have a natural dramatic structure, especially in the pyramidal forms Berg tends to favor; or it could be said that they have a natural sexual-dramatic structure, but that probably comes to the same thing. Berg's palindromes are obvious to the ear, in any case, and not dependent on memory of pitch order alone; it is not by accident that prime and retrograde serial orders are more conspicuous in his music than retrograde inversion. The turn-arounds themselves, and the withershins sides are invariably delineated by dynamic and coloristic means; but, then, a mirror image (enantiomorph) *is* "the other way around," and in that sense it *does* distort. One of the most accessible examples of the device, for new listeners, is the fusiform Sextet. It is obvious not only aurally, but also in its exemplification of a perfect correspondence between musical form and dramatic action.

Of the characters, Lulu herself poses the most problems. Like many beautiful women, she has a false reputation. While one faction of opinion contends that she is merely suffering from a bad case of the nymphs, another subscribes to the feminist view of her as an innocent *gamine*, ex-Girl Scout or Rebecca of Sunnybrook Farm, destroyed by men. Still another group argues that her destructiveness is not really her fault, as in the case of her manslaughter of Schoen, and in fact the most influential spokesman for this interpretation is Schoen's own son. "You turn all those around you into criminals without being aware of it," he tells Lulu.

It is time to put the legend aside. In spite of the mystique of her "profound innocence," Lulu is deceitful, mendacious, jealous, narcissistic ("I wanted to be my own husband"), cruel and callous ("and now Geschwitz is lying in prison in my place," she says, in an "amused tone" according to the stage direction), and by her own not necessarily reliable account, a premeditating murderess (Alwa's mother, by poison). This much comes to the surface, anyway, and the surface is where Lulu lives; or so one may justifiably conclude until her *Lied*, a musical jewel but dramatic stumbling stone that not only puts an obstacle in the way of our understanding of the heroine's own character, but also upsets our view of the opera as a whole. The Lulu of the *Lied* suddenly knows all about herself and proceeds to tell all directly across the footlights to the audience, virtually stepping out of the opera to do so, and obliging the opera to pause. Whereas the dramatic suspension is a calculated effect, roughly equatable to that of an interpolated aria in a Mozart opera, the content of the confessional soliloquy, if calculated, is imperfectly realized, being utterly unprepared-for.

Sex itself is a subject of the opera (as well as, it might be said, its *hamartia*). In fact, by the third act of this Bunyan-in-reverse, where the heroine is a Parisian *horizontale* in the first scene and a low-rent London tart in the second, she has nothing else to offer. The only "progress" open to her is the step she in fact takes, which is sex for nothing. But precisely here, when nothing else remains, she attains a purity and luminosity, the musical evocation of which is one of Berg's greatest achievements. Throughout the opera, Lulu floats off periodically (no joke) into what seem to be hallucinatory sexual seizures, and it is during these moments of venereal elation that we almost believe in her otherworldliness— her White Goddess as well as her Christine Keeler aspects—and her ultimate redemption. The musical representation of Lulu's prodigious libido is based partly on the "woman's nature" theme in the Prologue (ms. 43–45, and the violin solo in ms. 57). This theme is remarkable in being indelible on first hearing, as each reiteration confirms (II, 209–19, 213, 1080); judging from the Introduction to the *Lulu Symphony*,[1] it is used still more prominently in Act III.

Lulu's erotic nature is also evoked by vocal means, especially florid passages and fioriture at high altitudes; one dazzling example is the vocal trapeze stunt in the reprise of the Sonata, soaring to F in *alt*. Similarly ecstatic vocal flights occur already in the first scene with the Painter (Lulu: *"Ich greife in dem Himmel . . . Gott Schütze Polen"*), and thereafter throughout the opera, and

---

[1] An unworkable potpourri in my opinion; both the *Rondo* and the *"Freiheit"* aria make little sense as voiceless concert pieces, though at the same time, something is to be said for the *Hymne* without voices.

these rapturous states, taken together, form the most attractive side of Lulu's personality, both musical and dramatic. Other libidinous noises issue from her as well, I should add, including her screams at the climax of the *Monoritmica* (at least they affect *me* that way), and her connubial *"du, du"* in the second strophe of the *Duettino,* following the *coitus interruptus* of the doorbell. The *Duettino,* incidentally, is the opera's unique representation of cuddlesome married life; no like moment is shown between Lulu and Schoen, and at the beginning of Act II, where one might have been anticipated, Lulu is carrying on like Wallace Stevens's "fretful concubine."

Gräfin Geschwitz, the crocodile of the Prologue, is another sexual force, and a more powerful one than any of the straight men. Wedekind described her, not Lulu, as the tragic figure of *Pandora's Box* but defined her sexual role as complementary to the Athlete's. In Berg's dramatic scheme, one lover dominates each act, in the order Schoen, Alwa, Geschwitz. If that scheme had been reduced to a more classic form, eliminating Alwa—even though he is the only one of the three to appear in all three acts— the legs of the remaining triangle would be represented, and in isosceles proportion, by Schoen and Geschwitz. The dying Schoen's curse, *"Der Teufel,"* seems to acknowledge that the future belongs to her; it is delivered at the midpoint of the opera, moreover, marking the division between "his" first half and "her" second half. We know little of the musical content of that future, lacking Act III, but Berg, like Wedekind, may well have intended to portray Geschwitz as Lulu's most sympathetic suitor (sympathetic victim?). He was keenly interested in sexual psychopathology,[2] and progressivist in his attitude to sexual emancipation; it is not unlikely, as I have already hypothesized, that he harbored a subconscious bias in Geschwitz's favor. However that may be, the *Gräfin* is braver and more heroic than any of the men in the opera, and her *Liebestod* is undoubtedly its most affecting music.

[2] See footnote 5, p. 327.

Geschwitz's musical portrait [3] as it stands at the end of Act II, however, is not a complete success. For one objection, the pentatonic reminders at every turn border on caricature, as in the knelling of the death motive on her cue, *"Was uns unter die Erde bringt gibt ihr Kraft"* (II, 740). The pentatonic apparatus is variable only as to color. Thus a flue-like wind chord is struck when Schoen asks the mannish Countess whether she has come down the chimney, and a no-less-hollow string chord knells Schoen's demise (preceded by a long pause, possibly intended to clear the air of cordite fumes for the singers' sakes); but that is about as far as color goes.

Another objection is that Geschwitz's scenes are spoiled by an uncertainty of mood only partly caused by the "problem" of Geschwitz herself. In fact the mood of Act II is so different from that of the first act, and the action in comparison is so loose and confusing, that the opera seems to have veered. The mixture of tragedy and farce—the antics and the hugger-mugger of the Schigolch gang—never quite compounds. Geschwitz is compromised by her association with these Schigolch rompings because her Lesbianism is a matter of high seriousness that cannot survive even a suggestion of the comic spirit. Furthermore, if the motivation for the cavortings of the Schigolch *mafiosi* seems obscure, then the hospital episode and Geschwitz's clothes-switching are not only obscure but unseen, as well, except in a film which, though not yet produced as Berg intended, cannot, because of compression, involve the audience in the same degree as the staged drama. In sum, the stature of Geschwitz in the fragment of the opera by which we now know her suffers from impingement by the characters with whom she is thrown together, from some over-all untidiness in the dramatic frame, and from the relegation of her principal action to two minutes of cinema.

Dr. Schoen, the tiger of the Prologue and a *"Gewaltmensch"* to Lulu, is a Wotan in modern dress; or perhaps he *is* Wotan: the

[3] The visual portrait in the Santa Fe production is surely wrong, for it is too subtle to dress her as a woman on the grounds that she hated men too much to want to look like one. Berg's own instructions at the beginning of Act III are: *"Geschwitz, wie immer, mit männlicher Betonung."*

lecherous god was fond of disguises, after all. Like the god, Schoen is weak, henpecked, philandering, in bondage to Lulu as Wotan to Brünnhilde—and Emil Jannings to the "Blue Angel." Schoen resembles Wotan musically, moreover (*cf.* I, 530, and *seriatim*, and the Wagnerian motive in *Von Heute auf Morgen* at ms. 541–2, so like the first theme of the Schoen Sonata). But Schoen's *Übermenschlichkeit* has gone soft, bourgeois, respectable. At a later date this moral lamb in wolf's clothing would have been an ostentatious, if less than munificent, contributor to a certain Winter Relief Fund. Schoen's persecution fantasies (I, 935) fail to arouse our sympathy, and in Act II, by which time they have driven him over the border into psychosis, he is an absurdly melodramatic figure, farther from tragic proportions than ever. Even his death fails to move us, though it is exciting as action, like an old-time movie, which, by the way, is what a lot of the action in *Lulu* reminds one of.

Alwa is inferentially identified with the Animal Trainer, and in that sense with the author of the opera. But he is a bad author ("Your eyes shimmer like the surface of the water in a deep well into which a stone has been thrown"), and we are grateful not to hear the dithyramb he threatens to compose for Lulu. Unlike his father, whose musical temperament is apoplectic and whose characterizing serial unit is initialed by a major third—major and minor modes retain their conventional powers—Alwa is musically macaronic and his serial initial is a minor third. Thus the musical heredity, without entering into the detail of the serial chromosomes, follows the active-father, passive-son syndrome, the "empire builder to aesthete" in one degeneration. Alwa strikes me as phlegmatic beyond the call of tradition, however, and his "I worship you" seems to me vacuous musically as well as on all other counts; but then this is another of those places, like the end of the second act, in which I am unable to fathom Berg's gravity. Has he really identified with his character to the extent of sponsoring this insipid sentiment?

To continue with the roundup of the cast, the Painter appears to be merely foolish, no less so as a married man than in the first scene chasing Lulu around the room like a Keystone Cop. Yet one of the most feeling passages in the opera is entrusted to him, the *"Ich bin den Glück nicht gewachsen; ich habe eine höllische Angst davor."* The natural terror of this is as powerful as anything in the *Wozzeck* to which it is so similar.

As the most highly endowed of composers for the depiction of bronchial disorders,[4] Berg must have found Wedekind's Schigolch irresistible. The musical portrait of this bizarre character, complete with notated wheezings, is one of the most masterful in the opera, though not one to support the view of him as a symbol of eternal evil, an interpretation that, to my mind, is also not clinched by the fact of his existence both before and after the action of the opera, for he is the only major character to prevail (as Faulkner would say). In truth, he is a light "heavy," a bit sinister but not terrifying, a contact man in the Berlin Branch of Cosa Nostra perhaps, but nothing higher up. Nor is he altogether unlikeable, either in his sweaty first scene or later, lounging about the Schoen house. The forms of skullduggery he specializes in, whether pickpocketing, pilfering, blackmailing, are not specified, but he is deliberately made mysterious because of Lulu, whose first lover and first ponce he seems to have been, if not, as the Athlete hints, actually her father. And the aura of mystery saves him from mere sordidness.

[4] Does Berg's asthma contain a clue to his creative psychology? The affliction is physical in that whatever it is responds to ACTH, cortisone, steroid tablets, and in that the carotid body is sometimes removed by surgery. But it is also psychological, in that the parasympathetic nerve responds to psychological stress by contracting the air passages. And it is sexual in prototype: the breathlessness and suffocation in sexual climax (Conrad Aiken's "the unappeasable suffocation of desire"). In fact many doctors now believe it to be a refuge from true sexual gratification, a sign of suppressed homosexuality. By medical records, men are more prone to it than women, but these records are "masculine," history having been invented, enacted, and written by, men; besides which only the most prominent cases, Pliny to Gesualdo, Lichtenberg to Proust, are the ones that have attracted attention.

Postscript: In the January 1968 issue of *Nature*, Dr. R. K. Mason announced his discovery that the hearing of asthmatics is more sensitive than that of other people, and that asthmatics are peculiarly sensitive to the high frequency in their parents' voices in certain emotive words. Speculating from this, Dr. Mason thinks that hearing and breathing might have had the same area of brain control at some remote stage of evolution.

The pants-role Schoolboy represents another return to operatic convention. Operatic girl-boys are as old as opera itself, of course. (So are operatic boy-girls, though we have lost that side of the tradition, part of which was maintained by the knife, and can no longer make any sense of a role such as Handel's Cleopatra, which should not be sung by a woman.) Even Wagner did homage to the in-drag convention (Ariano in *Rienzi*), but Mozart's Cherubino and Strauss's Oktavian would have been the familiar examples for Berg. As Mozart with Cherubino, so Berg associates his amorous adolescent with military music, by having him sing in fanfares. Berg's Cherubino is no gormless youth, however, but a precocious juvenile delinquent, even a Borstal Boy. Is he *too* precocious for the mock lullaby that Schigolch and the Athlete, his companions in an unholy triumvirate, set in motion? I note that the text of this little piece anticipates Joyce ("O tell me all about Anna Livia! I want to hear all about Anna Livia. Well, you know Anna Livia? Yes, of course, we all know Anna Livia"):

Athlete:	He once wanted to marry her.
Schigolch:	I also once wanted to marry her.
Athlete:	You once wanted to marry her?
Schigolch:	Didn't you once want to marry her?
Athlete:	Certainly I once wanted to marry her.
Schigolch:	Who has not once wanted to marry her?
Schoolboy:	What? All of you once wanted to marry her?

The Athlete, the bear of the Prologue, is accompanied by a small brass band, bass drum, and piano, but he is also identified by the piano alone, which is "his" instrument as the saxophone is Lulu's and the woodwinds are Schigolch's. In fact, a mere two wads of notes, one of white keys and one of black, in a six-four meter that seems ideal for gymnastic exercises and weight lifting, suffice to evoke him. To suggest his handstanding and cartwheel-turning feats, Berg employs such other pianistic items as note-clusters, trills, and *glissandi*. But the most impressive athletic display is Berg's own juggling act, as he twirls in simultaneous orbit the Athlete's two-beat 6/4 music, the Schoolboy's six-beat 6/4 music, and Schigolch's cut-time 4/4 music. The Athlete is so concisely and easily drawn, however, partly because he is to begin with no more than a cartoon caricature (very suitable for Dick Tracy). He would make an excellent intellectual companion for Fafnir, but for a personality hardly more interesting than one of his own dumbbells, his part in *Lulu* is too large.

Of the minor roles, the best-drawn profile for its length is the Prince. But the part is trinitarian, and to exploit social ironies the performer must play compendiously the Butler and the Negro as well. As the Negro appears only in the third act, I can say nothing about the part as a whole.

The Wardrobe Attendant, invented by Berg for musical reasons, could be staged as if she were in league with Lulu.[5] The collusion is not implied by the libretto, but if the Attendant is in on the faking, as the Theater Manager is not, a little more can be made of her.

Contrarily, of course, the Butler must be played straight. It would be inconvenient for Lulu if Alwa were to discover yet another truth at this point, which is why she takes the Butler's defense.

The scene of the Medizinalrat, who does not sing but only curses and drops dead, both in strict rhythm, is one of the most perfect constructions in the opera.

Of the new characters in Act III, Casti-Piani, the *Puffmutter*, the Journalist, the Groom, the Professor, the Negro, Puntschu [6] the Banker, and Jack the Ripper, only Jack's music is known, but it offers a brilliant example of the exploitation of the dual-role relationship. Jack is Schoen's double and shadow-soul, and his revenge from beyond the pale; and just as Wedekind, playing the part himself, invoked the poetic justice of the author destroying his creation, so is the destruction of Lulu a retributive act, for Schoen is her author in the Pygmalion sense. Kill or be killed is

---

[5] Karl Kraus, who otherwise accepted Wedekind's Lulu as the ideal portrait of the *Vollweib*, objected to this scene on the grounds that a sensuous woman cannot be a dancer. See also Erich Neumann's *Amor and Psyche*.

[6] Described as a *"Saujude"* in Wedekind, but not in Berg, which throws doubt on the story circulated after Berg's death that Schoenberg had been offended by an anti-Semitic stage direction in Berg's hand. As nearly as I can establish, Schoenberg had never seen any of the *Lulu* music except the Symphony and the Prologue.

the meaning of that confrontation at the end of the opera, and the audience is suddenly aware, thanks to the music, that the same jungle law had obtained between Lulu and Schoen. Berg anchors Jack's double identity in the music by the device of accompanying his retreat after "ripping" Lulu, with the theme of Schoen's *Das mein Lebensabend* aria (II, 40). It is a master stroke, not merely of irony but of unification, extending back over two thirds of the opera.

No guidebook has yet been provided for *Lulu*, but since the only study of value that does exist (by George Perle) is devoted to analyses of pitch structures, it seems incumbent to mention some of the other aspects of musical novelty. In the domain of rhythm, for example, *Lulu* is one of the most richly innovatory creations of the century. In fact, the four-note rhythmic code, designated *Hauptrhythmus* (RH) on its first appearance (I, 9), is primary and paramount beyond any pitch construction. It could be labeled the "Man's Fate" motive, in the sense of the fate of the heroine's husbands and lovers, which is sudden death. This code recurs hundreds of times—not all of the reifications are marked—and is the most emphasized musical message in the opera. Its ubiquity is accounted for in that the rhythm can be attached to any intervallic or melodic material, and even to none, as in the "pitchless" beginning of the *Monoritmica* and in the reports of Lulu's revolver at the shooting of Schoen. By the same power, it follows that the rhythmic signal is a more comprehensive identifying tool than any combination or succession of pitches.

But the opera explores rhythmic functions of a wholly new kind, and to new and far-ranging dramatic effect. The tempo of the *Monoritmica*, for example, is in flux throughout, the first half of the scene being an *accelerando*, the second half, from Lulu's scream at the climax, a *rallentando*. The upgrade is stepwise. Eighteen changes of pace are effected, by prolations of the eighth note, the quarter, and the half. The downgrade, on the contrary, is a progressive braking, without plateaus or even two beats in the same speed. This rhythmic engineering is not an architectural abstraction, moreover, but a framework corresponding to the dramatic shape, and even to the vocal instrumentation, the dialogue that begins like Amos and Andy, in low tension, and shifts into higher vocal gears, parallel to the increases of speed, until both voices leap from *Sprechstimme* [7] to song. Dramatically and musically the *Monoritmica* is one of the most original inventions in the music of our century.

Another instance of a new in-depth rhythmic function is found in the scene of the pursuit of Lulu by the Painter. Here both the form and the dramatic description are determined by rhythmic devices. The Painter's chase, like many others, is represented by a canon. It is a progressive one in that the distance between pursued and pursuer shortens as the former loses ground. They are three beats apart at the outset, two beats apart in the second stage, one beat apart in the third stage. Finally, when caught, Lulu goes on warbling her resistance in her three-rhythm, while the Painter continues to express his fatuous infatuation in his two-rhythm,[8] the metrical conjunction—and differentiation—representing the two as both together and apart. This symbolism is further extended by the underlying of the whole scene with the RH code, which in this instance signifies the husband's music.

The concordance of thematic and other cross-references [9] is a computer-size project that must include identifications both in the "real world" (the trumpets at the beginning of the *Ostinato* imitating the police horns of Berlin's Black Marias of the time) and in the worlds of other works by Berg (the allusions in Lulu's *Lied* to the *Sieben Frühe Lieder* and *Altenberg Lieder*, for exam-

---

[7] The performance of *Sprechstimme* is the same, presumably, as in *Wozzeck*, which is the same as *Pierrot lunaire*, which no one knows how to do. The question remains: why did Schoenberg and Berg take such pains to notate exact pitch and then settle for a singsong inflected speech? If they did.

[8] A similar example of this rhythmic dualism occurs at the end of *Reigen* (*cf.* ms. 101–10), the second of Berg's Three Orchestra Pieces.

[9] As in the recurrence of the Painter's music in II, 466, at the words "suicide" and "destruction," and in the dying Schoen's echo of the Painter's death cries, "*O Gott, O Gott*" from I, 679.

ple). But the composer's search for such relationships seems to me so obsessive that a compilation of them should be as interesting to psychology as to music. Not being a psychologist or tabulating machine myself, I will say no more on the subject.

As I have already warned, it is impossible to form a just appreciation of the opera so long as it is deprived of its resolving act. Nor can we even appraise the main event of Berg's dramatic structure—as distinguished from Wedekind's—until some enterprising director fulfills the composer's instructions with regard to the film sequence; [1] this "blue movie" is the axis of the plot, after all, and the bridge between the two Wedekind plays.

But the music even as it stands has not been recognized for what it is, or for what is most truly new in it. I will not attempt a resumé but must nevertheless mention such other novelties as the canon of five percussion timbres (I, 755) followed by the canon of four one-timbre percussion pitches, which show that Berg is on the way to new serial uses; and, in the Athlete's muscle-flexing scene where the bulging wind-instrument dynamics in correspondence to the bulging biceps, show Berg discovering a polyphonic use of volume dynamics. Then, too, the use of instrumentation as an element of dramatic structure, already alluded to in the discussion of the characters, is an important novelty, in the degree to which Berg carries it; the instrumentation itself is enriched, I should add, by colors borrowed from jazz, nor is it Berg's fault that one of them, the pre-Lionel Hampton vibraphone (which may also have been suggested by the *Fanciulla del West*), became the "in" instrument *ad nauseum* of a more recent decade. Finally, *Lulu* abandons so many Schoenbergian recipes [2] the restriction to a single referential series, the equating of the four serial orders, the strict adherence to serial

[1] The use of slides, in substitution, in the Hamburg staging contradicts not only the cinematographic speed and movement in the music but also the type of cinematographic action that is part of the opera itself, for Berg's timing is closer to the cinema of Pabst than to the theater of Wedekind.
[2] Schoenberg could hardly sanction *Lulu*, let alone complete it, which speculation at the time considered a possibility.

order, the proscription of harmonic bass functions and triadic progressions and octave doublings [3]—that a case could be made for it as the end of "the 12-tone system"; or better, the beginning of its new life, reincorporated in a larger, less exclusive concept of music, for Berg's exploration of new resources and new structuring techniques avoids the evolutionary determinism of an ever-more-perfect system.

"Postskriptum," Lulu dictates, and Schoen pens her words in unsounding writing, which is notated in canon with Lulu and is thus a literal example of *Papiermusik*, as well as a further example of the composer's psychological obsessions. As a *"Postskriptum"* of my own, I ask the reader to follow the instruction preceding the ceiling-high pile-up of fourths on the first page of the score. It is the only instance of the word that I know of at the *beginning* of a work, but it is also highly characteristic of Alban Berg. The word is ATTACCA!

[3] Octaves are employed as terminal devices, nakedly, for example, at Schigolch's first entrance and Schoen's death, as they were in Berg's earlier music (*cf.* the end of the fourth variation in the Chamber Concerto).

INDEXES

INDEX I

Compositions by Stravinsky mentioned in the text

INDEX II

A NOTE ABOUT THE AUTHORS

IGOR STRAVINSKY

(born at Oranienbaum, Russia, June 18, 1882) has been recognized for sixty years as one of the great composers. His compositions are in the repertoires of instrumental and vocal musicians throughout the world. Stravinsky also is renowned for his extraordinary erudition and wit, both of which illuminate his published writings. He lives in Hollywood, California.

ROBERT CRAFT

*(born at Kingston, New York, October 20, 1923) is the first American to have conducted both of Alban Berg's operas—*Wozzeck *and* Lulu—*and is the author of monographs on Stravinsky's* Le Sacre du printemps *and* Les Noces. *He collaborated with Stravinsky on five earlier books:* CONVERSATIONS WITH IGOR STRAVINSKY *(1959)*, MEMORIES AND COMMENTARIES *(1960)*, EXPOSITIONS AND DEVELOPMENTS *(1962)*, DIALOGUES AND A DIARY *(1963)*, *and* THEMES AND EPISODES *(1966)*.

A NOTE ON THE TYPE

This book was set on the Linotype in Janson, a re-cutting made direct from type case from matrices long thought to have been made by the Dutchman Anton Janson, who was a practicing type founder in Leipzig during the years 1668–87. However, it has been conclusively demonstrated that these types are actually the work of Nicholas Kis (1650–1702), a Hungarian, who most probably learned his trade from the master Dutch type founder Kirk Voskens. The type is an excellent example of the influential and sturdy Dutch types that prevailed in England up to the time William Caslon developed his own incomparable designs from them.

The book was composed, printed, and bound by Kings-port Press, Inc., Kingsport, Tennessee. Typography and binding design by Betty Anderson.